BREAKING THE BONDS

The American Social Experience Series

GENERAL EDITOR: JAMES KIRBY MARTIN

EDITORS: PAULA S. FASS, STEVEN H. MINTZ,
CARL PRINCE, JAMES W. REED & PETER N. STEARNS

BREAKING THE BONDS

Marital Discord in Pennsylvania,

1730-1830

MERRIL D. SMITH

NEW YORK UNIVERSITY PRESS

NEW YORK AND LONDON

1991

Library of Congress Cataloging-in-Publication Data
Smith, Merril D.
Breaking the bonds : marital discord in Pennsylvania, 1730–1830 /
Merril D. Smith.
p. cm. — (The American social experience series ; 21)
Based on the author's thesis (doctoral—Temple university).
Includes bibliographical references (p.   ) and index.
ISBN 0-8147-7934-4
1. Divorce—Pennsylvania—History—18th century.   2. Divorce—
Pennsylvania—History—19th century.   3. Marriage—Pennsylvania—
History—18th century.   4. Marriage—Pennsylvania—History—19th
century.   I. Title.   II. Series.
HQ835.P4S57   1992
306.872'09748'09033—dc20   91-5061
CIP

c 10 9 8 7 6 5 4 3 2 1

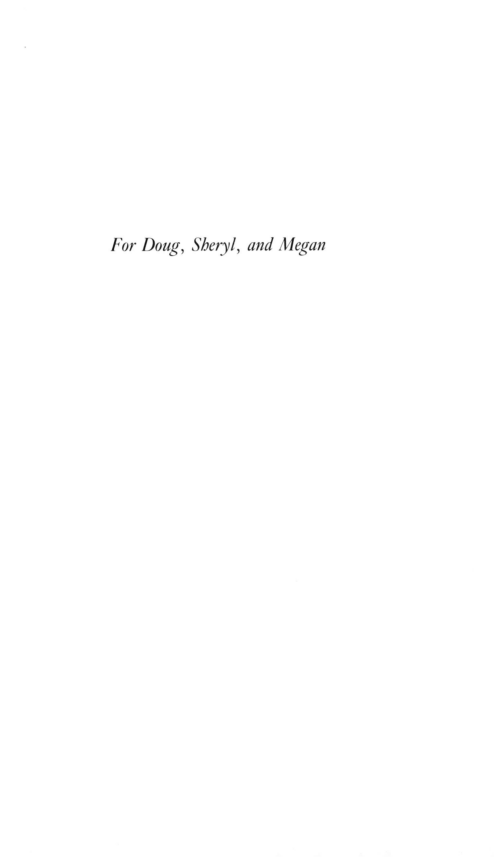

For Doug, Sheryl, and Megan

Contents

Illustrations and Tables

xi

Acknowledgments

During the writing and revising of this book, I have incurred innumerable debts. The first version of this work was my doctoral dissertation. The members of my committee at Temple University, Allen F. Davis, P. M. G. Harris, and Emma Lapsansky, in addition to giving editorial advice and guidance, always showed great interest in my topic, encouraging me to finally finish the project. Seminars at Temple University and at the Philadelphia Center for Early American Studies were also helpful. Participants there provided suggestions and comments on some of the early drafts. In particular, I would like to thank Jean R. Soderlund, Lisa Wilson, and Lucy Simler. Ric Northrup, Susan Mackiewicz, Judith Hunter, and Susan Klepp graciously shared their own work and supplied me with obscure citations.

Wayne Bodle encouraged me to publish my dissertation. James Kirby Martin, series editor, Colin Jones, Director of the New York University Press, and two unknown readers bolstered my confidence in this work. In addition, Colin Jones has always promptly returned my calls and courteously explained the intricacies of publishing. Despina P. Gimbel supervised the final editing of this manuscript and guided me through the process.

I received much needed assistance from the staffs of the Historical Society of Pennsylvania, the Philadelphia City Archives, and the Library Company of Philadelphia. Rosemary Philips of the Chester County Historical Society and Laurie Rofini of the Chester County

Archives went beyond the call of duty in providing me with references, documents, and friendship.

"Real life" sometimes gets in the way of writing. Baby-sitters extraordinaire, Stephanie and Jennifer Stefanow, deserve special thanks for entertaining Megan while I worked. Friends: Chris, Steve, Irene, Jim, and Josie helped me work and play. Michael J. Turzanski cheerfully provided long-distance computer advice. I also received encouragement and support from my father, Lee L. Schreiber, my mother, Sylvia L. Schreiber, and my in-laws, Walter and Sandra Smith. All of them were wonderful about not asking, "when will you be finished?"

My daughter, Megan, has been a help by just being. She constantly reminds me of what is truly important. Sheryl was born as this book was ready to go to the press. She has added a new and joyous dimension to our lives. Finally, my husband, Doug, proofread, worked on statistics, and printed the dissertation and the book. More than that, he has shown enormous pride in my work, and even more love for me.

List of Abbreviations

CCA   Chester County Archives, West Chester, PA
CCHS   Chester County Historical Society, West Chester, PA
HSP   Historical Society of Pennsylvania, Philadelphia, PA
PCA   Philadelphia City Archives
PMHC   Pennsylvania Historical and Museum Commission, Harris-
       burg, PA
PMHB   *Pennsylvania Magazine of History and Biography*
WMQ   *William and Mary Quarterly*

Introduction:
The "Open Question" of Marriage

Is not marriage an open question, when it is alleged, from the beginning of the world, that such as are in the institution wish to get out; and such as are out wish to get in.

RALPH WALDO EMERSON, "MONTAIGNE; OR THE SKEPTIC"

Nearly all adults in early America expected to marry at some point in their lives.[1] Husbands and wives fought and quarreled, loved and hated, and in many ways behaved much as they do today. What marriage— and the roles of husband and wife—meant to the people of early America, however, was much different from today. It was a time when Americans glorified marriage, which joined together husband and wife as a symbol of the bonds that held together the disparate aspects of republican society. Eighteenth- and early nineteenth-century Americans considered marriage a microcosm of a larger world. It was through marriage that men and women could learn to be virtuous citizens as well as to instill virtue in future generations.[2]

But not everyone was happily married, and those who were unhappily married came from all walks of life. It is impossible to know how many people were unhappy in their marriages. Most probably left no traces in legal records or other standard sources. The majority of unhappily married people in early America, in fact, did not divorce.

I

Instead, they found solace in socializing with family members and friends, in alcohol, or through involvement in extramarital affairs. Some vented their anger and frustrations by abusing family members or deserting their spouses and families. For those intent upon breaking free from their spouses, however, desertion probably remained the easiest and most frequent method.

This study will not try to discover how many people were unhappily married; rather its aim is to determine what kind of problems those in troubled marriages had, and to analyze how men and women coped with marital discord during a time of great social and political transformation. Throughout this time period in Pennsylvania, there was a sometimes bitter and ongoing clash between two opposing sets of marital ideals: the older one emphasized patriarchal authority, wifely obedience, rigidly defined gender roles, and it permitted a double standard of sexuality. The other set stressed love, companionship, a single standard of sexuality, and complementary gender roles. I begin with the following questions: Were married couples affected by these conflicting ideals? To what extent did the idealization of marriage in this period lead to unreasonable expectations in marriage? What subsequent problems arose? How did husbands and wives cope when tensions developed? Did the grounds for divorce change over this period?

I have limited the geographical scope of this study to Pennsylvania, particularly the southeastern region, encompassing Philadelphia and Chester County. Although the topic of marital discord has not been explored in great detail by anyone for any region of early America, what is known of Pennsylvania is probably more meager still. At the same time, Pennsylvania is unique in some interesting ways. The divorce law of 1785, for example, was the first divorce law in the nation to include cruelty as grounds for divorce, though this "divorce" was more of a legal separation than what we know today. Pennsylvania is also a profitable area of study because of the rich variety of sources available. The diversity of the state, both in its socioeconomic makeup and in the composition of its population make insightful comparisons possible. I believe that much of what I have found about marital discord in general, if not the impact of specific divorce laws and the like, will hold true for other colonies and states—and will add a much needed dimension to our knowledge of early America and the family. In the bulk of literature on women and the family in early America, marital strife has not been given the close scrutiny it deserves. Concentrating mainly on New England, studies of marital discord generally look only at divorce. Unlike New England, however, Pennsylvania had no clear procedure for divorce until 1785. Although the Assembly granted a few divorces, Parliament forbade this process in 1772. Thus, Pennsylvania granted no more divorces until after the Revolution. The Pennsylvania divorce act of 1785, influenced by Revolutionary ideas of personal freedom and republican ideals concerning virtuous citizenry, once again provided Pennsylvanians with a legal way to leave their spouse—but the people who took advantage of the law were only a fraction of those involved in unhappy marriages. Most did not divorce. Instead, as they did before the passage of the divorce law, they tried to endure their marriages, or left without the benefit of litigation. Consequently, studying the ways people reacted in troubled marriages when they did not divorce, as well as when they did, gives us a broader and more complete picture of marital discord.

In examining marital tensions and the ways in which eighteenth- and early nineteenth-century Pennsylvania couples coped with them, I am looking at both women and men. It is important to understand how each gender felt about marriage and about each other, their similarities and their differences in perception, their expectations, and reactions. Thus, such gender issues form a significant part of this work.

In addition, studying marital discord illuminates much about families and communities. Throughout the period, the support of family and neighbors remained important to those involved in contentious marriages. To a man or woman betrayed or abused by a spouse, they gave comfort and solace; to a man or woman deserted by a spouse, they gave economic support. The testimonies of family members and neighbors indicate, furthermore, the ways in which the community felt the couple upheld or violated its moral standards. In the eyes of the law and the community, what constituted a troubled marriage?

Records of marital disruption can be found in legal documents, newspapers, and almshouse dockets. These pieces of evidence expand upon the testimonies found in the diaries and letters of the middle class. I have used whatever sources I could find. Many of the examples I have compiled remain just tantalizing fragments. For example, in May 1732, *The Pennsylvania Gazette* reported that "one William Young, upon some Difference with his Wife, and being disguised in Liquor, went voluntarily into the Delaware, and drowned himself." Nothing else about his case survives, however. At another time, an entry in the Philadelphia Almshouse Daily Occurrence Docket reported that Margaret McGrotto, a former inmate of the Philadelphia Almshouse, returned to that institution because she could not "agree with her Husband."[3] On the other hand, I have discovered a rich lode of material about couples such as Rachel and James McMullin, discussed in Chapter 4, because they appear in court records several times over many years. In still other cases, correspondence or diaries discussing marital discord have been preserved. By examining a large number of diverse sources, I have studied people from all walks of life, and not just those unhappy marriages ending in divorce. My goal has been to explore the expectations of normal marriage, marriages under strain, and those split by desertion or divorce as part of a continuum whose tenuous boundaries often remain ambiguous and vague.

This study analyzes the years before, during, and after the Revolution to search for changes over time in the expectations and experiences of marriage. Scholars have examined divorce in some of these decades, or they have looked at the evolution of laws or changes in the status of women, but no one has produced a full picture of marital discord for the period under study here.[4] During this time, patriarchal forms and methods of "self-divorce" coexisted with new expectations about how marriage should work and more frequent legal divorce. Moreover, the changing American culture around them helped men and women to form gender identities that often opposed each other. Families, neighbors, and religious authorities, as well as prescriptive literature and laws, all influenced men and women on how to be husbands and wives, and on what a marriage should be like. Thus, men and women brought a wide range of expectations to marriage, and they reacted to tensions in their marriages in quite different ways. Yet, despite such evolution in marital anticipations, couples faced many of the same problems in the 1830s as in the 1730s. Typically, they quarreled over money, sex, drinking, abusive behavior, and in-laws.

People changed their ideas about marriage in the eighteenth century. Although seventeenth-century Americans expected husbands and wives to feel affection for one another, often this came after the marriage. In choosing a mate, they were supposed to be guided by their parents. Later in the eighteenth century couples expected to choose their own spouses and married primarily for love.

By the time of the Revolution, these new ideas about marriage had strengthened and were expressed in popular literature throughout the colonies. Republican rhetoric stressed partnership and mutual affection between husband and wife. In addition, as Linda Kerber and Jan Lewis have shown, the roles of wife and mother assumed more importance in the ideology of the new republic—concepts that continued to be stressed into the nineteenth century. Both male and female writers described the ideal wife as a loving friend to her husband. Guided by the concept of republican virtue in the eighteenth century and influenced by the evangelical and reform movements in the nineteenth, she would be pure and virtuous, and able to reform a drunken or unfaithful husband by her good example.[5] She would also be willing to submit to his authority, however. These contradictory ideas frequently led to friction between husbands and wives

Americans also expected husbands to behave themselves in particular ways. They, too, were supposed to be loving spouses and kind fathers. Nevertheless, both traditional outlooks and the law made them the breadwinners and heads of the household. Yet not every husband could achieve these standards of respectability.[6]

Although marriage, republican style, stressed partnership and mutual affection, it continued to emphasize the differences between men and women. The role of each was supposed to complement the other. The idea was not to regard one another as equals. These differences in roles contributed to separate cultures for men and women, and often led to discontentment between husbands and wives. In addition, the economic control which most husbands possessed gave them considerable power over their wives.

My thesis, simply stated, is that women and men were influenced both by the new ideals about marriage concerning how wives and husbands should behave, and by traditional patriarchal notions about men being the head of the household, especially in terms of earning and controlling the money to support the family. Conflicts arose when couples could not reconcile expectations about marriage with the reality of it, especially when one partner, usually the wife, anticipated a marriage based upon the new ideals and her husband expected a traditional patriarchal one. Both husbands and wives, moreover, often found that they could not live up to the image their society demanded of them. In order to receive help when a marriage failed, however, it was wives who had to prove that they were blameless, pure, and virtuous. The new ideology trapped them just as much as the old patriarchal norms had.

Yet women discovered ways to manipulate the legal system in order to gain some relief from their marital problems. By portraying themselves as virtuous wives and innocent victims, women were often successful in obtaining economic support, if not a final break from their spouses. Changes in the divorce laws also benefited women. Between 1785 and 1815, there were 236 women out of a total of 367 applicants who appealed for divorces from the Pennsylvania Supreme Court. The court granted 114 (48%) of their petitions.

Because Pennsylvania had no clear policy on divorce until 1785, it is impossible to use divorce records exclusively as a gauge of marital expectations in this state. In some ways, the law itself can be seen as a watershed. Before the law, divorces were mostly sought by men. After the law, more women than men petitioned for divorce. The emergence of a divorce law, however, should not be seen as the sole indicator of rising marital discord. There were men and women who found themselves caught in unhappy marriages earlier in the century, and many of them found ways to leave their marriages without a divorce law. At the same time, there were men and women, who for various reasons—lack of money or inclination, inability to travel to the Supreme Court, or entanglement in marital troubles unrecognized by the 1785 divorce law—continued to use alternative methods of leaving their marriages even after the divorce law was enacted.

Conditions in America made desertion a relatively easy way to quit a marriage. Many people left a spouse across the ocean, and remarried in the new world. Others abandoned their husbands or wives in

America in order to return to Ireland or France. In a port city, such as Philadelphia, it was relatively simple to take a ship to another colony/state, or farther—if one had the money for passage. As travel became easier, it was less difficult for the unhappily married individual to leave his or her spouse to go to the frontier.

Nevertheless, women often fared worse than men when their marriages collapsed. Being deserted by a husband frequently meant a woman was left without means of support. Many times she was pregnant and/or had young children. She might even have her home and belongings sold to pay an absent husband's debts. The physical act of leaving was probably easier for men, who would not be as conspicuous traveling alone, who would find it easier to obtain work, and who would not have to worry about pregnancy or nursing infants. Yet, despite the risks and difficulties involved, women did leave their husbands.

Chapter 1 examines divorce. Besides changes in public perceptions regarding marriage, laws and the public institutions bearing on it in Pennsylvania evolved significantly. They permitted more options for beleaguered couples. Prior to the 1785 divorce statute, divorce was possible in Pennsylvania only through submission of a private bill to the Assembly. Changes in the law were most profound for women— the new legislation permitted divorce on grounds of both desertion and cruelty, which was not possible prior to the law. Moreover, women could receive alimony in cases of cruelty. Thus, the act appears to have been influenced by new beliefs about what marriage should be. Nevertheless, it retained older patriarchal characteristics. These women seeking divorces were still seen as wives—part of the conjugal unit, rather than as distinct adult women who could function on their own. Only later did legislation in the 1830s and 1840s give married women more control over their own money and property.

Changing marital beliefs are explored in Chapter 2, which focuses on the marital expectations of eighteenth- and early nineteenth-century couples in Pennsylvania. This chapter examines how the new ideals affected men's and women's ideas about marriage, and the impact these expectations had on the marriages themselves. Subsequent chapters analyze particular problems that Pennsylvania couples experienced, and the ways in which they endured or resolved their marital difficulties.

Chapter 3 explores the sexual expectations and problems couples had in their marriages. As today, sometimes sexual tensions caused marital problems, and sometimes they were the result of problems already existing in a troubled marriage. This chapter finds that far from being "passionless," some women sought sexual encounters as a way of finding the love their society taught them they should find. A double standard remained, however. Although society supposed that both husbands and wives would remain faithful to one another, wives most of all were expected to practice the norms of sexual self-control, and to forgive and reform their husbands when they lapsed.

Violence between husband and wife is the subject of Chapter 4. This is not just a modern problem. Early Pennsylvanians, too, had to determine how, and how far, they would interfere between husband and wife when violence arose. Family members and neighbors were crucial in offering both physical intervention to curb conflict and testimony in court depositions, despite claims by many historians that the privacy of the family was beginning to be held sacred. Also within the period studied, laws began to change to help women who were abused by their husbands.

Chapter 5 is about wives and husbands who deserted their spouses. The reasons for and the results of desertion differed according to gender. The term "desertion" actually had a different meaning as applied to men and to women. Women who left their husbands or refused to cohabit with them were often labeled disobedient or immoral. Husbands who abandoned their wives were considered lazy or irresponsible, and they could be forced to provide support for their wives.

Chapter 6 explores how men and women coped after their marriages broke down. The dissolution of a marriage—whether through divorce, separation, or desertion—required economic readjustments. In these situations, both women and men had to adapt to living without a spouse. However, wives' economic status and conditions were more likely than husbands' to change for the worse, due to the restraints of coverture, the legal concept that placed married women under the protection and authority of their mates. For this reason, however, divorce laws and laws against desertion often benefited women over men.

The conclusion summarizes the dynamics of marriages, 1730–1830, a period in which couples attempted to fuse old and new beliefs into a workable system. Full fusion was not always possible, however, and tensions resulting from the clash of expectation and reality occurred. Changes in the nineteenth-century laws might permit more women to leave their marriages, but they did nothing to rectify the causes of marital discord.

Marriage in early Pennsylvania really was an "open question," with people wanting both to get into it and to get out of it. By examining unhappy marriages, we can learn more about marital expectations and how marriage worked during this time. For some, the bonds of matrimony linked two hearts in an affectionate union. For others, the same bonds became as weighty and confining as iron chains—from which they sought escape. We start with those who attempted divorce.

CHAPTER I

Dissolving Matrimonial Bonds: Divorce in the New Republic

But for what end was unhappy matrimony instituted or compelled to be born, when there is an easy remedy always at hand, and not denied to the meanest slave, that of changing his or her master?
"AN ESSAY ON MARRIAGE OR THE LAWFULNESS OF DIVORCE," ANON., 1788

In a divorce petition dated September 8, 1794, Elizabeth Sutter of Philadelphia charged her husband, James, with cruelty. She and James had been married for about twenty years, and, as Elizabeth related in her petition, he had treated her in an "affectionate manner" for most of that time. During the three years preceding her application for divorce, however, James had given himself up to "the intemperate use of spiritous Liquors," abandoning her and their two children, neglecting to provide for them, and treating her badly.

In 1794, Elizabeth reached a level of desperation due to the "abusive and insolent Behaviour" James inflicted upon her elderly mother, with whom Elizabeth and her children lived. Elizabeth stated that James frequently came to her mother's house "under pretext" of visiting his family. During his visits, his abusive language and threatening acts had often forced her mother to call for a justice of the peace. Although James was under a court order to preserve the peace with his wife, he continued his visits to his mother-in-law's house. As Elizabeth's mother became unwilling to tolerate James's behavior, Elizabeth feared that she and the children would be left without a home if James continued to make his disruptive calls. It was this situation that provoked her into asking for a divorce from bed and board with alimony.[1]

Three days after Elizabeth filed her petition, James received a notice from her attorney. The counselor observed that a deposition would be taken from Elizabeth's mother, Elizabeth Whitton, the following Saturday afternoon, and asked James to attend with "any Attorney you see fit to employ" in order to cross-examine the witness. Nevertheless, he made clear that if James did not attend, Elizabeth Whitton would still be questioned. As no depositions are extant in the court records of this case, it is not known whether James did attend, or even if Elizabeth Whitton was examined. The following April, however, James received a court order to file an answer within four days or the court would proceed to hear his wife's allegations *ex parte*.[2]

Unlike most defendants, James chose to answer the charges. In his defense, he denied abusing Elizabeth or her mother except when his mother-in-law barred the doors of the house, thus preventing him from "visiting his Wife and Children to whom he was attached by the Ties of Nature," and causing in him "a natural warmth of temper." Responding to Elizabeth's other charges, James argued that he had provided for them, and that he had vouchers proving that he had bought furniture and had had house repairs made. After Elizabeth filed the original charges, he went to sea, where he "had the Misfortune to be cast away, and lose all his Property, except the Cloathing [*sic*] upon him." Ever since his return he felt that they had treated him "with uncommon Indifference and Contemp." In addition, he believed that they were provided for sufficiently because Elizabeth's father had left his estate to Elizabeth's mother and Elizabeth for the terms of their natural lives. Declaring that his own losses were an act of God, and that he had committed no crime or impropriety, James asked for the libel to be dismissed. A year later, in April 1796, the case was abated by James's death without a decision having been reached.[3]

The Sutters' case illustrates the process of divorce in Pennsylvania. Marked by stages of marital dissatisfaction, economic worries, and family concerns and interference, it is typical in many ways of the divorce cases that came before the Supreme Court between 1785 and 1815. The majority of suits were filed by women on grounds of cruelty; and, as in the Sutter's situation, economic concerns were often of primary importance. Yet, couples often disputed the facts of the situation. In James' view, his wife had no monetary wants, while he was the innocent victim of circumstances beyond his control and plagued by a mother-in-law who kept him from visiting his family. Although not every case stated it as clearly as the Sutters', it is typical that husband and wife fought a battle in the courts to be believed. Bolstered by detailed petitions, and sometimes by even more elaborate accounts from witnesses, they paraded the outrages committed by their spouses before the judges.

There are several reasons why men and women intent upon ending their marriages went through the long and involved process of obtaining a divorce. A divorce from the bonds of matrimony ended a marriage and allowed both men and women to remarry legally. It also provided a way of settling economic problems. In addition to being able to remarry, a husband who divorced his wife no longer had to provide for her, although this changed with later alimony laws. For a woman, the availability of divorce was even more important. If granted an absolute divorce, she became a feme sole able to transact business as a single woman, or she could remarry. If granted a divorce from bed and board (essentially a legal separation), she could not remarry, but, under the Pennsylvania divorce law of 1785, she was permitted to apply for alimony. For some women the knowledge that they were to receive a regular income from their husbands was more important than being legally clear of them and without assistance. Moreover, because a divorce from bed and board did not dissolve the bonds of matrimony, she could still inherit as her husband's widow if she outlived him. For both men and women, a divorce from the bonds of matrimony permitted a clean break from an unpleasant situation. Not only was this important for economic purposes, but it was also significant for emotional reasons, as well. Many men and women probably felt a sense of relief at being free and clear of an unhappy marriage. Pennsylvania laws permitted a wider range of options for divorce than

The Seven Stages of Matrimony. Opposing the tenets of domesticity, this 1830s print is aimed at men. Although it appears from this depiction that all marriages ended in divorce, it does illustrate the process leading to divorce. Most unhappy couples fell in love, then quarreled after the realities of marriage—a crying baby, not enough money—clashed with their expectations. *American Antiquarian Society.*

did other states, many of which authorized only one type of divorce or none at all.

Just as Americans were trying to come to terms with two opposing sets of marital ideals: one set representing an older, patriarchal tradition, and a later and evolving set stressing love and companionate marriage, the law was affected by and reacted to these two competing norms. Pennsylvania's divorce law of 1785 incorporated new ideas about the meaning and purpose of marriage, while retaining its traditional aspects. Although more generous than the laws of other states, the law limited the grounds for absolute divorce to adultery, bigamy, desertion, impotence, and the false rumor of death of one's spouse, and for bed and board divorces to cruel and barbarous treatment. Because of this, the husband or wife wanting the divorce had to prove that he or she was the innocent victim of a spouse who was guilty of one of these outrages. The absence of love between husband and wife was not enough to legally end a marriage anywhere in the United States, but in Pennsylvania the timing and wording of the divorce law and the testimony of petitioners and witnesses indicates that the flaunting of new societal beliefs about marriage by one spouse could aid the other in lawfully quitting the relationship.

In this transitional period, the new law gave some women and men who were influenced by more modern ideas about marriage a way to leave their marriages. Women, in particular, benefited from the passage of the law, and women's petitions for divorce far outnumbered those by men. Yet for most couples divorce remained a last resort, attempted only after conditions became intolerable and reconciliation impossible. Although it became easier over time to divorce, the process involved expenses and complications that prevented many unhappily married individuals from trying to obtain one. At the same time, many more unhappily married people used the older and traditional means of quitting marriages through desertion or quasi-legal separations, or attempted to seek help through families, friends, or the criminal courts.

Although Pennsylvania had no clear policy on divorce until the passage of its 1785 Divorce Act, divorces were granted before that time.

Prior to the act, Pennsylvania followed some English laws and practices, such as in the grounds for divorces and in the granting of divorces through petition to the legislature. In other ways, however, Pennsylvania departed from English precedents. For instance, there were no ecclesiastical courts, and Pennsylvania granted more divorces to its citizens than did England. Divorce, while possible in England, was neither very easy nor very common.

England granted few divorces in the seventeenth and eighteenth centuries, and those only through the ecclesiastical courts or by an act of Parliament. A total divorce from the bonds of matrimony (*divortium a vinculo matrimonii*) could be granted only if the marriage was declared null to begin with because of sexual incapacity, bigamy, or consanguinity. A partial bed and board divorce (*divortium a mensa et thoro*), which did not allow remarriage, could be granted for adultery, cruelty, or desertion. Parliamentary divorces allowing remarriage did not became available until the late seventeenth century, and then only for men. According to Parliament, a husband's adultery was not sufficient grounds for divorce, although a wife's unfaithfulness was. The law was designed to protect the property rights of the English nobility by preventing unfaithful wives from passing off the offspring of another man as their husbands' heirs. Thus, only the upper classes could afford this expensive procedure, which involved the petitioner first receiving a divorce *a mensa thoro* from the ecclesiastical courts. Although civil courts would accept the testimony of one witness, if no more could be obtained, the ecclesiastical courts always demanded two witnesses. Divorces were not granted to women until 1801. These factors limited the number of divorces granted in England.[4]

Puritan thought, however, developed a strong defense for divorce for both men and women that never appeared in English statutes. In seeking to cleanse the church, Puritans opposed the abuses of the ecclesiastical courts and the canon laws. The process of cleansing the church of these abuses included the reform of divorce procedures. At the same time, divorce was also defended for its own sake, and as a means of maintaining orderly homes and communities. John Milton, for instance, called divorce a "law of moral equity." He believed that in the restraint of divorce one "may see how hurtful and distractive it is to the house, the church, and the commonwealth." In addition to adultery, Milton thought that cruelty, idolatry, "headstrong behavior," and desertion were valid reasons for divorce.[5]

In the American colonies, the settlers of New England developed a new system of divorce, which was outside the jurisdiction of the church. Here divorce was a civil procedure, as, too, was marriage. In Massachusetts, the governor and his Council reviewed divorce proceedings between 1692 and 1786. In 1786, jurisdiction moved to the Supreme Judicial Court held in each county. Prior to the changes made in 1786, grounds for annulment included consanguinity and bigamy; grounds for dissolvement included long-term desertion and adultery with or without desertion, neglect or cruelty.[6]

In Connecticut, grounds for divorce were even more liberal, as defined in a 1667 statute. Besides adultery and fraudulent contract, petitioners had only to prove desertion of three years time. Divorces were also easier to obtain there because they went before the Superior Court, which was held twice yearly in each county. In contrast, southern states did not allow absolute divorces. Virginia courts were not authorized to grant bed and board divorces until 1827, and were not authorized to grant complete divorces until 1848. In South Carolina, no divorces of any kind were granted until 1868.[7]

The regulation of marriage and divorce occurred early in Pennsylvania laws. Here, as in New England, marriage was considered a civil contract, although the law permitted the tradition of marrying before a clergyman to continue. Within William Penn's Great Law of 1682 was a statute permitting divorce for the injured husband or wife upon his or her spouse's conviction of adultery. A subsequent act passed in 1700 permitted divorces in cases of sodomy, bestiality, and bigamy. Under the terms of this statute, a married man who committed sodomy or bestiality was to be castrated; the punishment for bigamy was life imprisonment at hard labor. These statutes, however, were overturned by the Queen and Parliament because of their cruelty and divergence from English law. New statutes, passed in 1705, permitted divorce from the bonds of matrimony only in cases of consanguinity, but they did allow divorce from bed and board for the injured spouse in cases of adultery, sodomy or buggery, and bigamy. Punishment of the convicted spouse entailed whipping and either fines or imprison-

ment. In order to be eligible for a divorce, application to the governor
and Assembly had to be made within one year of the husband's or
wife's conviction.[8]

These divorce options may have been intended as economic measures to protect wives, or they may have been intended to protect
communities from having to support deserted or betrayed wives, since
remarriage was not allowed except in cases of consanguinity.[9] Apparently Pennsylvania lawmakers believed that the injured husbands could
fend for themselves, but upheld the patriarchal view of them as heads
of the household who were responsible for maintaining their wives
and families. In a bed and board divorce, the wife could receive alimony, and upon the death of her husband inherit as his widow. Support payments would come from the sale of property and goods by
authorities for the wife's maintenance, as an imprisoned husband would
not be earning money by his labor. With a divorce from the bonds of
matrimony, there was neither alimony for the wife nor inheritance as
the widow because the divorce nullified the marriage, as if it had never
existed.[10]

Although these statutes empowered the governor to grant divorces,
they neglected to prescribe the necessary procedures. The earliest example of an attempted divorce is Anna Maria Boehm Miller's unsuccessful plea to Lieutenant Governor Patrick Gordon and the Court of
Chancery in 1728. She did not use the word divorce, but she did ask
to "be relieved from her unhappy Marriage."[11]

There do not appear to have been any divorce attempts between
the Boehm case in 1728 and 1766. Between 1766 and 1773, five husbands filed private bills for divorce in the Assembly. The friends and
relatives of the widow, Rebecca Vanakin, whom they called insane,
also made an unsuccessful attempt to have what they considered a
fraudulent marriage dissolved. Rebecca's supporters accused two relatives of John Martin, "almost an Idiot," of arranging the marriage in
order to obtain control over her money. Of the other five bills, only
two were granted.[12]

One of these unsuccessful divorce attempts reveals the plight of
husbands who could only obtain bed and board divorces under the
colony's laws. John Goggin submitted a petition to the House asking
for a divorce in 1766. He stated that his wife, Catherine O'Brien, had

an "extravagent Fondness for strong Liquors," led a dissolute life, and had run him into debt—making life with her intolerable to him. After he made some sort of written agreement with her in which she promised not to make any further claims on him and he gave her a sum of money, he went to sea. On his return, about fourteen months later, he found she had given birth to a bastard child. Making him responsible for the support of his wife and the child, the Overseers of the Poor put an attachment on him. "To avoid Contention," he paid, and then again went off to sea. Following this episode, Catherine "became a Prostitute to Negroes" and gave birth to a mulatto child. When Goggin returned, he was made to pay the costs of the birth. Goggin stated that under the current laws, he could only receive a bed and board divorce from the governor for his wife's adultery, but that his wife would then remain "at Liberty to sue for Alimony or Support." Under the circumstances, he asked that the House pass a law in his favor granting him a divorce from the bonds of matrimony, and not just a divorce from bed and board.[13]

Only one side of the story is represented because the records do not contain depositions of either Catherine or of witnesses. In addition, there are no comments by legislators on why the divorce was not granted. However, three years later, another petitioner, Curtis Grubb, did secure a divorce. Grubb was an iron master from Lancaster, who asked for a divorce from his wife, Ann Few, after she had "been delivered of a Bastard child" and married Archibald McNeal in 1763. Grubb had not cohabited with his wife since 1756. The Assembly granted Grubb the divorce with permission to remarry, and the bill was then signed into law by John Penn. Perhaps the fact that Goggin left his wife—no matter how justified he may have been—then returned and paid his wife's lying-in expenses was a factor in his not receiving a divorce. In addition, if Goggin had received his total divorce, his then ex-wife would have become a public charge. On the other hand, Grubb's wife deserted him. Although she had also had a child by another man, that man was willing to support her, and so, in the thinking of the Assembly, she was not likely to become a burden to the community.[14] Again, this reasoning is in line with the economic and patriarchal concepts of marriage that remained in Pennsylvania laws even after the new divorce law was passed.

In the second successful plea, the Assembly granted George Keemle a divorce in 1772. Keemle was a barber from the City of Philadelphia whose wife, Elizabeth, had been convicted of adultery.[15] This conviction probably made it easier for the Assembly to approve the divorce. This time, however, after the Assembly sent the bill to the Board of Trade and Plantations, as was required, it was sent on to the Privy Council. Although the Board of Trade had questioned the Grubb bill at the time, it had been approved. This time, there was more fear that such an exercise of authority by a colonial assembly during those unsettled times could lead to other displays of power. England disallowed Keemle's divorce, and forbade governors of colonies to grant divorces. No divorces were granted in Pennsylvania then until after the Revolution.[16]

Prevented from divorcing, unhappily married individuals found other means to escape discordant marriages. In cases where a woman had been deserted or turned out of the house, she could apply to the courts to have her husband's goods seized or have him ordered to pay her alimony.[17] In other instances, couples made mutual agreements to separate and had legal papers drawn up, sometimes later seeking divorces. These legal separations occurred both before and after the passage of the divorce law. Meanwhile, other couples relied upon less formal methods of separation by taking long visits to family members, by moving in with parents, or deserting. Still others drank, attacked their spouses, or made the best of a bad situation.[18]

Between 1777 and 1785, Pennsylvania granted only eleven divorces, although the House heard thirty-five appeals. Twenty-three men applied for divorces, and nine were granted. Only two of twelve women succeeded in obtaining a divorce. In the twenty-four instances where grounds for the divorce were stated, all but two listed adultery as the primary complaint, and all were granted from the bonds of matrimony. The two cases that did not cite adultery were wives complaining that their husbands had deserted them. Neither women was granted a divorce, but as there was no law granting divorces in cases of desertion, it is difficult to see this as an example of sexual bias in the Assembly.

Most of the petitions are poorly detailed, stating only that the spouse had committed the "heinous sin" of adultery. A few were more specific. For example, not only did Catharine Summers' husband, Peter, commit adultery, but he also "boasted" of his crime. In another case, Giles Hicks, a captain in the Tenth Pennsylvania Regiment, stated that at the age of fifteen he was "seduced by the artifices of a certain Hester McDaniel . . . at the time a common prostitute." She then separated from him and lived "in open adultery with divers other men, by means where she became so diseased . . . as to be declared incurable after seven months in the Pennsylvania Hospital."[19]

The procedure for legislative divorce was lengthy and involved. Although a few applicants managed to obtain divorces in three or four months, most proceedings took between one and two years. First, the aggravated husband or wife had to be granted permission to bring in a bill of divorce. Then the Assembly read the bill, referred it to a committee, read it several times more, revised it, and debated it, before possibly enacting it as law. Sometimes the Assembly required the petitioner to advertise the proposed divorce in the newspapers. Not only did this require an expenditure of time and effort on the part of the claimant, it also occupied valuable Assembly opportunities. Feeling that too much attention was being spent on divorce legislation, the Assembly passed the Divorce Act in 1785.[20]

The passage of this act came at a period when writers were declaring the importance of marriage and the fact that they should be happy and affectionate unions. The only two magazines published in the American colonies in 1774 and 1775, *The Pennsylvania Magazine* and *The Royal American*, "extolled the joys of a good marriage even more than they magnified the horrors of a bad one."[21] Both magazines ran regular articles and essays on troubled marriages in which men and women were locked in unhappiness or suffered under "domestic tyranny." Marriages instead were supposed to be happy and affectionate unions. For as "The Old Bachelor" of Thomas Paine's *The Pennsylvania Magazine* noted, "I had rather be a solitary bachelor than a miserable married man."[22]

Many of the eighteenth-century essayists writing in these magazines, as well as in newspapers and pamphlets, believed that an individual had a right to freedom and happiness in and of itself. This included rights within marriage. Historians have noted the ties eighteenth-century essayists drew between Revolutionary freedoms and domestic ones. In some cases, the demand for freedom from unhappy marriages took on a decidedly Revolutionary cast. The individual's right to freedom from domestic tyranny mirrored the colonies' right to freedom from the tyranny of England. As the anonymous author of "An Essay on Marriage or the Lawfulness of Divorce" declared:

America has been famous for her love of liberty, and hatred of tyranny of every kind; She has not only by arms expelled her foreign foes, but generously extended her liberality, in a great measure, even unto the African slave. Therefore, it is hoped, the same spirit of indulgence will extend still further —to those unhappy individuals, mixed among every class of mankind, who are frequently united together in the worst of bondage to each other.[23]

Throughout this time period, beliefs about marital and family relations were evolving. Many historians believe that changes in family life intensified in the second half of the eighteenth century. Some scholars view these transformations as part of an overall revolution against patriarchy, affecting both the American family and the culture of the eighteenth century.[24] Others note that a new trend toward "companionate" marriage beginning in the eighteenth century led to rising expectations and accompanying disappointments when those expectations were not met. This led to a new emphasis on marriage being not just a civil contract, but also a private compact based on the consent of both parties.[25] In Pennsylvania, the desire men and women felt for marital happiness and freedom from "tyrannical" marriages resulted from a combination of these tendencies. Variations in marital expectations began before the time of the Revolution, but escalated around mid-century as men and women espoused the idea that marriage should be the joining of two loving partners. At the same time, the passage of laws in Pennsylvania made leaving unhappy unions somewhat easier.[26]

In Pennsylvania, divorce law became a part of the new state's republican reforms. Yet the new divorce law continued to display patriarchal characteristics. For instance, it required a woman to have a "next friend" (usually a male relative) act on her behalf in submitting the divorce petition because she was a feme covert. On the other hand, men still had to support wives granted divorces from bed and board, if they applied for alimony. This provision, however, often benefited women who would have found it difficult otherwise to maintain themselves and their families in a society where women and men were not equal, despite the new emphasis on the mutual interests of wives and husbands. Revolutionary rhetoric combined with new marital expectations led to changes, while patriarchy, in the form of alimony and certain legal conventions continued.

Only in Pennsylvania was divorce part of republican changes in government. Other states, such as South Carolina, heard impassioned pleas for divorce, but to no avail. The passage of the divorce law may have been easier in Pennsylvania because, unlike South Carolina and the rest of the South, there was a history of divorce in the state. Apparently Pennsylvania legislators agreed on the need for such a law, which clearly outlined the grounds for divorce, allowing the law to pass with little debate.[27]

Those who sought divorces in Pennsylvania found them easier to obtain after the passage of the 1785 act. This law authorized the Supreme Court of Pennsylvania to grant divorces (although it was still possible to receive one by legislative act), and, more important, spelled out the grounds necessary for divorce and the procedures to be followed in obtaining one. Following its passage, divorces in Pennsylvania increased significantly, with women's petitions far outnumbering men's.[28]

Although much of the language in the new law came directly from Boyd's *Judicial Proceedings in Scotland*, published in 1779, the law was a product of republican reforms introduced in the state after the Revolution. Its language reflects the reformers' nod to republican ideology and what they felt were the functions of a "well regulated society." In this well-regulated society, virtuous citizens were entitled to relief, if they were harmed or unable to care for themselves. Couples could not divorce merely because they wanted to marry another person; one person had to be the injured party and the other had to have violated his or her vows. In the wording of the law, divorce was not to be "made out of levity or collusion."[29]

The 1785 act did not promote equality between the sexes. Husbands and wives had specific duties, and the lawmakers' views on this can be seen in the law. For example, they believed that it was the husband's duty to provide financial support for his wife if he abandoned her or so mistreated her that she was forced to leave him. Thus, they permitted women to apply for alimony in these situations. Men, however, could not apply for alimony under any circumstances because it was not a wife's obligation to support her husband.

In addition, the law was stricter for women in cases of adultery. A woman who was divorced for adultery and then lived with the man with whom she had committed the adultery could not make deeds, wills, appointments, or conveyances; her lands or tenements would descend as if she had died intestate. How often this provision was enforced is questionable, but there was no such stipulation in the law for husbands who committed adultery. Under the divorce law, adulterers of either gender, however, were not to marry their lovers after the divorce.[30]

Nevertheless, the passage and wording of the 1785 act indicates that members of the Pennsylvania Assembly espoused the current beliefs about marriage, as well as the roles of wives and husbands. Marriage was supposed to be a lifelong union based upon mutual affection between husbands and wives. It was a compact made between two individuals, but it was more than that. It was also a contract over which the law and public officials maintained control in order to regulate society.[31] Husbands provided economic support and wives moral stability. Couples were supposed to discuss their differences and work them out. Loss of love, therefore, was not enough to obtain a divorce, presumably, the partners could always try harder. However, if one spouse injured the other by neglecting his or her duties or sufficiently violated the marriage vows so that they could not live together, then lawmakers believed the innocent partner should be granted a divorce.

Despite the gender differences in the law, the intent of the legislators seems clear—they were granting men and women freedom from marriages that caused them moral or physical harm or in which they were unable to cohabit as a married couple due to desertion or sexual incapability. They were not, however, condoning moral laxity or licentious behavior.[32] Marriage between virtuous citizens was a key aspect of the well-regulated society.

Citizens of Pennsylvania also understood the importance of the well-regulated and virtuous society. One petitioner, Eve Page, stated these views in her 1801 divorce plea. She claimed that her husband, Robert, had committed adultery with numerous women. His conduct, she declared, was "so flagitious the object of the marriage contract is entirely defeated," bringing shame and scandal upon "that sacred ordinance" and upon her. She asked for a divorce "that the innicent [*sic*] victims of the baseness of the said Robert may find comfort and that an example may be made to deter others from offending in a manner so fatal to the order of society & the happiness of individuals."[33]

Besides adultery, the grounds for a total divorce were bigamy, desertion for more than four years, and impotence or inability to procreate at the time of the marriage. It was also possible to receive a divorce from bed and board for these causes. An additional clause added the grounds that if a man or woman remarried after a "well founded" rumor of the former spouse's death, he or she would not be liable for an adultery conviction if the rumor then proved to be false. In this instance, the former spouse could choose to have his or her husband or wife restored, or could seek a divorce. In addition to the above grounds for a complete divorce, a wife could receive a divorce from bed and board with alimony, if her husband abandoned her, turned her out of the house, endangered her life "by cruel and barbarous treatment," or offered "such indignities as to render her condition intolerable, or life burdensome," and thereby forcing her to leave him.[34]

Besides stating the grounds for divorce, the law outlined the procedure to be followed. First the plaintiff, either the husband "in his own proper person," or the wife by her next friend, exhibited his or her petition to the justices of the Supreme Court, at the same time attaching an affidavit swearing that the libel was not "made out of levity or by collusion" or by the desire merely to be free of the marriage. After that, the court issued a subpoena directing the defendant to appear before the court to answer the libel. A copy of the subpoena was left at the defendant's last residence at least fifteen days before the next court term. If the defendant did not appear, the court issued an alias subpoena. If he or she still could not be found, the sheriff of the county made a public proclamation on three market days at the court house. In addition, newspapers printed notices for four successive weeks. Either side could demand a trial by jury, and could appeal the decision to the High Court of Errors and Appeals (upon submitting a recognizance in a sum double the amount of the cost of the Supreme Court decision). Finally, the petitioner had to be a resident of the state, and to have resided in the state for at least one year prior to filing the libel.[35]

Yet one letter suggests that applying for a divorce involved politicking, as well as following the outlined procedure. In 1789, Robert Whitehill, an assemblyman in western Pennsylvania wrote a letter to George Bryan, a Pennsylvania Supreme Court Justice. After discussing other matters, he wrote that the bearer of this letter, Patrick Dickson, was man of "upright character" from his neighborhood, who was seeking a divorce. Whitehill concluded "how for you with the other honorable Justices of the Supreme Court may give relief, you can best judge. I have written to [Chief Justice] Mr. McKean and given a general character of Dickson." Despite his introduction to the judges, however, Patrick Dickson's name does not appear in the Supreme Court divorce records.[36]

Only two people submitted libels in the remaining three months of 1785. The next year, nine persons filed for divorce. After that the rate remained fairly steady until 1795, when the number of libels submitted jumped to nineteen. The frequency of petitions peaked in 1801 at thirty-one, dropping to fourteen in 1804, twelve in 1805, and one in 1806. In 1804, a revision in the law permitted petitioners to submit their petitions to their local common pleas court. This helps account for the decrease in Supreme Court divorces after that year, because people could travel more easily to the common pleas court held in the county of their residence instead of having to travel to Philadelphia in order to go to the Supreme Court.

The 1785 Divorce Act and subsequent early nineteenth-century revisions did not include provisions for the custody of children involved in the cases. The only mention of children in the law is the declaration that those born during the time of the marriage were not declared illegitimate by the divorce. When children were mentioned in divorce cases, it was usually by wives trying to prove that their husbands did not support their families. Wives also indicated the difficulties involved in trying to sustain themselves while attempting to feed, clothe, and educate their young children. Young children never testified in the divorce cases, although occasionally, older teenagers and adult off-spring did.

Laws on child custody in Pennsylvania were not passed until the late nineteenth century. Prior to that time, the courts ruled on a case-by-case basis. Under the common law, fathers had the right to custody of their children, but this right was not always guaranteed in Pennsylvania. Sometimes custody was determined by default—men who deserted their wives rarely took their children with them, although women who left their husbands due to ill treatment often did take their children, especially infants and young girls and boys.

The earliest reported case in Pennsylvania regarding the subject is *Commonwealth v. Addicks* (1813). In this case, the wife gained custody of the two children, daughters aged ten and seven, on the grounds that young children needed to be with their mother. The court rendered this opinion even though the father had divorced the mother due to her adultery. Although the mother then married the man with whom she had been unfaithful, it does not seem to have influenced the court—at this point. Three years later, however, the father was given custody of the children. It was felt that, by this time, the older could be harmed by exposure to bad morals. Rather than separate the two children, custody of both was given to the father.[37]

Pennsylvania was the first state to include a provision for granting divorces from bed and board on grounds of cruelty. In 1817, the law was changed to allow women to choose between a bed and board divorce or an absolute divorce when suing abusive husbands.[38] Massachusetts did not include spouse abuse as a reason for a court divorce until the passage of its new divorce law in 1786, when it permitted women to obtain bed and board divorces on the basis of cruelty. Connecticut did not allow divorces for cruelty until 1843. Between 1785 and 1815, Pennsylvania wives who pleaded for divorces before the Supreme Court cited cruelty more than any other reason.[39]

Women applied for 236 (64%) out of the 367 cases filed between 1785 and 1815; the court granted 114 (48%) of their petitions. Women most often sued for divorce citing cruel and barbarous treatment from their husbands (see Table 1). Yet, of the seventy-five cases filed by women under this plea, only twenty-three (31%) were granted. The

TABLE I

Divorce Cases Filed by Women before the Supreme Court, 1785–1815

Grounds	Total (M/W)	Number and Percent of Total Filed by Women		Number and Percent Granted	
Adultery	127	43	34%	26	60%
Cruelty	76	75	99%	23	31%
Bigamy	8	6	75%	3	50%
Desertion	75	54	72%	34	63%
Impotence	3	3	100%	0	Na
False Rumor	1	0	Na	Na	Na
Adultery/Bigamy	4	2	50%	1	50%
Adultery/Cruelty	12	12	100%	6	50%
Adultery/Desertion	32	16	50%	8	50%
Bigamy/Cruelty	1	1	100%	0	Na
Bigamy/Desertion	9	6	67%	3	50%
Cruelty/Desertion	14	14	100%	10	71%
Unknown	5	4	80%	Na	Na
Totals	367	236	64%	114	48%

result of the court was not noted in all cases, but in these instances, they were probably not granted.[40]

The number of cases filed under the complaint of cruelty indicates that many women were unwilling to endure abusive treatment from their husbands. Wife abuse occurred throughout the time period, as other records such as newspapers, almshouse entries, and court documents show. The statements of both the women and their witnesses reveal husbands who treated them cruelly and sometimes violently. Although some women had their husbands arrested, this was not a very effective method of stopping the abuse, since husbands were not usually confined for long. The chance of obtaining alimony might have given abused wives a definite incentive to attempt divorce, instead of deserting or enduring a violent situation. The low rate of favorable decisions for divorces on these grounds suggests that it was more difficult to prove "wilful and malicious" cruelty than either adultery, bigamy, or desertion. A woman with other options would probably choose to exercise them, unless she either had actually suffered abuse, or desperately wanted to obtain the alimony.[41]

The clause permitting divorces on cruelty grounds applied only to women. Nevertheless, these were the grounds cited by Alexander McArthur in his petition. The McArthurs originally came from Ireland. Alexander emigrated to Philadelphia with the hope of making a more prosperous living. After working as a cordwainer for twenty-one months, he felt that he had earned enough money to support his wife, and wrote asking her to join him. Soon after her arrival she "alienated her affections from him," destroyed his property, and injured his credit. He noted in particular, however, that Sarah struck him "with Sharp Forks" and threw "Bottles hammers and other dangerous weapons" at his head. His petition concluded with the formulaic phrase, usually seen only in women's petitions that her "cruel and barbarous" treatment had made "his condition intolerable and Life burthensome." Alexander did not win his divorce.[42]

Desertion was the next most often cited grounds by women. Women claimed desertion in fifty-four cases, and in thirty-four of them (63%) the court granted their pleas. Desertion probably was easier to prove than either cruelty or adultery, especially if the deserter did not live in the area. Since desertion had to have been for at least four years, it was probably not difficult to find witnesses able to testify that husband or wife had been alone for at least that period of time, especially if the defendant had moved far away. In many cases, family members and friends were called upon to help the deserted spouse with economic and emotional support, and in these cases would certainly know if the couple were cohabiting together. If the deserter still lived within the same community as the libellant, matters could be more complicated. In this event, the libellant had to prove that he or she did not cohabit with the spouse at all within the four years preceding the divorce attempt, despite having seen the defendant, and perhaps having conversed or had other contact with him or her.

For men, desertion was the second most cited grounds (see Table 2). Out of the 131 cases they filed, twenty-one cases were for desertion, but the court granted only seven (33%). Because women were often left in much more precarious circumstances when their spouses

TABLE 2
Divorce Cases Filed by Men before the Supreme Court, 1785–1815

Grounds	Total (M/W)	Number and Percent of Total Filed by Men		Number and Percent Granted	
Adultery	127	84	66%	44	52%
Cruelty	76	1	1%	0	Na
Bigamy	8	2	25%	1	50%
Desertion	75	21	28%	7	33%
Impotence	3	0	Na	Na	Na
False Rumor	1	1	100%	1	100%
Adultery/Bigamy	4	2	50%	0	0
Adultery/Cruelty	12	Na	Na	Na	Na
Adultery/Desertion	32	16	50%	8	50%
Bigamy/Cruelty	Na	Na	Na	Na	Na
Bigamy/Desertion	9	3	33%	2	67%
Cruelty/Desertion	14	Na	Na	Na	Na
Unknown	5	1	20%	Na	Na
Totals	367	131	36%	63	48%

left, they were probably more successful in obtaining divorces on these claims. For both sexes, desertion was probably the easiest way to leave an unhappy or tiresome situation, although it was easier for men than it was for women.[43]

Women and men differed in the frequency of claiming adultery. Men overwhelmingly cited adultery as grounds for divorce in the Supreme Court cases, filing eighty-four (66%) on these grounds, of which forty-four (52%) were granted. William Keith won divorces from two wives on grounds of adultery within five years. On the other hand, women only cited adultery in forty-three cases (34%), but twenty-six (60%) were granted. Because men traditionally sought divorces or separations after their wives were unfaithful, but women did not, this pattern probably persisted in the first years after the passage of the 1785 law. Nevertheless, although the wording of the law expresses a sexual bias in adultery cases, men and women who filed for divorce on grounds of adultery seemed to have been treated equally by the court, judging by the proportions granted.[44]

In cases of adultery, there had to be proof of the actual crime, although this proof ranged from court convictions to circumstantial evidence. According to the law, conviction on a charge of adultery was admissible as evidence, but it was not necessary. In cases where a conviction of adultery was admitted as evidence, a transcript from the court of Quarter Sessions was affixed to the court papers. For example, Catharine Wright deserted her husband, Joseph, in August 1785. While living apart from him, she had a child, and was convicted of adultery in the Court of Quarter Sessions of Dauphin County in May 1788. That same month, Joseph filed for divorce, citing his wife's conviction. The conviction worked to Joseph's advantage—he would have been unable to divorce her for desertion for another year.[45]

In other cases, where the spouse was not convicted of adultery in court, eyewitnesses described seeing the husband or wife in sexual acts or compromising positions with members of the opposite sex. Sometimes, men were described as being seen in the company of prostitutes, or women were described as being prostitutes. A witness for Catherine Pemble testified that he saw the stained and still damp "linnen" of her husband, David, after he had been with a "lewd girl" in a house of ill fame as proof that David had committed adultery. Under the law, however, divorces for adultery would not be granted if the defendant could prove the plaintiff also committed adultery, if a man knew of a wife's adultery and resumed or continued marital relations with her (no mention is made of a woman's knowing of her husband's extramarital affairs), if a man allowed his wife to be a prostitute or received money from her hire, or if he had exposed his wife to "lewd company" so that she "became ensnared to the crime."[46]

Unlike adultery, divorce for "false rumor" was not a traditional basis for divorce, and only one person applied for a divorce for that reason. The case concerned Thomas and Elizabeth Kyle. The Kyles married on March 8, 1783. They lived together in Washington Township in Fayette County until December 16, 1796, and had seven children. On this date, Thomas left Elizabeth with "Intent as he said to go over the Mountains to the Eastern part of Pennsylvania." Elizabeth never received word from him, but she did receive what she felt was a reliable report of his death. She and her neighbors believed the report to be true—so much so that she was granted Letters of Administration, and plans for the deposition of his estate were made. Elizabeth noted that these measures were undertaken by the advice of the most respectable people in the county. On February 2, 1797, she married John Jones, and subsequently had two children by him. Elizabeth revealed her astonishment and despair upon Kyle's return home:

The particular day on which Thomas Kyle returned I do not recollect but believe it was before Christmas in the year 1799. his return was to me & to the whole Neighborhood as astonishing as would be the resurrection of the dead. the fact is however that he is alive and now at his [illeg] home. But after the Testamony I had received of his death and after the universal belief entertained by the whole country that he was no more altho I must forever lament the the misfortune which has befallen me, yet I cannot condemn myself for [illeg], nor blame Mr. Kyle for pursuing as he now does the legal course for dissolving that sacred connexion which has subsisted between us.[47]

The problems of distance and communication affected the legal process in other ways as well. Apparently some defendants did not receive the subpoenas, or subsequently issued alias subpoenas. Although notices of the divorce action were placed in newspapers to alert defendants in this event, there were still some problems. William Sheaver did not get his subpoena in time for the court case. He wrote the court that one subpoena he received on the twenty-fourth of September was for court on that very day. He asked that the court be held in Washington County, where he would be able to present his evidence because he claimed that the expense made travel to Philadelphia impossible for him. The case was discontinued, so perhaps his wife returned to him as he requested in his petition, or perhaps she also felt the expenses involved in pursuing the case were too high.[48]

In other cases, too, traveling to court and paying expenses presented a problem. John Crawford complained that he could not get to court—because he was in prison for counterfeiting. Since he did not have funds for counsel, he asked that the court be delayed until the following session. In addition, he noted that his wife, Ann, really did not want a divorce. According to John, in his absence, Ann had been persuaded by her "pretended friends" to divorce him in order to marry a richer man. They hoped then to benefit through the connection.

The court did award Ann a divorce in 1803 on the grounds of her husband's adultery.[49]

The expenses of travel not only affected the couple involved in the divorce, but also witnesses in the trial. In one case, the witnesses, who lived in Erie County, in western Pennsylvania, complained about having to travel without compensation. The commissioners, men appointed to take the witnesses' depositions, promised to try to get the witnesses repaid, if possible. They then requested in a letter to Charles Smith, the lawyer, that he attend to it. The outcome is unknown.[50]

Some men and women were probably prevented from pursuing a divorce because of the necessity of retaining an attorney. Yet, in some instances, lawyers could be almost an obstacle to justice. There were lawyers who did not consider their clients and divorce cases of great importance. In one example, the above mentioned lawyer, Charles Smith, wrote a letter to Edward Burd, Prothonotary of the Supreme Court, in which his legal work appears to be almost an afterthought:

Having so much running about when in the city, I became so much fatigued & exhausted that I was prevented from calling for the *alias subpona* [sic] in Thompson v Thompson & the Commission which I directed to be made out. I now beg to trouble you to forward them to me by *Post*—as the time is fast running by. . . . Below you have the interrogatories—you will please to fill up the Christian Names, as I have forgot them—the subpoena is not yet paid for, but I will send down the whole together by Mr. Yeats or sooner if you desire it . . . please to endorse the Whole sum due to you.[51]

Respondents did not usually reply to the subpoena; most divorces were uncontested. Those who did respond usually denied guilt, as James Sutter did. In some cases, however, the defendants admitted guilt. James Miller, a yeoman from Northumberland County, acknowledged that all the facts in his wife's libel were true; Bartholemew Corvaisier also admitted his adultery and "that he hath violated the duties of the marriage state," in an answer to the court. When Jacob Engleman sued for divorce, the confession of his wife, Magdelen, to her adultery was attached to the court papers.[52]

Occasionally, couples tried to divorce each other. John Lesher filed court papers in 1786, charging his wife, Margaret, with adultery, and stating that she was named as a respondent in an adultery case in Berks County. His wife denied her guilt, but claimed that John had been unfaithful. She then sued for divorce in 1787, accusing him of adultery, and noting that he had left her without any support or provisions. According to the petitions, the couple had been married twenty-three or twenty-four years, and had lived in harmony for twelve, before their troubles started. John died before the case could be decided.[53]

The information in the divorce papers gives us limited knowledge about the occupations and incomes of the litigants. Sometimes subpoenas indicated the occupation and area of residence of the defendants. In other examples, these things can be ascertained through remarks made by witnesses. Yet, many times a witness or female petitioner referred to the husband's occupation along with the notice that he was not successful in his endeavors. These categories then *might* indicate class, but not income, and may not indicate either for wives.

One hundred twenty-five mens' occupations can be identified from the 367 petitions (see Table 3). Thirty-six men were yeomen or farmers, with another five classified as farmer or yeomen combinations (i.e., yeoman-tavernkeeper, farmer-miller). Five men considered themselves gentlemen and five were merchants, probably members of the upper class. There were a number of cordwainers, storekeepers, and house carpenters, a French master, a sculptor, an assortment of craftsmen and artisans, all of whom would have been in the middling bracket. The four laborers and two carters were of the lower sort. In addition, there were fourteen in seafaring occupations. Most of them would be mariners, members of the lower sort, but some of them might have been captains, and thus in the middling group. This limited information suggests that those involved in divorces—both the libellants and defendants—came from a wide range of social classes and income levels. Divorce was not confined to the wealthiest. In fact, most of those involved in divorce cases were probably in the "middling" range.[54]

This information is based upon men's occupations only. Although some women worked outside the home, or took in additional work, such as laundry and sewing, these were not jobs that paid very well. In addition, even women who came from middling backgrounds could be left destitute if their husbands deserted them and they had no separate income of their own.

TABLE 3

Occupations of Men Grouped by Class

Class and Occupation	Number	Percent Listed
UPPER		13
Gentlemen	5	
Professional	6	
Merchants	5	
MIDDLE		38
Metal Crafts	3	
Woodcrafts	10	
Leather crafts	8	
Textile crafts	3	
Other crafts	4	
Shopkeepers/Innkeepers	8	
Clothing Producers	7	
White collar	3	
Army Officer	1	
LOWER		17
Carters, Coachmen, Laborers, Mariners	21	
UNSPECIFIED		33
Farmers, Yeomen	41	
Known Occupations	125	100
None Listed	242	
Total	367	34

In the same fashion, court papers sometimes indicated the area of residence, although the person filing may have filed in Philadelphia, for example, but originally have come from another area. For example, Jane Corvaisier came originally from Charleston, moved to the West Indies with her husband, and finally settled in Philadelphia. Others came from France and the West Indies. Some moved back and forth from Philadelphia to the surrounding Pennsylvania counties of Bucks, Chester, and Montgomery, and the counties of Gloucester, Salem, and Burlington, in New Jersey. In order to obtain a divorce, however, the petitioner had to have been a citizen of Pennsylvania, and had to have resided in the Commonwealth for one year prior to filing the complaint. Those divorce papers that note residence indicate that slightly over half of the Supreme Court petitioners came from the county of Philadelphia, although not necessarily the city itself. In reality, probably more filed from Philadelphia than from elsewhere in the state because the court was more accessible to them, and because those in frontier areas may not have felt the need to go through the legal formalities of divorce.

Although the petitions are not standardized forms, they usually include certain standard phrases, such as "wilfully and maliciously deserted" and "cruel and barbarous treatment." These formulaic expressions, taken directly from the statute conformed to the legal practice and spirit of the law. The wording of the petitions did not change over the 1785 to 1815 period, nor were there many differences in Chester County libels filed between 1804 and 1840.

There were, however, several changes in the divorce laws over this period. As noted above, after 1804 individuals could take their petitions to their local common pleas court. This 1804 law also established divorce from the bonds of matrimony for marriages within forbidden degrees of consanguinity or affinity. Since anyone seeking a divorce under this provision was also liable for prosecution under the law against incest, it is not surprising no records exist of anyone seeking a divorce under this provision.[55]

In 1815, additional changes were made in the divorce law. The term of desertion was changed from four years to two, as was the term for false rumor. Under the 1815 law, there was no provision for bed and board divorces; a divorce from the bonds of matrimony could be obtained on the grounds of cruelty. The other charges and stipulations remained the same as in the 1785 and 1804 laws. A further amendment to the law in 1817 permitted wives to choose divorce from bed and board or from the bonds of matrimony in cases of cruelty. However, on a libel for divorce *a vinculo* the court could not decree a divorce *a mensa et thoro*.[56]

The existence of unusually complete and available divorce records in Chester County allows historians to examine and compare divorces between 1804 and 1840 (or beyond) with the earlier Supreme Court cases. This offers scholars a chance to observe what changes, if any,

TABLE 4

Divorces Filed by Women before the Chester County Court of Common Pleas, 1804–1840

Grounds	Total (M/W)	Number and Percent of Total Filed by Women		Number and Percent Granted	
Adultery	12	7	58%	4	57%
Desertion	31	23	74%	16	70%
Cruelty	6	6	100%	3	50%
Adultery/Desertion	5	3	60%	1	33%
Cruelty/Adultery	1	1	100%	1	100%
Bigamy/Desertion	1	1	100%	1	100%
Adultery/Bigamy/ Desertion	2	1	50%	1	100%
Unknown	8	6	75%	3	50%
Totals	66	48	73%	30	63%

occurred in divorces over time within a rural area. By examining these divorces, it is possible to draw some observations about marital expectations, both among the couples involved and in society at large.

With the passage of the 1804 law, the Common Pleas Court of Chester County began to grant divorces. Once again, women filed most of the divorce cases before the Chester County Common Pleas Court. Most of them were requested on desertion grounds (see Table 4). Of the forty-eight cases filed by women between 1804 and 1840, twenty-three petitioners stated that their husbands had deserted them, and five cited desertion plus adultery, bigamy, or cruelty. Seven asked for divorces on accusations of adultery and six charged cruelty only. In six instances the extant papers did not indicate the reasons. For the most part, the Chester County women did not ask for bed and board divorces or alimony.

In contrast with the Supreme Court divorces, Chester County men also mostly accused their wives of desertion in their divorce pleas (see Table 5). Eighteen Chester County men filed for divorce between 1804

TABLE 5
Divorces Filed by Men before the Chester County Court of Common Pleas,
1804–1840

Grounds	Total (M/W)	Number and Percent of Total Filed by Men		Number and Percent Granted	
Adultery	12	5	42%	3	60%
Desertion	31	8	26%	6	75%
Adultery/Desertion	5	2	40%	2	100%
Adultery/Bigamy/ Desertion	2	1	50%	0	Na
Unknown	8	2	25%	1	50%
Totals	66	18	27%	12	67%

and 1840. In eight cases, they sued for divorces due to their wives' desertion. Three men asked for divorces on the grounds of desertion and adultery or bigamy. Another five cited adultery, and two were for unknown reasons.

Divorce petitions in Columbia County, in western Pennsylvania, followed similar trends. In these cases, women again outnumbered men in the number of petitions granted, and desertion similarly was the most commonly cited grounds for divorce for both sexes. Between 1814 and 1836, twenty-eight women and thirteen men filed for divorce there. Women petitioned on grounds of desertion in nineteen cases. Men in nine cases filed on grounds of desertion, although some of these cases involved adultery and bigamy as well.[57]

There are similarities between Pennsylvania divorces and those occurring in other times and places. Scholars studying eighteenth-century Connecticut, for instance, found desertion to be the most frequently cited reason for divorce. Others have discovered this to be the case in late nineteenth- and early twentieth-century California, as well. Finally, this was true also of Pennsylvania between 1867 and 1886. As well as being both the simplest and the traditional method of quitting a marriage, desertion was the easiest to prove in a divorce court. It is likely, too, that as travel methods improved, desertion may have become more tempting for an unhappy husband or wife.[58]

A realization that the court did not often grant divorces on the grounds of cruelty probably influenced the nineteenth-century Chester County women who filed for divorce. A comparison of women known to be from Chester County who petitioned for divorce before the Supreme Court to the Chester County women who pleaded before their Court of Common Pleas supports this hypothesis. Of the seven women known to be from Chester County who filed for divorce before the Supreme Court, four pleaded for divorces on the grounds of cruelty, one on grounds of desertion, and two on grounds of adultery. Although this is a small sample, in general, most women who applied to the Supreme Court accused their husbands of abuse (see Table 1). Nineteenth-century Chester County women were less likely to ask for a divorce on cruelty grounds. Only six out of forty-eight applied that charge, compared to twenty-three citing desertion. With the change in the law for desertion, making the wait only two years instead of four, combined with the greater chance of having the divorce granted, it seems reasonable that women would seek a divorce most often on desertion grounds. This does not mean that men and women did not commit adultery or acts of violence, but it is more likely that those pleading for divorces cited the grounds they thought would be most easily granted.[59]

That men would also try to win divorces by claiming desertion seems just as reasonable, as it was easier for them to prove desertion by their wives than adultery. Of the five Chester County men who filed before the Supreme Court, three sought divorces on the grounds of their wives' desertions, while two asked for divorces citing their wives' adultery. However, in two of the three desertion cases, the husbands claimed that their wives had committed adultery and bigamy as well. Many times, in both the Supreme Court petitions and in the Common Pleas cases, plaintiffs charged their spouses with several offenses.[60]

Despite the relative ease of obtaining divorces in the courts after passage of the 1785 law, however, Pennsylvania continued to grant legislative divorces until 1874, when the new Constitution prohibited

Petition of Ruhamah Evans, July 1823. This is the first divorce petition that Ruhamah Evans submitted. She filed a second libel in 1829. Both were dismissed. It is an unusual petition in that both times her "next friend" was a woman. Also unusual is that unlike most Chester County women, Evans filed for divorce on the grounds of cruel and barbarous treatment, and she described in detail her husband's violent behavior. *Chester County Archives, West Chester, Pa.*

the procedure. Between 1785 and 1874, Pennsylvania granted 291 legislative divorces. In most cases, these were for reasons not covered by statutory law, although some were granted on grounds of adultery, desertion, and cruelty.[61]

The legislature ruled in several cases that a woman did not have to live out her life with a criminal, even though this was not grounds for divorce under the law. Rebecca Adkinson, whose husband, Thomas, had escaped from the Fayette County Jail and then had been sentenced and convicted in Allegheny County to five years in the Philadelphia penitentiary, won a divorce from the bonds of matrimony in 1805. Although the legislature acknowledged that existing laws did not authorize the courts to grant her a divorce, it declared that "the conduct of the said Thomas . . . has been one continued scene of vice evincing a total dereliction of morality, and an entire neglect of his wife and tender infant," and enacted the bill of divorce.[62] Mary Dewees was granted a divorce from her husband, Thomas, after he was sent to prison for the second time in two and a half years. The 1804 act declared that "the unfortunate woman ought to be released from any connection with a character apparantly so irreclaimable." In 1810, the Assembly granted Mary Carmack a divorce after the court committed her husband to prison for four years for committing forgery.[63]

In other cases, the legislature legitimized the children born of second marriages by granting divorces to individuals who had "self-divorced." Jacob Sell of Adams County and his wife, Eve, made a mutual agreement to separate after she gave birth to a daughter five months after their marriage in 1777. Three years later, Jacob remarried, and had six living children by his second wife. He and his wife worked hard to acquire a large property, but he feared that Eve might have a claim to it. Being elderly and in declining health, he asked the legislature to distribute the property to his present wife and family. The legislature annulled his first marriage and legitimized the children of his second. In a similar case, Elizabeth De Franqueen Le Clerc was legally divorced and had the son of her second marriage legitimized in 1811. Elizabeth had felt herself free to remarry after her first husband, Philip J. G. De Franqueen, wrote her from Europe that he was not returning to her and that he considered their marriage ended.[64]

In still other cases, petitioners won divorces after they claimed traveling to court and paying court costs would present a hardship. In the case of John Vanlear, however, his not being a citizen of Pennsylvania would have prevented his divorce under the divorce laws. Vanlear, who was a citizen of Washington County, Maryland, was granted a divorce, as if he were a citizen of Pennsylvania. In another instance of legislatively granted divorce, Lewis Albertus won a divorce from the legislature from his wife, Zilla, claiming that she was insane. Her father, he noted, was willing to support her, and had consented to the divorce.[65]

Although nineteenth-century Chester County women and men requested divorces more often on the grounds of desertion rather than cruelty and adultery, in most respects, divorce petitions remained the same throughout the years examined here. Even the petitions submitted to the Governor and Assembly before the Divorce Act were very similar to those submitted later to the Supreme Court and the Common Pleas Courts. Language did not vary much in the petitions, although there was more emphasis on mutual love and affection in the later ones, in keeping with the spirit of the new divorce law and changes in marital expectations. However, throughout the period the petitioners' primary emphasis was on proving that their pleas for divorce fell under the grounds stated by law. Husbands and wives attempted to demonstrate that they had behaved properly, to show that they had not provoked their spouses' offenses, and that there was no collusion in trying to win a divorce. They then detailed the specific offense or offenses committed by their spouses.

Throughout, witnesses' testimonies remained of prime importance. Besides revealing interconnections of family and community, they uncover the actual family life of the litigants—whom they visited and slept with, how they supported themselves, whether they kept lodgers or servants, and how they coped with the discord in the marriage. In addition, witnesses revealed what they considered to be proper behavior on the part of husband and wife. Deponents in cases represented the plaintiffs as good husbands or wives because the husband supported his family and the wife took care of the house and did not provoke her husband's rages. In terms of the legal procedure, their reports were crucial, and could determine the outcome of the case. Neighborhood observers disclosed the litigants' conduct during the entirety of their married lives together, as well as demonstrating the knowledge that the couple was legally married. For many unhappily married people, both the words and deeds of bystanders helped to give them much needed support during and after the breakups of their marriages.

Men and women expressed dissatisfaction with their marriages both before and after the passage of the divorce law. What did change were the various options opened to unhappily married persons, especially in the divorce laws. Divorce in Pennsylvania was restructured as part of the state's republican reforms and tied to new beliefs about marriage and the family, even while the law maintained older patriarchal standards. Men and women continued to marry, seeking the marital bliss promised them by new ideals of behavior. But when those who were influenced by these evolving ideas about marital love found themselves at odds with their spouses, they were able now to make use of formal methods to end their marriages permanently instead of relying upon traditional means of "self-divorce" or less permanent actions, such as having their spouses arrested.

Women most frequently sought divorces because the law benefited them more than it did men. Although hampered by legal codes and customs that restricted their rights, married women nevertheless sought redress through the legal process. While making divorce easier, however, the law continued to legislate upon morality. Divorce required a victim in the marriage. That many were desperate by this point is clear—divorce usually came only as the final step after numerous outrages had occurred, or attempts at both reconciliation and separation had failed.

The decision to divorce was a difficult one to make. Men and women had to decide if they had the proper reasons and if they could afford the costs. They had to seek legal counsel, and, finally, they had to endure the whole process. For some, divorce was worth the problems and pain because it was the end of what had been a long and bitter struggle. For others, however, the seeking of a divorce did not end their problems. Predicaments in the form of divorces not granted or alimony unpaid would continue to cause them complications in the future.

With the Divorce Act of 1785, divorce became a more available option for the unhappily married people who were able and willing to pursue a legal route. Although those who divorced came from a wide variety of backgrounds, divorce still remained the province of the few, and usually an option only for those with some money. Those who received divorces obtained the legal right to remarry, and in the case of some wives, the opportunity to receive alimony. For most, however, divorce was never an alternative to their marital dilemmas.

CHAPTER 2

Weaving the Bonds: Husbands' and Wives' Expectations of Marriage

Dear Daughter, since this is your judgement,
Your notion I do recommend,
    for a good honest man
    will save all he can
While a rake he will willingly spend,
Abusing his family quite.
Dear daughter you're much in the right I will not
    deny you
Let Roger stay by you
Since he is your joy and delight.
And when you are married I'll make it well known
I'll give Roger a plow and a farm of his own.
        ELIPHABET MASON, "YOUNG ROGER,"
        The Complete Pocket Song Book (1803)[1]

"Even you My Brother . . . could not desire for a Husband one more perfectly formed to make me truly happy," declared Harriet Chew Carroll in an 1801 letter to her brother, Benjamin Chew, Jr.[2] These words, written shortly after her marriage to Charles Carroll, expressed Harriet's contentment with her husband and with her married state. With marriage she began a new phase of her life that involved moving from her home and family in Philadelphia to a new abode in

Maryland with her husband. Despite this physical separation from her parents and siblings, however, she was happy. Harriet began marriage with the knowledge that she and her husband were embarking upon a new life together. No longer simply daughter and sister, Harriet was now a wife as well.

As a wife, Harriet began a new life as mistress of her own household, loving companion to her husband, and mother of their children. Similarly, Charles' role and duties also changed after marriage. In becoming a husband, he was now responsible for supporting his wife and any children they might have. Family, friends, and the world around them influenced and prepared Harriet and Charles, as they did other young couples, for their new roles and for what they should expect from marriage. Marriage brought new responsibilities to both partners, but it also brought the promise of great fulfillment. For late eighteenth- and early nineteenth-century American society assured young men and women that "marriage is that mystical union of soul and body which produces happiness superlatively great."[3]

Letters written by family members indicate that both Harriet and Charles seemed content in the early years of marriage. After ten years, however, the image Harriet held of Charles as one who could make her "truly happy" began to waver. Because of his excessive drinking and violent rages, Charles did not live up to the role Harriet, their families, and their society expected of him—that of family provider and loving partner. Moreover, Harriet, who struggled to be a loving and dutiful wife, and who tried to change her husband's behavior through her love, influence, and example—as society expected of her —finally abandoned her efforts, and resigned herself to a formal separation.[4]

What happened between 1801 when Harriet described herself as being "truly happy" and 1813 when she wrote of being "more resigned to my unhappy fate"?[5] Her disillusionment arose from more than Charles's drinking. As their marriage disintegrated, the couple's perceptions of each other and of their own roles as husband and wife underwent a process of redefinition, and they were forced to reevaluate their marital behavior and expectations. Most couples probably learned early in marriage that there was a difference between their original hopes and the day-to-day substance of their marriages, and they adapted without too much difficulty. For others, such as the Carrolls, the adjustment between expectation and reality caused fundamental tensions in their marriages.

Influenced both by new ideas about marriage and traditional beliefs about the roles of husbands and wives, men and women of the eighteenth and early nineteenth centuries frequently found themselves in the midst of a paradox. Marital expectations were changing, but the old ways persisted. Both partners hoped for happiness, but precisely what they desired and looked for in their unions often differed substantially. As they entered matrimony with contradictory viewpoints, some couples were unable to reconcile their differences. This chapter explores both the formation of marital expectations and the effect the clash of expectation and reality had in the disruption of some marriages.

In troubled marriages, there are two stories—the husband's and the wife's. By terming marriage "parallel lives," a biographer of five Victorian marriages addresses, but does not adequately reflect, this dual image of marriage. In her view, each partner constructs his or her own narrative of their shared marital experiences. These narratives express two points of view of a single marriage. Although the two storylines share some similarities, since each develops from a separate imagination, there are gaps between them.[6]

Marriage is not altogether like that. Although there are indeed two stories in each marriage, they are not parallel. Unlike parallel lines, which mirror each other but never intersect, husbands' and wives' stories do not always mirror each other. They often *do* intersect. Intersecting, yet distinct, the lives of married couples twine together like the fibers of a loosely woven fabric. Husband and wife enter the marriage with a variety of hopes and fears, weaving them into this marital cloth. Although their expectations may change as the substance and texture of the marriage develops, the men and women involved continue to weave their strands independently. Each partner perceives and tells a different tale that evolves throughout the marriage, and yet, like warp and weft, their lives and their stories connect at many points. How they intersect depends upon the weavers; the strands of their lives together may cling at one point, unravel at the next, forming patterns of harmony or discord.

Long before they are actually united in marriage, husbands and wives begin to create their distinct stories. In part, differences between husband and wife may develop due to early training, opportunities for socialization, and the formation of a gender identity. In part, these differences are due to the experiences of women and men within their particular social context. As a result, by the time they marry, most men and women broadly understand what it means to be a man or a woman in their society, or a husband or a wife. Central to the formation of gender roles are the relationships of power and dependency within a particular culture.[7]

In the mid-eighteenth century, influenced by vast changes in politics, technology, and the growing belief in individualism, the concept of marriage, both as a private relationship between a man and a woman and as a public institution, underwent basic changes. Consequently, the roles of wife and husband also evolved. Increasingly throughout the eighteenth century and into the nineteenth, the belief developed that husbands and wives should marry because they loved each other. Spouses were supposed to be friends and partners linked by mutual affection rather than by duty, as in previous decades. Love within marriage was not a new idea, but during the mid-eighteenth century a new emphasis was placed on this idea of "companionate" marriage. As part of the new emphasis on individualism, young people planned to choose their mates themselves for love rather than to have their parents choose them for status, ability, or to cement relationships with another family.[8] This belief placed marriage in a new perspective, challenging the expectations of both men and women entering marriage and those already married. Nevertheless, old customs and traditions persisted.

Though covered by a patina of new affectionate ideals, marriage remained in many ways an economic and reproductive institution. Legally, men continued as heads of their households, with the right to control their wives' inheritances, property, and wages. Ideally, the loving partners jointly made the decisions concerning family money matters. In reality, although the economic instability of America in the post-Revolutionary years often forced both husbands and wives to contribute to the support of their households, this did not mean they always shared in the control or distribution of the money earned.

At the same time, the image of the loving, virtuous husband as family breadwinner developed as a middle-class ideal. This stereotype viewed the wife as being responsible for ministering to her family's emotional needs while running the household and being the partner and confidant of her husband. Because these distinct gender roles developed as middle-class ideals, they did not necessarily exist for most people in the reality of everyday life. Nonetheless, these ideals did influence many husbands and wives to expect a particular form of marriage in which the partners were mutually affectionate and committed to their children, yet where husbands often had a subtle control over family finances and a degree of power over their mates, and where wives felt an obligation to submit to their husbands when discord arose.[9]

Among the lower sort, the economics of marriage may have produced more of a power struggle between women and men than it did with couples who had more money. Since both husband and wife needed to contribute to the family economy in order to survive, they each desired a say in how money would be budgeted and spent, and they argued over who would have the final word over its distribution.[10] Although middling or wealthy husbands and wives sometimes clashed over the control of family finances, both partners did not have to provide revenue to fight against immediate poverty. However, the difficulties of trying to achieve parity with their peers, to maintain the standards set by previous generations, and to live up to the ideals of support and obedience expected of them—as wealthy ladies and gentlemen—caused a different set of strains in their marriages when they were unable to do so.

Few women of any class, however, were totally locked into the female "sphere" of home, family, and pious submission to God and husband.[11] Women without husbands, whether single, widowed, abandoned, or divorced, commonly took on roles not normally associated with the feminine ideal of popular early American culture. Poor women and rural women worked outside their homes in order to support themselves and their families, or at least to provide them with

The Wife, *Godey's Lady's Book*, December 1831. This portrait illustrates the model wife of the 1830s. She obviously lives a comfortable life, and is presumably so organized that she has time to sit serenely in her well-appointed parlor. She gazes adoringly at her husband and waits to attend to his slightest wish. Although this was an ideal, illustrations such as these influenced the women and men who saw them. *Courtesy of the Chester County Historical Society, West Chester, Pa.*

much needed supplemental incomes.[12] Many women of means were well aware of their family financial situations and understood the running of family businesses.[13] Nevertheless, the ideology of separate spheres for men and women, expounded by contemporary thinkers, was reinforced in the realities of defined physical space for both genders, prohibiting women, for instance, from walking city streets alone without fear or from speaking in public. Meanwhile the restrictions placed on them by law effectively limited women's role in the outside or "men's world"—and accorded men, in general, more power.[14]

This male world was a larger world. It extended outside the home and the concerns of family. Men brought their observations of the wider world, which included distinct gender differentiation, to their marriages. Because early American society encouraged men to be the economic providers for the family, this differentiation included the husband's perceived role as head of the household. Thus men at all levels of society were influenced to see marriage differently than women did. Yet because it was not always possible for husbands to support their wives and families totally, this image of economic provider frequently generated increased marital tensions, whether it was because a husband could not or simply refused to provide for his family.[15]

The differing expectations with which men and women entered their marriages helped to create tensions after they wed. Among Pennsylvania Quakers, for example, the idea of marriage as a loving partnership had existed since the early days of the colony.[16] With the coming of the Revolution, this particular concept of marriage spread throughout an American society infused with republican spirit. Although republican ideology encouraged both men and women to think of their marriages as partnerships, Americans still considered men to be the "head" of the household, and the one ultimately responsible for the economic support and social standing of wife and family. When differences arose between husband and wife, most believed that the wife should give in gracefully. Many husbands therefore perceived their position as one of power—economic power, physical power, and emotional power. Even when a husband valued the opinions and contributions of his wife, he believed he had the final power to make all decisions—his was the preeminent position within the marriage. As Philadelphia merchant, Thomas Cope, wrote in June 1814:

There must be grades of authority: Sovereign & subject, a head & a foot. Where differences—even in matters of opinion—occur between husband & wife, it is the duty of the latter, if she cannot think with, at least to succomb to the wishes of the former, unless conscience forbid. . . . A wife is never degraded by a dutiful submission to her husband.[17]

Many men and women, no doubt, continued to view the roles of husband and wife as Thomas Cope did. Problems arose, however, when husbands maintained this patriarchal outlook about marriage, while their wives, imbued with new republican ideas, viewed marriage as a relationship between equals. In Pennsylvania divorce petitions written between 1785 and 1815, some wives claimed that their husbands were "tyrants" instead of friends.[18] By stating this in the language of republican ideology, these women revealed not only their belief that in the new republic husbands and wives should be equal partners, but also that women had a right to leave marriages when this was not the case. Tyranny was not to be condoned in public or in private life, and marriage was now to be a republican contract between wives and husbands, a contract based on mutual affection.[19]

Because most early American women and men expected the husband to be the head of the household, however, problems developed in marriages when he did not take the expected lead. In this time of transition, the roles of husband and wife were often evolving and fluctuating between the new affectionate and companionate ideals and the older patriarchal traditions. Mary Seale's 1792 divorce petition expressed her affirmation of both these beliefs. First she stated her conviction that her husband should love her by declaring that: "John forgetting the duty he owed to the Libellant withdrew his affection from her without any cause but his own evil minded disposition." Then after stating that he had abused her, deserted her, and repeatedly refused to provide for her, she noted that he "is able to contribute to the support of the Libellant as by his marriage vow he is bound to do."[20]

Even a wife who believed that most husbands continued to perceive their role as that of master might still desire friendship from her mate. The unhappily married Nancy Shippen Livingston expressed this belief shortly after separating from her husband, Henry:

that men are generally tyrannical I will own, but such as know how to be happy, willingly give up the harsh title of master for the more tender & endearing one of Friend. Equality is the soul of friendship: marriage to give delight, must join *two minds*, not devote a slave to the will of an imperious Lord.[21]

Nancy learned in hindsight that it was important to marry a man who would value her as a partner and whom she could value as a friend.

William Shippen had convinced his daughter, Nancy, to marry the wealthy Henry Beekman Livingston of New York. Nancy, who was popular and vivacious, had a number of admirers. Although she fell in love with Louis Guillaume Otto, a French diplomat, she agreed to allow Henry Livingston to court her. Her father wrote to her brother, Tommy, "Nancy is much puzzled between Otto & Livingston. She loves ye first & only esteems the last . . . L has 12 or 15,000 hard. O had nothing now, but honorable expectations hereafter. A bird in hand is worth 2 in a bush."[22]

Nancy, who was just sixteen, gave in to her father's wishes and consented to marry Livingston. The wedding preparations were made quickly, and Otto was kept from seeing Nancy to prevent her from changing her mind. Unfortunately, the marriage was a failure almost from the beginning. Livingston often became unreasonably angry and jealously accused Nancy of being unfaithful to him. Nancy returned home to Philadelphia, but Henry forced her to return their daughter, Peggy, to New York. As a compromise, Henry allowed Peggy to live with his parents, and in order to visit her Nancy moved back to New York. Unable to get a divorce there without losing the custody of her daughter, Nancy remained unhappily married, but lived apart from her husband. Finally, Livingston obtained a divorce in Connecticut.[23]

Though influenced by their parents, as Nancy Shippen was, increasingly throughout the eighteenth century, most young men and women expected to choose their future mates. While they often sought and valued the opinions of their mothers and fathers, they did not expect them to veto the choices they had made.[24] People took note of occasions when parents forced their offspring to marry persons not to their liking. Rebecca Shoemaker wrote to her daughter, Anna Rawle, about a young woman who shot herself through the heart because her father disapproved of her engagement to a British officer, and pressured her to marry "a person in the Neighbourhood of Very Unequal years & every way disagreeable." She concluded the anecdote with the observation, "How truly miserable must those parents be who will reflect on themselves as the cause of so tragical & melancholy a disaster."[25]

It may be that young men living on their own felt more freedom to choose their spouses without input from parents or family, although they desired their approval. In 1767, Robert Parker wrote an affectionate letter to his sisters telling them of his forthcoming marriage to a woman whom they had not met. He stated, however, that he did not want to appear disobedient, and asked that "Mammy or the rest of my friends throug [sic] you would write to me if you see propper to give your approbation."[26]

Besides parental viewpoints and wishes, newspapers and magazines also described the ideal husband and wife, advising men and women on how to be one and on how to choose one. Articles in newspapers and magazines stressed the importance of selecting a proper spouse. Although these ideals may not have had as much meaning to the men and women of the lower sort, it is useful to look at them as models circulating through the middle-class culture of the time.

Throughout the eighteenth century and into the nineteenth, the authors of essays and advice manuals recommended that men and women not marry for money. Love matches certainly existed before this time, and marriages made for money continued to be made after then, but an emphasis on marrying for love began to appear in newspaper and magazine articles after about 1750.[27] In part, this reflects a new concern with individual happiness and freedom, a freedom that extended to an individual's right to marry for love, rather than marrying the person chosen by his or her parents. In their advocacy, the writers of newspaper and magazine essays did not propose marrying for the romantic and passionate love of our present day, but rather urged marriage to a morally upright man or woman who would make a good parent and with whom one could find love based upon mutual respect and friendship.

Indeed, the right to select one's own partner without parental interference loomed large in the literature read by eighteenth-century Americans. In reality, young men and women had chosen their own partners before then. But it was at the time of the Revolution that newspapers, essays, and even novels reverberated with echoes of individuals fighting tyranny in all forms, including parental tyranny. However, the reality of standing up to parental pressure could be difficult, as Nancy Shippen found, and most couples probably desired to marry with the blessings of their parents.[28]

Besides advocating love, essays written in the second half of the eighteenth century cautioned readers to beware of the immoral practices and pleasures of the world. If marriage was the hope of the new republic, it was necessary that both partners be virtuous in order to raise future virtuous citizens.[29] In one such essay, the author advised planting love "in Truth and virtue" in order to keep it from withering. It recommended prudence in selecting future mates, being careful to avoid those who were only interested in seeking their own pleasures. In addition, the essay condemned the practice of parents marrying their offspring to the highest bidder noting that, "when we daily observe Controversies, Animosities, Elopements, and Divorces, the Consequences of such Junctions, it is evident Act of Inhumanity and Barbarity."[30]

Together, real-life examples and newspaper and magazine articles promoted the idea of choosing one's mate and marrying for love, not money. Reading the stories no doubt inspired some young men and women to seek love matches, while newspapers and magazine essays on the subject proliferated with the number of people supporting that view. For a few months, *The Royal American Magazine* presented a column called "the Directory of Love," an eighteenth-century advice series. In February 1774, "Nancy Dilemma" asked for counsel. Her parents wanted her to marry a man who had money, but whom she did not love. She loved another man. This second man did not have much money, but Nancy Dilemma stated that he did have more sense than the first man. In response, "Polly Resolute" noted that sense was a valuable commodity and advised her to *"marry the man you love"* — provided he had enough money for them to get by.[31]

As Polly Resolute indicated, it was important for couples to have *some* money. The *amount*, however, was not supposed to be the determining factor in deciding upon a husband or wife. The "Old Bachelor" of the *Pennsylvania Magazine* declared that "we should not wonder that those who either marry gold without love, or love without gold, should be miserable." In "Thoughts on Old Maids," the essayist advised women and men to accept the first reasonable offer of marriage, and not to wait for a suitor with more money. These sentiments were typical of most of the essays published in newspapers and magazines of the time.[32]

By the nineteenth century, prescriptive literature seldom used republican rhetoric in underscoring the characteristics of either an ideal or troubled marriage. Books and articles, however, persisted in advancing the notion that marriage was the goal for all young men and women. As with earlier works, later essays continued to emphasize mutual affection as a precondition for marriage. Above all else, husbands and wives were supposed to be friends.

Although the belief persisted that men and women should seek virtuous mates, a new emphasis in the literature focused upon the wife's ability and *duty* to reform an errant husband.[33] Influenced by American Protestantism, Lockean and Scottish moral philosophy, and literary sentimentalism in the decades following the Revolution, the concept of virtue became linked with women who "were increasingly deemed the moral instructors of men."[34] In the nineteenth century, women were in the forefront of the religious revivals of the Second Great Awakening, and evangelical mothers asserted control of this type over their offspring, later extending their sphere of influence to include the world around them by forming moral reform societies.[35] Prescriptive writings insisted that women were naturally virtuous and unhampered by animal passions, which made them morally superior to men. Thus, for this reason, women and men faced an additional burden in adjusting to the realities of their married lives when they did not meet these prescribed ideals. In a paradox created by the interaction of old and new beliefs, women were urged both to take the lead in moral guidance, and yet to submit to their husbands when necessary, while men were supposed to follow the spiritual advice of their wives, but remain the head of the household.

In addition to the urgings of newspaper and magazine essays, religious and community leaders offered marital advice and counseled women and men on how to choose an appropriate spouse. These authority figures told men and women to choose a spouse with similar tastes, background, and interests. This meant the prospective spouse should be of or about the same age, of the same race, of the same religion, and of the same class.

Of course people of different backgrounds did marry, and changes at mid-century may have contributed to this. By the time of the Revolution, for example, Philadelphia was the largest city in the American colonies and contained a diverse population, including immigrants from many countries and men and women from the surrounding rural counties. It also incorporated a significant number of free blacks. Philadelphia records indicate that interracial unions did take place. The minister of Gloria Dei (Old Swedes) Church in Philadelphia noted that he had refused to perform interracial marriage ceremonies because he believed the union of blacks and whites to be against public opinion. "Nevertheless," he wrote, "these frequent mixtures will soon force matrimonial sanctions. What a particoloured race will soon make a great portion of the population in Philadelphia."[36]

Although he was against interracial marriages, the minister did not appear to condemn the individuals. In one instance, he referred the couple, who were cohabiting and who had had a child, to a black minister.[37] Not everyone shared his views, however; another opinion appears in the following entry in a docket of the Philadelphia almshouse:

Mary Spry . . . a dirty white Hussey Trul to a Negro man Jacob Spry—she laid in here, of a white Child—so must have Cuckold poor blackey.[38]

The age at which individuals married was also an important consideration. Friends of Philadelphia Monthly Meeting expressed concerns about "their great age" when one couple proposed to marry in 1700. On the other hand, in the next century the minister at Gloria Dei regularly refused to marry young couples because he feared they did not have the approval of their parents. In one case, he refused to marry a man "above 20 years" who had supported himself for several years, because his widowed mother had not consented to the marriage.[39]

Others looked askance when couples with large age differences married. Charlotte Wilcocks noted in her diary the disapproval of some of her family members when her Uncle Joe, aged sixty-five, married thirty-five-year-old Sally Waln. In another case, the almshouse records reported the admittance of "Elizabeth Moffett upwards of sixty years of age; this poor, foolish, inconsiderate old woman married a young blade twenty five years of age, who gave her the foul disease." Popular literature also expressed the opinion that marriages should be between men and women of approximately the same age. The author of a "Curious Sermon on Marriage" advised young women not to marry old men because people would assume that they were just marrying for money.[40]

Experts advised men and women not to marry a person who held a different religious belief. Yet, men and women did choose partners who did not share their faiths. Finding a religious authority to marry them, however, often proved difficult. One Philadelphia minister refused to marry a well-to-do middle-aged widower to a Jewish woman, even though the man claimed she would be baptised. The minister stated that he could not perform such a service until after she had been baptised.[41]

Most typically, couples who intermarried were of different Protestant sects. Even then problems could arise. As was customary among Friends, when Joseph Carver married Hannah Cary in 1792, Wrightstown Monthly Meeting dismissed him because she was not a Quaker. Later, however, after the couple separated, a committee of Friends met with them to try to settle their differences.[42]

Religious obstacles could be overcome, especially if the couple was otherwise suitably matched. When Harriet Chew, a Protestant, and Charles Carroll, a Catholic, married, Charles' father declared he had no objection to Harriet picking a clergyman of her choice to perform the ceremony, as long as the couple was married first by a Roman Catholic priest. Charles, meanwhile, pledged never to try to change Harriet's religious views.[43]

Parents, authority figures, and prescriptive literature all advised couples on how to choose a proper mate. It was important to be about the same age, of the same background, and the same class, although some did not follow this advice. More confusing to young men and women, it was important to marry for love, but to have enough money on which to live; to choose one's own mate, but to have parental blessings. Men and women brought these sometimes conflicting ideas both to their search for a spouse and to their expectations about marriage.

Along with parental and societal influences, laws also influenced and challenged marital expectations. For instance, the early legal codes of Pennsylvania confirmed the viewpoint that it was the husband's duty to provide financially for his wife. Poor laws demanded husband support wife. This was almost a necessity because Pennsylvania denied married women (femes covert) the right to own property or control their own money and estates unless the matter was arranged by a prenuptial trust.[44]

An act passed in 1771 permitted the overseers of the poor to seize the goods of a husband who deserted his wife or children. The seized goods could then be used to support her or them.[45] The purpose of the law was to prevent deserted wives from becoming a burden to the community, but implicit in this legislation was the idea that a husband who did not support his wife was neglecting his duty. There was no provision made for husbands whose wives left them. Acknowledging that deserted wives often had no way to maintain themselves, the law declared that husbands were responsible for them and their offspring. But also realizing that an abandoned wife was often left with children to support and not wishing those children to become a charge to the community, the law further stated that mothers had an obligation to maintain their children. In this way, the law preserved a patriarchal view of marriage as the legal standard, but also recognized eighteenth-century economic realities.[46]

In order to prevent wives from being left destitute, some couples, or their families, made prenuptial agreements to guarantee that if the woman was widowed, she would not be denied her share of the estate. Charles Carroll of Carrollton, Harriet's future father-in-law, agreed that Harriet Chew would receive the sum of three thousand dollars in "current money" if his son died before her. He made his own manor, Carrollton, security for the money.[47]

The agreement made between the farmer, George Roe, and his intended bride, Hester Bizard, was more detailed. The document provided that Hester would be adequately situated in the event of George's death by furnishing the ingredients necessary for a comfortable life in the country. Thus while she was given money and a place to live, she was also given the cow of her choice, a fifteenth share in the yearly amount of flax and wool, the liberty of the apple orchard, and one-fourth share in the kitchen garden. In addition, she was to be provided with firewood, the cow was to be kept in the stable for free in the winter and the pastures the rest of the year, and her share in the flax and wool was in the already combed product.[48]

Prenuptial agreements underscored the economic realities of marriage. Often these agreements permitted any money or property the woman brought to the marriage to remain hers. Until the end of the eighteenth century, Pennsylvania courts of equity enforced separate estates for married women only if the agreements were made in the form of a trust. Thus, these women needed the agreement of their husbands or relatives acting on their behalf in order to effect the trust, and therefore, they were not in total control of their estates. Nevertheless, this does not change the intentions couples had when making these agreements.[49] Men and women who made prenuptial or post-nuptial contracts had particular expectations about marriage and the roles of husband and wife. George Roe's document stipulated that the items Hester brought to the marriage were to remain hers. Moreover, he stated that she was to share equally in his estate with the children of his first marriage.[50]

Yet, for the most part, wives remained dependent upon their husbands for economic support. Although the beginnings of industrialization in Philadelphia in the early nineteenth century and the commercialization of the market economy in the surrounding area even earlier opened up new opportunities for women, as well as for men, the money they earned was rarely enough to support a family. Indeed, the wages earned by working men often were not enough to support a family. Yet, the norm remained that men should and would support their wives and families.[51]

A wife's expectation of economic support from her husband went back to the earliest days of the colony and England. A husband's neglect in providing shelter, for example, could become a contentious issue within a marriage. In 1695, Philadelphia Quakers became aware of a married couple who were not living together. The Meeting decided that the husband should provide a house for his wife so that she would have no excuse to live apart from him. In 1697, the husband appeared at Monthly Meeting to report that he would try to have a room or two finished within a few months, if his wife would then live with him. By January 1698, she had still refused to live with him, but in December of that year the mediating Friends noted that they expected that the couple would soon be living together.[52]

The provision of shelter may not, in fact, have been the cause of this couple's living apart, but it became an issue in their living together. In the expectation of their community (at least their *religious* community) husband and wife lived together. If they wanted to remain a part of that religious society, they had to meet those expectations. Thus, it was up to the husband to provide a suitable dwelling for his wife. By doing so, he fulfilled his duties; it was then up to his wife to fulfill hers by cohabiting with him. Drawing on the conventions of their community and based upon their own wants and desires, husband and wife engaged in a sort of marital bargaining with Monthly Meeting serving as the mediators.

Marriage, of course, involved more than financial arrangements. The hopes and fears with which men and women entered marriage reflected this. Before beginning a formal courtship of Hannah Logan, John Smith experienced feelings of unworthiness. He even made an unsuccessful attempt at turning his attentions to another woman, but found that he had little in common with her. In writing of that experience to Hannah years later, he told her:

Soon after that I had some opportunities of Converse where thou was in Company, which much Enhanced my Esteem. I plainly saw that though the Cabinet was Exquisitely framed, the mind lodged in it far Excelled; and thus as it renewed and strengthened my formerRegard, so it increased the difficulty I saw it was obtaining what I so much wished for. Many were the Racking thoughts occasioned by the different Sensations of desire and doubt.[53]

Distressed by feelings of inferiority, John questioned whether he should make his feelings known to Hannah, until in a casual conversation a friend suggested that Hannah would make him an excellent wife. Since the friend had not known John's feelings about Hannah, John took the suggestion as a good sign for him to begin courting her. By the time he began to court her seriously, his mind was made up —he wanted to marry her if she would have him.

Even though John had been troubled by feelings of self-doubt, he did not envision that marriage would change his way of living to any great extent. Hannah, however, had more difficulty making the determination to marry; she feared marriage would interfere with her desire for spiritual growth and awareness. She kept John Smith alternately elated and despondent for months while she attempted to make her decision. After first telling him that she did not want to marry, she then allowed him to call on her. Shortly after that she once again decided against marriage and declared that he should not visit her so often. Finally, she did marry him in 1748.[54]

Hannah Logan was not alone in her uncertainty about whether to marry. For women, marriage brought more profound changes to their lives than it did for men. Not only did some fear that they would not continue to grow spiritually; they also had to be prepared to manage a household and to have children. Facing the responsibilities of being both a wife and a mother and the fears of sex and childbirth might make any woman pause to reconsider a marriage proposal. In addition, marriage meant relinquishing the independence of being a single woman or widow, or delaying the opportunities for authority. For example, among colonial Quaker women in Pennsylvania and New Jersey, those who held positions of authority were usually married, but most of them were in their mid- to late thirties, and at the end of their childbearing years before they began committee work in their meetings.[55]

Anna Rawle, for instance, expressed some uncertainty toward her forthcoming marriage. That she missed her mother, who was in exile from Philadelphia because of her marriage to a loyalist, was part, though not the total source of this ambivalence. Anna indicated that though she felt marriage was inevitable, she did not necessarily look forward to it with pleasure. She appeared resigned, rather than happy. In a letter to her mother, she wrote, "It is not improbable, had my situation been other than it was, that a preference would have been given to the single state, altho' I know no person (here indeed there is no great choice) who I could view in the same light."[56]

Not all women approached marriage with reluctance or resignation, but most could not help realizing that they would be embarking upon a new life. Harriet Manigault and her daughter, Charlotte, each kept diaries when they were young, single women. These documents reveal a similar awareness that marriage would be a new stage in their lives. The last entry of Harriet's three-volume diary recorded her marriage in 1816, and ended with the statement: "I think we have the prospect of passing a most delightful summer, & with that thought I shall end my *memoirs*, for it is not customary for the story to go on after the heroine is married." Charlotte wrote, after becoming secretly engaged in 1842, "Oh! No! quite too strange for such a harem scarem thing as I am to be engaged."[57]

The expectations which eighteenth- and nineteenth-century Pennsylvania women brought to their marriages were also tied to their perceptions of themselves both as women and as members of their particular society. In many ways, they were much like women in the rest of the nation, although they had different options open to them. For example, unlike women in many states, after 1785, they were able to file for divorce under a relatively liberal divorce law. They were urban women, living in Philadelphia; they were rural women living in the fertile counties surrounding Philadelphia, as well as in the remote counties further away. They were both rich and poor women. Influenced by family, friends, prescriptive literature, and the society around them, they learned what was expected of them as women and wives. In addition, women's shared experiences formed a pervasive female culture bounded by the rituals of courtship, marriage, pregnancy, and childbirth, and the concerns of housewifery and child care.[58]

Men, too, were influenced by society and they learned how to behave as men and specifically as married men. They also had rituals that helped to form a male culture. Just as women formed bonds with other women through their shared experiences with home and family, men formed bonds through their socialization at work and in the tavern.[59]

It was only after marriage that divisions between women and men became so sharply drawn. Not only did women go from being daughters to wives with all the added responsibility; they also went from feme sole to feme covert with all its limitations. This made the decision to marry a difficult one, and it contributed to increased tensions once couples actually were married.[60]

Legally, the husband remained head of the household, and even strong and independent women had to work within these constraints. Thus a woman who took the extreme measure of suing her husband for divorce often consciously used a submissive and pious tone in the language of her petition. She portrayed herself as a dutiful wife and innocent victim of an irresponsible or immoral man. Men, on the other hand, emphasized their roles as good providers to ungrateful wives in their divorce petitions. This combination of gender awareness and concerns over what society expected combined to form and strengthen separate male and female worlds.[61]

Consequently, men and women brought to marriage not only expectations based on societal ideals, but also anticipations and perceptions based upon their own awareness of themselves as men and women, husbands and wives. After marriage, spouses continued to perceive their marriages in differing ways. It is possible that these differing expectations and perceptions of husband and wife caused tensions in marriages, but most couples learned to adjust or cope with their situations and the conflicting views with which they entered them without destroying their marriages.

The need to fit prescribed roles often made it difficult for men and women to adjust to marriage. Some women found that they could not always live up to the image of submissive and obedient wife. A number of newspaper advertisements placed by deserted husbands noted their wives' "unwifely" behavior. George Miller reported that his wife had eloped from him, taking various goods, "contrary to her duty, and to the evil example of other women." George Douglas stated that his wife, Althalanah, had behaved "in a very unbecoming manner" to him, while Lydia Mitton "greatly misbehaved herself," according to her husband James. These women may have only rebelled against their strictly defined roles and their husbands' strict standards. This may also have been Mercy Henderson's situation, when her husband in seeking to divorce her noted "her perversion of mind" after months during which "she [had] regulated her conduct by the strictest rules of prudence and propriety."[62]

Some men, meanwhile, found it difficult to live up to the image of economic provider, whether it was from bad luck, incompetence, or laziness. Thomas Feeley apparently went to Ireland, leaving his wife and child behind because he could not support them. Hannah Carpenter's uncle, William Pennington, noted that her husband, Abraham, had "behaved to her in a very Cruel and disgraceful Manner, entirely Contrary to the duties of a husband to a wife." Other men, such as Charles Carroll became dependent on alcohol and therefore unable to be loving and supportive husbands.[63]

Although laws and public opinion decreed that the family's money belonged to the husband, the actual control of the family finances could become an explosive issue. In one case, Sarah Lloyd filed for divorce from her husband, Benjamin, a mariner. The couple lodged in a house in the Northern Liberties of Philadelphia. In a court deposition filed during their proceedings, Catharine Page, who lived in the same house, recounted a fight between the couple. According to Catharine, Benjamin wanted the couple's money, in order to put it in a bank. Sarah, however, told him that, "as she had kept it so long, she thought she was Bank enough to keep it safe some time longer, that she could not get any money but what she worked for herself and did not wish to go to him for every five penny but she wanted or to take in work while he was giving away so much money to his father."[64]

Clearly, Sarah resented both the fact that she was forced to earn her own money and that Benjamin was giving so much of it to his father. In her view, their relationship as a married couple entitled her to both support and some measure of control over the money. Sarah was obviously used to earning money. Yet, her desire for economic independence in not wanting to go to her husband "for every five penny" clashed with her expectations of economic support. She did not agree that Benjamin had the power to decide what to do with the money since he had not provided the couple's sole support. On the other hand, Benjamin believed that though he might allow Sarah to hold the money, he need not consult her in its distribution. Unlike Sarah, he saw himself as the final decision-maker in the marriage.

What they were really fighting over, however, was power and control. Whatever love or affection Sarah may have felt for Benjamin at the time of the marriage was gone. Witnesses testified that Benjamin had in the past beaten his wife and committed adultery. Sarah had endured this behavior for four years before filing for divorce in 1801. Although it is impossible to know exactly why Sarah chose that time to file for divorce, possibly for the first time she saw that her husband's beatings could actually kill her, or that he would never change. Or it may be that in taking the money, Sarah understood that Benjamin was taking away the one thing over which she had some control. Without possession of or authority over the money, Sarah was totally dependent upon her husband for economic survival, as even the money she earned, he took and spent. Keeping the couple's money allowed her some measure of independence and power within their marriage. Using her husband's definition of marriage, Sarah fought to maintain a position of power.

For a woman this effort was no small measure. Until Pennsylvania passed legislation in the 1830s and 1840s, a husband could control all of his wife's money and property, unless it was protected by a separate trust.[65] Although some marriages were love matches and worked as equal partnerships, marriage as a whole retained this patriarchal structure. Living up to such standards imposed by society, moreover, could be difficult for both men and women: not every man could be a patriarch, nor could every woman live comfortably within a patriarchal system.

Because most women married with the expectation that their husbands would provide them with some measure of economic support, it was troubling, even for a poor woman, to find that her husband would not support or provide for her. To discover then that her own resources were so limited was just as distressing. This is what happened to Sarah Lloyd. Neither husband nor wife met the standards imposed upon them by their society. Benjamin was not providing adequately for his wife; in addition he abused her and was unfaithful. Sarah, however, was not totally the submissive wife—she fought back. She did win her divorce, probably because of Benjamin's numerous transgressions, and because she had endured his behavior for a number of years before seeking a legal remedy.

Discord arose in many marriages over economic support and the way in which it related to the struggle for power within the marriage. Yet, husband and wife saw their versions of this power struggle differently. Husbands frequently placed notices in the newspapers when their wives left them, making clear that they would not be responsible for their debts. In one of these advertisements, Benjamin Ashton of

Lower Dublin township stated that his wife, Ann, had eloped from him. Ann replied and told a different tale. Her advertisement in the *Pennsylvania Gazette* noted that Benjamin had promised before witnesses to "put away the red hair'd Girl," but that instead he had locked himself in the room with her, forcing the pregnant Ann to sleep in the kitchen. Ann declared that she was willing to live with him, especially as her condition prevented her from supporting herself. Benjamin renounced his duty to support his wife after she left him. To Benjamin, her action was an act of insubordination. By leaving him, Ann was showing that he had no power over her, and if he had no power over her, then he had no need to support her. In Ann's version, she was forced to leave her husband because of the treatment he accorded her. To Ann, her husband's power was tied to his duty to support her and to treat her as his wife. In a way similar to Sarah Lloyd's perception of marriage, Ann saw herself and her husband as part of a relationship in which each partner had a duty to care for the other. It was only after Benjamin abused this reciprocity that Ann left him.[66]

Both rich and poor women expected some measure of economic support from their husbands. A poor woman, such as Sarah Lloyd, usually attempted to find ways to supplement the money earned by her husband, but the loss of a husband's income could lead to complete destitution, and even the almshouse. For a rich woman, the loss of a husband's economic support could also lead to poverty, but she would be more likely to have wealthy family members or friends who could come to her aid. Nevertheless, the loss of a husband's maintenance could lead to a change in lifestyle and status for a wealthy woman. This change, in turn, affected her perceptions about her marriage, her husband's role, and her own role.

Many women found their lifestyles and status shattered by the political and social upheaval of the American Revolution. Soldiers died, families were broken and divided, and loyalists often faced exile and the loss of properties and fortunes. Married women, whether they considered themselves loyalists, patriots, or completely apolitical, were affected by these events because, according to the state, husband and wife were one person with a single will—that of the husband's.[67] Women who did not share their husbands' point of view about the

Revolution, however, may also have found that they likewise had little else in common. Other women who did share their husbands' beliefs could discover that material changes caused by the war affected the stability of their marriages.

For Grace Growden Galloway, the Revolutionary War served as a catalyst in the disintegration of her marriage. Her husband, Joseph Galloway, served as Speaker of the Pennsylvania House from 1766 to 1775, and was a powerful force in Pennsylvania politics until the Revolution, when he sided with the British. Although her diary reveals that she had a clear understanding of Pennsylvania politics and had no love for the patriots' cause, Grace resented the Revolution's intrusion into her life. To Grace, politics were part of a man's world, and there was no reason why they should affect her life.

Grace was born to wealth, and expected it in her married life. She became embittered and unhappy when she was left to cope with trying to hold on to their property in Philadelphia, while her husband and their only child, Betsay, fled to England. Finding that her husband had put some of her holdings in his own name without her knowledge increased her resentment of him. When forced to give up this property, she went from great affluence to what she considered great poverty. As a result of her husbands' loyalties and actions, she lost her property and possessions. Consequently, she lost her status as the wife of a powerful man, and this caused her considerable distress.[68]

Grace's perception of herself was tied to the position she had held as the powerful Joseph Galloway's wife. Marriage to her meant the continuation of a particular way of life. Though she had not been particularly happy before the Revolution, her husband's actions after the outbreak of hostilities contributed directly to her disagreements with him. She felt betrayed. In Grace's mind, Joseph had failed in his duty to support her and maintain her as a person of importance. Equally important, he had robbed her of her role as mother by taking away her precious Betsay. Without her powerful husband or her daughter, Grace's day-to-day existence conflicted with the image she held of herself; left to cope with relative poverty, the expectations she had held of marriage did not fit the reality of it, causing her bitter resentment. Unable to return to either her husband's estate, which had been confiscated or to the estate left to her by her father, which was being kept from her while her husband was alive, Grace Galloway died in 1789, without being reunited with Joseph or Betsay. Joseph outlived her by fourteen years.[69]

Joseph Galloway may not have consulted his wife when making decisions about their money, but he did not deliberately oppress her. In some instances, however, husbands clearly used their legal control of the couple's money to dominate or punish their wives. Edward Blaney who told his mother-in-law that "he would never have married, if he thought his wife could not support him," habitually mistreated his wife over money-related matters, even pawning her clothes, "except those which she had on," to pay the debts he owed a tavern-keeper. Other men, such as Thomas Minor, used wills to ensure that even after their deaths, their money and property would be kept from their wives. In all of these ways, they demonstrated their belief that they had economic power over their spouses.[70]

When husbands exercised the right to make decisions on how the couple's money was to be spent and how the couple was to live, it could cause problems between husband and wife. Bela and Susannah Badger moved from their New Bern, North Carolina, home to their more rural plantation because Bela believed it would be less expensive to live there. After the move, he put the horses, formerly used for his wife's carriage, to the plow, and put two of the five house servants to work in the fields. When Bela became ill, Susannah left him, and returned to New Bern. After his recovery, Bela moved to Philadelphia, filed for a divorce in 1806 and charged his wife with desertion —a charge she denied.[71]

This couple's marital expectations and the way they envisioned their lives together did not agree. Far from being parallel, their ideas of marriage were totally skewed; they seemed only to agree that they were married. Susannah expected a particular lifestyle, and she felt justified in leaving her husband after he decided that they should live more simply. In this situation, Bela's decisions were within the bounds accepted by their society. By leaving him, though, no matter how justified she felt it to be, Susannah was not fulfilling her role as obedient wife and helpmeet in the eyes of her community. Susannah's sister-in-law noted, for example, that instead of nursing her husband, as befitted a wife, she left him in the care of black servants [slaves?]. Ideally, husband and wife discussed such changes, but whether or not the couple actually agreed upon the changes, Bela expected his wife to comply with the decisions that he made.[72]

The sense of separation from each other that some men and women felt added to their difficulty in making compromises and adjusting to their marriages. Even when they were in love, men and women sometimes found it difficult to adjust to living together. There was often both an emotional and physical separation between the sexes. A month after her marriage, Anna Rawle Clifford wrote to her mother, Rebecca Shoemaker: "I used to say if I ever married I hoped my spouse & I would not be forever together, And I have my wish, for we never are but at meals and in the evening."[73]

By the end of the eighteenth century, women increasingly began to expect love in their marriages. Through a variety of factors such as changes in the economy and the movement of men to the frontier, the age at which men and women first married rose, and "single blessedness" for women became somewhat more acceptable.[74] Given the fact that they might not find it as easy to marry as in earlier generations, one might assume that early nineteenth-century women would place less insistence on love. In fact, the opposite appears to be true. Love had become the standard for marriage. Even though they did not always marry for love, some expected love to appear once they were married, and they believed, even if the law did not, that its absence was sufficient reason to leave a marriage.

In some cases, women fell in love with men other than their husbands. When Joseph Guemeteau filed for divorce in 1805, he accused his wife of adultery. Their family physician stated in court records that Julia Guemeteau had told him she did not love her husband. His deposition reported that her lover was the father of the child she had three and a half or four years ago, that she was pregnant by this man again, and that she had declared "she could not consent to live with one man and have children by another."[75]

In other cases, it was simply the absence of love and not the presence of a lover that compelled a woman to desert her husband. After leaving her husband, Hannah Carver of Bucks County told a neighboring farmer that "she was sorry she had ever married him [her husband], as she never loved him as a woman ought to do to marry a man." Hannah told the farmer that she had married Joseph Carver because she thought his affections for her would enable her to have a comfortable life.[76]

Ellen Coile Graves stated her case even more forcefully in a letter written at her husband's request, after he initiated divorce proceedings. Ellen had deserted her husband, who lived in Chester County, dropped her married name, and opened a "variety and trimmings store" in Philadelphia. In this excerpt from her letter one can sense a difference in the way in which the couple perceived marital love. Henry believed that his wife would grow to love him enough to be content, but Ellen was disappointed in finding that she did not develop a deep and passionate love for her husband after their marriage. In Henry's mind, it was not necessary that his wife love him, but, for her, love became the necessary and unachievable goal of her marriage. Although her letter stated that she wished her husband well, she made it very clear that she would not return to him. She even wrote that she hoped to hear he was happily married.

I do not and could not Love you I am not one of those lukewarm Creatures who can bestow their affection upon all alike where they please . . . I *cannot compel* myself to love where there is no congeniality of feeling I did wrong very wrong in marrying you without feeling a sincere attachment but believed you was capable of attaching me to you by kind and affectionate treatment you encouraged me in this beleif for you was not deceived in this respect.[77]

Examples such as the ones above became more numerous in the nineteenth century, as greater expectations sometimes led to greater disappointments. Some women married husbands whom they did not love, but who loved them. Women during this time were supposed to make love matches, equal partnerships, but were urged to be submissive toward their husbands when there were difficulties. For certain women, these conflicting directions caused confusion and doubt. Perhaps feeling that her prospective spouse knew best, the woman, in some cases, went ahead and married him. When the expected love did not materialize, women such as Ellen Graves and Hannah Carver felt trapped and unhappy—and sometimes guilty because they did not love their husbands.

Letter by Ellen Coile Graves to Henry Graves, 1806. This independent Chester County woman left her husband because she did not love him. Ellen wrote this letter at Henry's request to state her feelings and intentions—it was included with the depositions submitted to the court in their divorce proceedings. *Chester County Archives, West Chester, Pa.*

The men in these two examples apparently did love their wives. Joseph Carver was extremely upset when his wife left him, and, according to his father, "he was indifferent what became of him." Ellen Coile's letter to her husband indicated that he loved her; she wrote that she was "sorry that you still love me," and hoped her letter would remove his attachment to her. Nevertheless, his idea of marital love and her idea did not agree.[78]

It is impossible to be certain what men and women really believed in these emotionally charged situations. Based upon these limited examples, however, it appears that some men thought their wives could learn to love them and would find contentment in being their wives and the mothers of their children. Apparently they convinced their prospective wives of this. This suggests that both men and women were influenced by their expected roles of power and dependency. Some women, conditioned to dependency, listened to the voices of suitors who seemed strong and convincing, or as Nancy Shippen had, heeded their strong and convincing fathers. At the same time, some men, influenced by the earlier patriarchal aspects of their society, asserted themselves as head of the household whether or not that was adequate for satisfying the expectations of their wives.

In a letter written to Elizabeth Ingersoll, the woman he later married, Sidney George Fisher declared his love and adoration of her. At one point, however, he revealed his thoughts on the role of women: "You were born to make some man happy, your life is a failure, the purpose of your existence is unaccomplished if you do not. Why not then one who is devoted to you—as no other can be." Although he then declared that he should not try to influence her, and that she should be guided by her own feelings, he clearly believed that it was her purpose in life to marry. Since he adored her, it seemed obvious to Sidney that Elizabeth should marry him.[79]

Some women did resist marrying men they did not love. Fearing that they would never find a true love match, a "union of hearts, not of hands alone," some women chose not to marry.[80] Identifying with women who had had unhappy marriages discouraged some women from being wed. This might have been the case with Margaret Beekman Livingston, who at age sixteen left her grandmother's house, where she had lived most of her life, to live with her mother, Nancy Shippen Livingston. Nancy's marital problems had begun almost from the start of her marriage. She spent most of her married life in Philadelphia, where she had grown up and where her parents lived, while her beloved daughter lived in New York with her husband's mother. This separation between Nancy and her daughter continued even after Nancy's husband divorced her. Mother and daughter once reunited were never apart, and lived together in seclusion, as daughter devotedly cared for her mother. Margaret identified closely with her mother, and she never married.[81]

Other women tried to find love, but were unsuccessful. Elizabeth Graeme Ferguson, for example, was unhappy in love twice in her life. She was engaged to William Franklin, although neither her father nor William's was happy about the match. The two men, Thomas Graeme and Benjamin Franklin, were bitter political foes, but Elizabeth's father grudgingly allowed William to call on his daughter. In 1757, William went to London at his father's request. Although William was not eager to go at first, Benjamin made him his heir and executor in a new will, and offered to pay for his legal education in England. Apparently William could not refuse these incentives; however, he and Betsy Graeme became engaged before he left, although she declined his idea of eloping.[82]

Shortly afterwards the couple became estranged through distance and their political differences. William considered their engagement broken; he felt himself free to become involved with other women. He fathered an illegitimate child after a brief affair in 1759, and then married another woman, Elizabeth Downes, in 1762. Unfortunately, Betsy Graeme did not consider the engagement broken. When William married, she suffered a nervous breakdown, recovering only after several years and a trip abroad to forget him.[83]

Finally, in 1772, Elizabeth Graeme married, but her expectations of a lasting love were not to be. From the beginning, her husband, Henry Hugh Ferguson, spent most of his time in England, while she remained in Pennsylvania. During the Revolution, his loyalist sympathies forced him to flee permanently to England. Indeed, after Henry became General Howe's commissary of prisoners in Philadelphia, he was attainted and proscribed by the Americans. Elizabeth suffered from his actions, and the estate left her by her father, Graeme Park, was confiscated.[84]

Elizabeth and Henry never saw each other again. Despite that, Elizabeth apparently still felt something for her husband years later. In a letter to a friend, she wrote: "Indeed I am treated beyond all hopes of reconcilment no Body on the other Side of the water feels for me." Remembering then that it was the anniversary of her marriage to Ferguson, twenty-four years before, she continued, "a man one once loved and expected to have passd ones Life with to such a temper as mine cannot be the object of Indiference tho he may be of extreme Resentment."[85]

Through the effort of influential friends, Graeme Park was restored to Elizabeth Ferguson after the Revolution. She held a literary salon there, and died in 1801, after spending many years working on a translation of Fenelon's *Telemaque* into heroic verse.[86]

Both men and women searched for a perfect spouse, one who would fulfill the role of husband or wife, and increasingly one whom they could love. Although guided by family, friends, and those in authority on what to look for in a husband or wife, young men and women increasingly insisted upon choosing their own mates. Sometimes the decision to marry was a difficult one. Yet, it was after marriage that the husbands and wives had to adjust and make compromises. When couples could not adapt their viewpoints, slight tensions became chasms, and sometimes destroyed marriages.

Differences arose when wives viewed their marriages as the reciprocal relationships promised them in the literature of the new republic, while their husbands continued to see marriage in patriarchal terms. Both men and women were influenced by the distinct gender roles of a society that alleged that husbands and wives were equal partners in marriage, but that continued to give husbands economic power over their wives. This anomaly would not change substantially, until the mid-nineteenth century with various acts concerning married women's money and property.[87]

Beginning wedlock with contrasting expectations and with opposing views of life and themselves, wives and husbands often continued throughout their marriages to perceive their marital relationships differently. Husband's and wife's stories changed as the marriage developed; they intersected and connected in the weaving of their marital story, but there always remained a separate tale for wife and husband. It was the clash of expectation and reality in terms of husbands' and wives' differing perceptions, rather than simply the expectations themselves, that caused trouble in their marriages.

CHAPTER 3

"If We Forsook Prudence": Sexuality in Troubled Marriages

Masculine ethics, colored by masculine instincts, always dominated by sex, has at once recognized the value of chastity in woman, which is right; punished its absence unfairly, which is wrong; and then reversed the whole matter when applied to men, which is ridiculous.

CHARLOTTE PERKINS GILMAN, 1911[1]

In December 1805, a distraught Jacob Collady confessed that he was unable to consummate his marriage "by having carnal knowledge . . . and performing the duty of a man towards his wife."[2] Jacob's shamed admission revealed his belief that he had failed as a husband. Behind that belief was the understanding that sexual relations between husband and wife were a fundamental aspect of marriage. Although discussions of sexual dysfunctions such as the Collady's only occasionally appear in eighteenth- and early nineteenth-century Pennsylvania documents, they were certainly not the only married couple in early Pennsylvania to encounter sexual problems.

Both men and women began marriage expecting that they would have sexual relations with their spouses, and both men and women expected their spouses to be faithful to them. Whether the problem was impotence or adultery, sex caused tensions in the marriages examined here.[3] Yet the sexual problems these couples encountered often

76

were not the only difficulties they confronted; frequently the problems were reactions to tensions already existing in the marriage. How individuals reacted to their own particular marital problems differed. But by examining the testimonies of those who appeared before the court, as well as those few who put their thoughts in letters and diaries, it is possible to observe what some unhappily married men and women, their families, friends, and neighbors considered acceptable sexual behavior within marriage and how sexual tensions contributed to discord in many marriages.

In the Collady's case, both Jacob and his wife, Sophia, sought help from family members and professionals. Jacob admitted his sexual impotence to William Wonderly, a Philadelphia victualler whose late brother had been married to Sophia. Wonderly had heard that there was "considerable uneasyness and dissatisfaction" between the recently married pair, and he had noticed with surprise that Jacob left his bride's house early in the morning after their wedding night. When the couple came to Wonderly for advice, he pressed them to explain the cause of their unhappiness with each other. Jacob first answered that "the fault" was his. Then he explained that he was impotent. Wonderly responded angrily to Jacob's admission, declaring that he would not have expected a man of Jacob's character to have behaved in such a fashion. He then asked him "what he supposed a woman so healthy and young would marry him for; that it could not be for a maintenance, as she did not want for that." Jacob did not answer, "but seemed much distressed and mortified."[4]

Wonderly, however, was not the only person who observed that the Colladys were having problems. Sophia's mother noticed her daughter's distress three days after the wedding. On discovering the nature of the problem, she counseled her daughter to give Jacob more time, "that perhaps on further trial he might succeed," and to keep the matter quiet.[5] When the problem continued, the couple went together to Sophia's mother for advice. The mother asked Jacob why he had married Sophia "if he was not fit to know her." He replied "because she was a handsome woman, and he thought they could live together." He repeated again that the fault was all his.[6]

Jacob then went to see the couple's minister, who referred him to Dr. John C. Otto, a thirty-three-year-old "Practitioner of Physick."

Otto examined Jacob, and found him to be healthy, noting "that he had not arrived at that period of life when the sexual feelings are extinct," that he had fathered several children by a previous wife, and "that there was nothing repulsive in the person of his wife." Jacob told the doctor that "he felt the sexual desire as usual, but that when he went to gratify them [sic], his powers suddenly failed him, and that he could not consummate his marriage." After considering the case, Dr. Otto decided to give Jacob "some medicine merely to inspire him with confidence in himself, and to impress him with an idea, that he would become perfectly well." In addition, he told Jacob to refrain from attempting sexual activity with his wife for a week. Shortly after this, Dr. Otto met Jacob in the street. Jacob informed the doctor that he had not been able to wait the prescribed week, but had consummated the marriage "to his own satisfaction, and he believed to that of his wife."[7]

Unfortunately for the Colladys, Jacob once again became impotent. He returned to Dr. Otto, but this time the "medicine" was either ineffective or its effects short lived. In March 1806, Sophia filed for divorce, citing Jacob's impotence as grounds. She noted in her petition that as she was a young and healthy woman, her husband's impotence rendered her life "miserable and uncomfortable."[8]

Because she had been married before, Sophia probably brought certain sexual expectations to her marriage with Jacob. According to Wonderly, she did not marry Jacob for economic support. Apparently Jacob appealed to her for other reasons; perhaps she married him because she found him sexually attractive. If this were the case, her frustration may have been more acute when she found Jacob was unable to consummate their marriage than if she had married him primarily for money, especially if she had enjoyed sexual relations with her previous husband. In Sophia's mind, and that of her family and neighbors, she had a right to a sexual relationship with her husband. She had apparently behaved as a proper wife and had come willingly to the marriage bed. Nobody, not even her husband, blamed her or indicated that she had behaved improperly.

On the other hand, Jacob blamed himself and was blamed by others for failing in his duties as a husband. It is impossible to know two centuries later why Jacob experienced sexual impotence.[9] He admitted to finding Sophia attractive and to feeling sexual desire. He felt shamed and guilty at not being what he considered a proper husband, and his wife's unhappiness probably added to his own misery.

Under the Pennsylvania divorce law passed in 1785, impotence at the time of marriage was grounds for divorce.[10] But in order to obtain a divorce on any grounds during this time, one person had to be innocent of blame and injured by the conduct of his or her spouse, while the other clearly had to be at fault. In an age when the causes of sexual dysfunctions were not understood (although Otto's prescription of a placebo is interesting), Jacob, his wife, and those they consulted for advice all placed both the burden of guilt and the failure of the marriage solely on him. Yet, it was only after advice from family and professionals proved ineffective that Sophia took the desperate measure of divorce.

In its unusual frankness concerning a sexual dysfunction, the Collady's case is worthy of close examination. The Collady's plight, revealed in these court documents, goes beyond the examination of impotence to illuminate both what one married couple and their community expected from married intimate relations, and what was considered by them to be acceptable carnal behavior for married adults. The testimonies of the Colladys and their witnesses reveal that they expected sexual intercourse to be a natural part of marriage, and implied that a young woman might even marry to have her sexual desires gratified. (The witnesses seemed to assume that men and women past a certain age no longer experienced sexual desire.) For Sarah Collady to have sought a sexual relationship outside of her marriage would not have been unheard of in her time, but it would have been condemned by those around her. Nevertheless, her family and neighbors considered her desire for physical relations with her husband to be perfectly normal.

The outcome of this case is unknown.[11] Of the 367 divorce cases brought before the Supreme Court of Pennsylvania between 1785 and 1815, no men brought divorce suits accusing their wives of sexual incapacity, and only two other women cited impotence in her husband as their reason in applying for a divorce.[12] Documentation of one earlier case, discussed below, also exists.

It is not surprising that there are few examples of sexual incapacity in the divorce records. The disclosure of the condition to officials, by either husband or wife, permitted and required the public scrutiny of what would normally be a private act between the couple. A husband might suffer from feelings of shame, guilt, and inadequacy, as Jacob Collady did, but not seek help, even denying that there was a problem. A wife might also believe that the condition resulted from something she was or was not doing, and suffer silently. A newly married bride could be tense and anxious, or "frigid," especially if her partner was not a patient or skilled lover. Both men as well as women could suffer from wedding-night jitters. There was also the difficulty in proving that the condition existed. More than any other divorce grounds, sexual incapacity relied upon the testimony of husband and wife, for it is unlikely that others would know if sexual intercourse actually took place between the couple. In addition, since sexual incapacity had to exist at the time of the marriage in order to meet the wording of the law, a divorce would not be possible if a husband became impotent in later life, or if a wife refused to have intercourse after experiencing pain due to a physical condition developing later in the marriage.[13] Then again, a man or woman who loved his or her spouse or found the marriage otherwise satisfactory might not be willing to end it, or might not be willing to expose the couple's private life to the public because of a sexual problem.

A husband who experienced sexual incapacity could also take out his frustration on his wife. According to Anna Maria Boehm Miller, who petitioned the lieutenant governor of Pennsylvania for a separation from her husband in 1728/29, this was true in her case.[14] Unlike Sarah Collady, Anna Maria noted that although she felt her husband had done her a great wrong, she had been willing to live with his impotence, but feared he would "hurt her Life to conceal his own Shame." He had also threatened to sell everything he owned and "by Vertue of his Authority of a Husband" take her "to Parts remote," or alternately to sell everything and leave her. If he took her far away, her family and friends would not be able to help her, and she would be totally dependent upon this frustrated, violent man. If he left her, she would have to rely on family and friends to support her. Without his physical presence, however, she would not be able to prove his impotence, and she would have to remain a married woman.

The Collady and the Miller cases were quite different. In trying to obtain a separation from her husband over fifty years before Pennsylvania had a divorce law, Anna Maria stressed that her husband, George, had a physical deformity that made him incapable of consummating their marriage "for the procreation of Children."[15] Nowhere in her petition does Anna Maria indicate that she wanted sexual relations with her husband simply because she was a woman with sexual needs.

Given the nature of her argument, Anna Maria had to supply proof of her husband's deformity. George agreed to a physical examination, and he and Anna Maria each appointed two physicians to examine him. The doctors found that although he seemed to be missing one testicle and his other one appeared smaller than normal, he could maintain an erection and ejaculate semen, and therefore was capable of consummating the marriage. The doctors were concerned only with the fact that he was physically capable of having sexual intercourse.

The difference between George's physical examination and Jacob's are striking. Whereas Dr. Otto seemed to recognize that emotions might play a role in a husband's sexual relations with his wife, the doctors who examined George appeared to be concerned only with his physical attributes. On the evidence of two cases, it is impossible to know whether these differences indicate a change over time in knowledge of causes of impotence. What does seem clear, however, are the way the types of examinations complement the differences in the petitions. In Anna Maria's case, she stressed her husband's physical imperfections, and he denied them. Medical confirmation was therefore necessary. Sophia, on the other hand, never said that Jacob had a deformity, but only that he had not consummated the marriage, to which he agreed.

The fact that there was no divorce law in Pennsylvania when Anna Maria sought a separation from her husband also divides the two cases. Anna Maria necessarily worded her petition in a way most likely to get her a separation prior to the enactment of a divorce law. Under English law, sexual incapacity nullified a marriage. However, proof was necessary. Whether she truly believed her claims, or was as sexually frustrated as Sophia but unable to admit it in a petition, we cannot know. Because there are no testimonies of other witnesses we can not know what they thought either—did they also believe she had a right to a sexual relationship with her husband simply because she was young and healthy? In other words, we are unable to tell from these two cases how much individual perceptions of married sexuality changed. It appears, however, that in the seventy-five years between the cases, public perceptions in the form of a divorce law did change. This is not to say that the divorce law enabled any couple with sexual problems to divorce—clearly it did not. Yet the very existence of a divorce law at this time along with the dissemination of new and changing ideas about marriage beginning in the latter half of the eighteenth century may have combined to make some sexually frustrated wives and husbands more ready to demand a change in their marital status.[16]

The evidence from court records suggests that the types of sexual problems that Pennsylvania couples experienced did not change throughout the eighteenth and early nineteenth centuries. Since men and women seldom expressed in court documents or even in letters and diaries what they expected sexually from their spouses, it is more difficult to measure a change in sexual expectations over time. Nevertheless, available sources indicate that sexual behavior was often the battleground between a view of marriage stressing a patriarchal "double standard" and a feminine view stressing love and companionship. In addition, for some couples a conflict arose between the mens' persisting belief that they owned their wives' bodies and their wives attempts at independence. In addition, some women at least were influenced by new ideas about companionate marriage to form extramarital relationships with men they found closer than their spouses to their ideal concepts of a husband.

Ann Carson, for example, was unhappily married to a ship captain. She had wed him at age sixteen because her parents desired it. Although she did not love him, she was flattered by the attention the dashing captain paid to her. The couple had little in common: she was young and used to being petted and spoiled; he was accustomed to being obeyed. Whenever he was home, they fought. Ann wrote in her memoirs, "Can any thing on earth equal the misery of matrimonial infelicity? to find a tyrant where we expected a soothing companion, and to know that dire suspicion is corroding the bosom on which we depend for protection, sympathy, consolation and confidence. If not to a husband, where can a woman look for happiness?"[17]

After a few years, Captain Carson began to drink, declining job offers and neglecting those he took. Ann had a number of admirers, but was faithful to her husband until she fell in love with another man. Of her relationship with "Mr. M—," Ann later wrote, "I for the first time felt the soft passion of love. . . . My unfortunate marriage procluded all probability of our ever forming an honourable and legal connexion; can it be wondered at, if we forsook prudence, and forgot her precepts of virtue, for the enjoyment of a mutual passion, as tender, ardent, and sincere, as it was rash and imprudent . . . I was true to the object of my affections. How different would have been my fate, had my husband been that object." The unfortunate Ann traced all her later troubles to her unhappy marriage with Captain Carson.[18]

Ann knew that her society would condemn her sexual and romantic involvement with another man. Although she, too, believed it was wrong, she attempted to justify her affair by declaring that it was the first time that she had felt love. Married to a husband she did not love and with whom it appears she had little communication, she may have felt further justification for her actions because of his drinking and lack of economic support. He had ceased to live up to the ideal that society expected of husbands.

Ann, however, also failed to live up what was expected of wives. While the picture of the ideal woman came from the prescriptive literature read mostly by middle-class men and women, it circulated to some extent in the lower classes, too. Influenced by evangelical Christian thought, this literature, stressing "the ideology of passionlessness," emphasized virtue and purity in women. Women, according to this literature, were morally superior to men because they lacked sexual desires. Certainly there were models of sexually active women in novels available to middle-class readers, but the new *ideal* was that of the passionless woman. This image was spread through republican thought in the eighteenth century, and by the Second Great Awakening in the nineteenth. Women who felt themselves powerless suddenly had a mission to reform society. Some women probably did internalize these new sexual ideals as a result of their religious beliefs, or as a way to maintain some control in their lives by limiting conjugal relations and thereby limiting the number of children they had.[19] Fear of childbirth also explains why some women may have been "passionless." In addition, much of the literature and advice manuals produced by clergymen and doctors instructed nineteenth-century men to restrict and control their own sexual activity. For many couples, a lack of sexual knowledge and experience may have limited the wives' sexual pleasure by making sex perfunctory or even painful.[20] However, the new standard of passionlessness continued to conflict with older ideas of a woman as sexual temptress. Both were stereotypes, but this representation of perfect womanhood was what much of society expected wives to be. Women who flaunted their sexuality, or who *appeared* to be flaunting it, perhaps by even being on the street alone, were considered lewd or unrespectable.[21]

In reality, the activities of many couples both before and after marriage reflect their belief that women did feel sexual urges. For instance, eighteenth-century courting couples in the North engaged freely in premarital sex. What did change by the nineteenth century was that the act of sexual penetration became off limits to unmarried couples who otherwise engaged in a wide range of sexual activities. From their letters, however, it also appears that despite their sexual desires, couples believed more and more that it was up to the women to exercise self-control and restrain their lovers from going beyond acceptable sexual boundaries.[22]

Thus, beliefs about what constituted acceptable sexual limits were changing just as Americans were defining new roles concerning husbands and wives. This combination led to tensions in some marriages. Women, disappointed after not finding the expected love from their husbands, did discover it with other men. In some cases, this love propelled them into sexual relations with their new lovers. These women were not unaware of society's views concerning women who engaged in clandestine sexual relationships. Yet, their desire for love—something society promised they would find in marriage—persuaded these wives to go ahead and defy society's strictures. Even Ann Carson wrote of another woman, "She is but an erring female, the victim of a man, to whom love had made her subservient. I will not cast her off, for am I not too the slave of that seducing passions? and shall I condemn her, who am myself an erring mortal? Our blessed Saviour says, 'Let them that have no sin, cast the first stone.' I therefore was by humanity induced not to expose her and her family to public contempt."[23]

Yet respectability was once again possible if yielding women admitted to their evil ways and appeared to change willingly. Even a woman who had strayed from her husband and the respectability of wedded life was not beyond salvation. The Magdalen Society, a private charitable organization founded in 1800 in Philadelphia, sought to reform prostitutes. Some of these women had been married at one time, and married again after their rehabilitation. Magdalen No. 12 was married, but had become a prostitute. Noting that fact the minutes stated that, "she saw the evil of her former course of living, and being desirous of returning to a virtuous life, made application to your visiting committee."[24] Other women involved in fulfilling, if adulterous or bigamous relationships, however, were willing to risk ostracism or move to areas where nobody knew of their prior marriages.

Adultery cases appear more frequently than those of sexual dysfunction in early Pennsylvania records, both in court documents, and in other sources, such as almshouse records, newspapers, letters, and diaries. By examining accounts of adultery, we can learn more about what expectations married men and women in eighteenth- and early nineteenth-century Pennsylvania had in regard to sexual relations with their spouses, and we can discover what lead them to commit adultery. In doing so, we can also see how men or women contrasted in their expectations, motivations, or reactions concerning sexuality.

Reactions to unfaithfulness in one's spouse differed to some extent between men and women. Under the 1785 law, men sued for divorce on adultery grounds more often than women did. William Keith, for example, obtained divorces from two different women because of their unfaithfulness. Although it is possible that women believed they would be unsuccessful in gaining a divorce on the basis of their husbands' infidelity alone, they were, in fact, slightly more successful than men in winning divorces on adultery grounds when they did petition.[25]

Because husbands usually controlled the money and property in households, husbands were also more likely than wives to exact an economic revenge on unfaithful spouses. Such revenge could reach beyond the grave. Jacob Barr, a Philadelphia laborer, wrote in his will:

Secondly, I desire, that it is my full will & pleasure that my wife Margaret Barr shall have & fully paid to her for her Share of Legacys or any claim to my Estate one English Half Crown Commonly known by the Name of Two Shillings & Six pence Ster—& the Reason of So Small a donation to her bequeathed is on the Looss & Scandelous behavour from her Since our Marriage.[26]

To some extent, the economic revenge that men exacted upon their unfaithful spouses was part of a traditional belief that they owned everything in the household, including their wives' bodies.[27] By choosing to "give" their bodies to other men, however, their wives challenged this concept. Many men, however, then felt angered by their wives' insubordination, and felt justified in withholding all financial support.

Motivation is more difficult to pinpoint than reactions. For example, there were both men and women who probably committed adultery merely because they were looking for sexual adventures. Shortly after her marriage to Lawrence Huron du Rocher in 1798, Agatha Angelina Helena du Rocher seduced his sixteen-year-old nephew and fled with him to France. While in France, she carried on liaisons with several men, as well as with the nephew—much to the disgust of the servants. With depositions obtained from the French witnesses, her husband obtained a divorce. In another example, Eleanor Lightwood told a neighbor that there were a number of faces she liked better than that of her husband, Jacob's. The Northern Liberties farmer for whom she worked after she left her husband reported that Eleanor's "general character was that she would go after men and did not care whether they were black or white, so long as she could have connection with them."[28]

Casual sexuality was probably easier for men than it was for women, however. A double standard on sexual behavior continued to exist, although nineteenth-century society advised men, too, to limit sexual activity. Americans valued self-control in both men and women, but men did not carry the moral burden of being "exalted above human

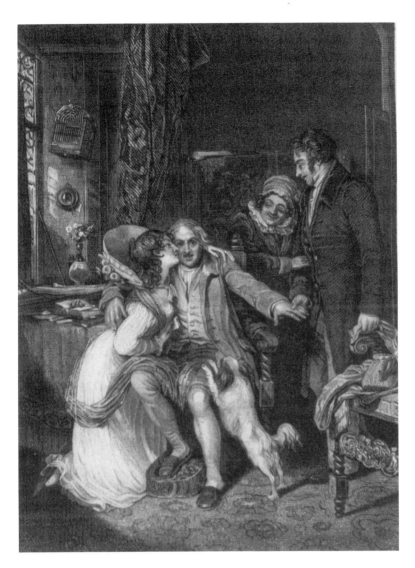

Reconciliation, *Godey's Lady's Book*, September 1831. The perfect wife welcomes her erring husband with open arms. Americans expected wives to forgive and forget their husband's transgressions unless their behavior was truly extreme or violent. *Courtesy of the Chester County Historical Society, West Chester, Pa.*

nature," nor did they have to worry about becoming pregnant. For Philadelphia men the apparent availability of prostitutes was one way in which they could have casual sexual encounters. For example, Henry Wilkinson frequently invited Samuel Addes, a Philadelphia attorney, to go with him "to houses of ill fame, where girls of easy virtue were." In addition, he often propositioned the female tavern servants while traveling to and from Philadelphia and Pittsburgh.[29] Witnesses in another divorce case testified that William Burk also had sex with prostitutes. Griffith Jones, a storekeeper in Philadelphia, reported that when he met Burk and "four other Gentlemen" on the street one night, Burk informed him that they were going "to a Whore-House" and invited Jones to go with them. Jones went along, but left after observing that there were more men than women. At a later date in 1797, he and Burk discussed the "girls of the town."[30]

As a result of these encounters, men sometimes became infected with venereal diseases. One husband, Lewis Thomas, confessed to his mother-in-law that he had had sexual intercourse with another woman and had caught a venereal disease from her, but he added, "that the same woman had also given it to another married man who had five children." In another instance, Simon Gore, a Philadelphia butcher, told his brother-in-law that he "was afraid he was Clapp'd" from having sex with a woman he met at a tavern "near the Playhouse." Still another unfaithful husband, Joseph Brown, "became incapable of performing his Business & confined to his Bed" with venereal disease due to his connection with "lewd women." His wife, Catharine, caught the infection from him.[31]

For many women, the discovery that their husbands had communicated a venereal disease to them provided confirmation that their husbands had been unfaithful. This knowledge was usually more than enough to put strains on what was probably already a troubled marriage. Esther Thomas, for example, had left Lewis several times due to cruel treatment, but she finally refused to return to him, saying "that she could forgive him everything but his connections with other women, from whom he had caught the venereal disorder."[32]

Even the treatment of the disease could cause tensions.[33] The Philadelphia physician who diagnosed venereal disease in Eliza and Jacob Steenburg in 1811 prescribed mercury, the standard treatment. A few months after the treatment, Eliza gave birth to a stillborn child. According to the doctor, this may have been from the mercury. After her confinement, Eliza went to the doctor to discover if she was still infected. He once again treated her with mercury "until it slightly effected her mouth." During this time, Jacob had been under his care twice for treatment of venereal disease, and the doctor believed his condition resulted "from his looseness and irregularities."[34]

As the examples above indicate, there were both men and women who simply desired sex with partners besides or in lieu of their spouses. In most cases, this put some sort of strain on the marriage. In other instances, however, tensions already existing in the marriage led husband or wife to seek sexual encounters with others. In analyzing these cases, it becomes clear that although there were similarities between men and women, there were also some differences in motivation, as well as in reaction.

For both men and women, alcohol seemed to be a catalyst—certainly it loosened inhibitions. Harriet Chew Carroll discovered that her husband, Charles Carroll of Homewood, whose excessive drinking had already caused her to leave him temporarily, was also seeing other women. At first Harriet refused to believe the stories, but when Charles' father produced a bill for seventy dollars indicating a hack had been hired for women, she had to believe the stories were true.[35]

The petitions of those seeking divorces and the testimonies of their witnesses frequently mentioned the combination of drinking and "lewd behavior." In an 1805 petition, Jane Houston referred to her husband, Samuel, as "a dissolute drunken & abandoned Man" who beat her after coming home intoxicated and who also committed adultery "with sundry Lewd Women." Thomas Evans, a witness in Robert Irwin's 1796 divorce case, testified that he knew Catharine Irwin had been taken to jail by a constable for lewd and disorderly behavior. After that time he frequently saw her drunk and consorting with black and white persons of "ill-fame." Lodgers in her house also testified that they had seen her drunk and had heard men in her room late at night while her husband was away with the militia.[36]

Yet alcohol was not a decisive factor in all cases. Some men and women apparently had affairs to "get even" with their spouses, or to make themselves feel better, more confident or more important. Rachel

McMullin told witnesses that she had affairs with other men because her husband had affairs with other women. Jacob Steenburgh complained to his wife about her staying out late at night and coming home by herself. Eliza became angry when he said he would escort her because he would only do so if she would tell him where she went. She then walked out on him. After she left, Jacob apparently did not know what to do with himself. He talked about entering the army, and visited women "of loose character." Apparently, however, he had contracted venereal disease prior to that, so perhaps Eliza went out at night as revenge.[37]

For men such as David Jones of Chester County, having sex with other women was one way of exerting power and control over their wives. David told his mother-in-law in 1803, a year after his marriage, that he did not marry his wife "to live with her" but only to spite his in-laws and "to prevent her from marrying anybody else." To another witness who had heard him speak disrespectfully of his wife before their marriage and asked why he married her, David said much the same. He then admitted to having sexual relations with "a certain married woman" more frequently than with his own wife, Sarah. By marrying Sarah, David made her dependent upon him; he believed he owned her, and then proceeded to treat her with contempt.[38]

Robert Murray also flaunted his power this way and used his adultery to control his wife. A nurse employed to attend his wife, Mary, during her confinement in 1797 reported that Robert did not allow her the necessary items she needed. "Most of the articles were kept and sparingly dealt out by an old woman who lived in the House, and whom the Defendant called his Mother." The nurse believed Robert had committed adultery with this old woman because "they sleep in the same room, where there is only one bed, and . . . he has often said that he slept with the said old woman." By humiliating and sometimes threatening their wives, men such as David Jones and Robert Murray maintained a sense of power and dominance over their spouses.[39]

This sense of dependence may in turn have led some wives to begin adulterous relationships. Married women relied upon their husbands for economic support due both to laws and their husbands' need to be head of the household.[40] Women who were unhappy in these relationships, and perhaps also emotionally dependent on their husbands, may have felt unable to leave their husbands without the protection of another man. For some women then, relationships with other men afforded them a way to escape husbands who may have been brutal or inconsiderate. When Philip Shriner of York County filed for divorce in 1794, he reported that his wife, Elizabeth, "for upwards of twelve months past has volutarily & perversly forsaken & abandoned the bed of your Petitioner without any reasonable cause." Since their marriage in 1786, however, Elizabeth had had three children by Philip, and all of them had died. It is possible that Elizabeth was reluctant to bear and bury another infant, and felt pressured in the marital bed. When she left Philip to live with Joseph Watkins "in a State of adulterous intercourse," she may have taken what she felt was her only opportunity to leave her husband. She married Joseph while still married to Philip, and they moved to Northumberland County. It is equally possible that Elizabeth and Joseph fell in love. Although we will never know, perhaps Elizabeth felt she needed a new start far away from the sorrow of her previous life, and in leaving with another man, she proclaimed her independence from her husband.[41]

More involved is the case of Richard and Eliza Whitting. Richard filed for a divorce in 1831, charging Eliza with adultery. Eliza had deserted Richard in 1825, and gave birth to a child three years later. Eliza clearly was guilty of adultery, but she became involved with another man only after she left Richard. In addition, it appears likely that Eliza left Richard because he beat her. After escaping a brutal husband and supporting herself, Eliza became dependent on another man when she became pregnant. Apparently Eliza intended to marry Samuel Dicky, who had a sick wife when the affair began, but he deserted Eliza after the birth of their child. Richard's application for divorce may have been prompted by economics, since he never bothered to pursue a divorce until Eliza became pregnant by Samuel Dicky, although he could have filed for divorce on desertion charges two years after Eliza left him. Perhaps Richard did not want to have to support a child his wife had had by another man. Whatever his motives, Richard received the divorce, but it is unknown what happened to Eliza.[42]

Many of the motives and reactions discussed above can be seen in the detailed divorce proceedings of Susannah and John Miller of Chester County. Although their divorce proceedings were long and compli-cated with witnesses testifying for both sides, it is clear that the mar-riage was in trouble long before John sued for divorce. Susannah and John seem to have been trying to "get even" with each other for hav-ing affairs, Susannah may have been trying to gain economically by her affair, and John apparently was a man who sought power over women by forcing himself on them sexually. The couple married in 1801. John, a tanner, brought up a petition for divorce in February 1811, noting that Susannah had lived apart from him for more than four years and had committed adultery with Isaac G. Gilpin.[43]

The one thing that all of the witnesses agreed upon was that Su-sannah did leave John to live at Isaac's. The testimonies differ in stat-ing whether Susannah and Isaac were having an affair, or whether she kept house for him. Although Susannah gave birth to a child after she left her husband, some witnesses claim he had visited her at Isaac's nine months before, and had slept with her in a room that contained only one bed. Susannah filed an answer to John's petition in August 1811, saying that she was not guilty, and noting that after John had filed for divorce, he took her back and admitted her to "his conjugal Society and embraces."[44]

Most of the witnesses testified against Susannah. Several of them described how Susannah used to meet Isaac before she left her hus-band. Martha Brown, for example, testified that she lived with the Millers "and Susanna Miller would frequently ask her to go with her to Isaac G. Gilpin about twelve oClock at night and she would go together Sometimes about three quarters of a mile and at other times not so far . . . until She could see Isaac G. Gilpin Settin in the bushes then Susan would send her home and tell her to knock about and John would think the [sic] were both there and John Miller would be in bed at the time and Susan would stay out until near or about day light and this affirment would stay up untill Susan would come home."[45]

Other witnesses testified to seeing or hearing of Isaac coming to the Miller's house. Even when John was home, witnesses reported, Isaac would come to the house and whistle to let Susannah know he was there. She would then go out to meet him. Ann Cornag testified that Susannah told her Isaac would come to the house pretending to be sick. John would have to leave his bed and give it to Isaac while Susannah stayed, ostensibly to nurse him. She would then get into bed with Isaac.[46]

Several witnesses declared Susannah told them that her third child was Isaac's. Elizabeth Hannum said Susannah told her that "her third child was Isaac Gilpin's and Isaac Gilpin told her that he would leave it an Equal share of his estates to[?] with the rest of his Children." Elizabeth reported that she had often known Susannah and Isaac "to be locked up in the Room together in the day time." She said Susannah told her she had left her husband because she thought it was wrong for him to support Isaac's child.[47]

Probably the most bizarre testimony is that of Joseph Estworthy. In a conversation at a tenant's house Susannah reportedly said:

Here is my Little Bugg [Her term for her third child.] that will ferther its Self She further Said that Her old Bugger Isaac G. Gilpin was Good for nothing Got [?] for many a knight She had to Gett up and warm a Stocking By the fire and Bath him with that and Dangle it for him Before He Coud Do anything for Her She said the Knight He Got Her that young One meaning her Little Bugg She had Made the Stocking warmer than ever.[48]

The deponent, observing that the child looked like Isaac, remarked that if Isaac took "so much Warming it could not be well done." Susannah replied that it was no use for Isaac to deny that the child was his because she would name the times and places of their meetings and would cost him "some thousand of pounds Before She had done with him."[49]

One of the witnesses for Susannah was Susanna Pennington, another housekeeper. She presented a very unflattering picture of John Miller. In her deposition, she stated that about two years earlier, John came to Isaac's looking for his wife. When Pennington answered that she was at the Market, John asked if he might then speak to Pennington in the barn. As she was milking a cow at the time and it was beginning to rain, Susanna agreed to go into the barn.[50]

After entering the barn together, John threw her onto the floor, telling her "he only ment to do a little job of Joiner work for her the deponant told Miller he was a mean son of a bitch & asked him if he intended to force her he said he must have a little old hat as Suzy Miller was not at home he could not wait." Although Pennington struggled, John raped her. Afterwards Pennington told him she would tell his wife. "Miller said he did not care as he had got a bit of fresh meat for his Cat." Pennington, however, felt ashamed and did not tell Susannah about the incident at that time.[51]

At a later date, Miller again accosted Pennington, this time in the woods. He told her "He had to do with two of his housekeepers in the same way . . . that he cared but little about Susy Miller in that respect as he could get his ends anwered by other women but at the same time Miller told this deponent to tell Susy Miller to come home and live with him he would use her well he cared nothing about what she had done or what had been said of her & Isaac G. Gilpin nor whether it was true or false all he wanted was to tare Isaac's character to pieces and get some more of Isaac's money if he could get that done he did not care if Isaac G. Gilpin & his wife lay together every night."[52]

Pennington then said that John urged her to swear falsely against his wife. She told him she would tell of "his dirty tricks." After that she told Susannah Miller what John had done.

As Isaac was a very wealthy man, it appears that both Susannah and John may have been using him to get his money. According to Susanna Pennington, John cared little for his wife, but was interested in damaging Isaac's character, and getting money from him—perhaps blackmail? Susannah may or may not have begun the affair with the idea that Isaac would support her and any children they had, but she did have an economic motive for continuing the affair, as she believed their child would inherit part of his estate. It is unclear whether she loved Isaac. Nevertheless, her marriage with John was undoubtedly a troubled one, and John was not above having his own affairs and boasting of them. Some of the witnesses indicated that Susannah and John had differences before she left him. However, he did apparently see her while she was living at Isaac's. Although neighbors acted as intermediaries between the couple, an attempt at reconciliation failed. After proceedings lasting a couple of years, John obtained a divorce.

Although John was not faithful to Susannah, he was willing to live with her as her husband. On the other hand, Susannah actually left him to live with another man. Whether she was unfaithful or not, the fact that she had a baby after she left John further complicated the matter. In the judgment of her neighbors who testified against her, and of the court that awarded John a divorce, Susannah—not John—was guilty of adultery. Neither Susannah nor John came close to representing the more modern concept of ideal spouse, but it was Susannah who fell victim to the older tradition condoning a double standard of sexuality.

As with the Millers, both husbands and wives in the other examples studied in this chapter appeared to have sexual desires. Despite the images promoted in prescriptive literature, witnesses in these divorce cases do not indicate that this was unusual in any way. What they condemned were cases of adultery and bigamy. However, neighbors rarely brought men and women to court for adultery. It was up to the spouse, although occasionally an exception was made when a woman became pregnant and officials feared the child would become a burden on the community.[53]

That neighbors did not haul adulterers to court did not prevent them from testifying and declaring their disapproval once an injured spouse brought charges. Nor did it prevent them from gossiping about the sex lives of others. Divorce cases involving adultery indicate that in most instances neighbors knew that husband or wife had been unfaithful. The testimony of these witnesses was crucial in the divorce proceedings. In examining these cases, we learn what they considered proper behavior for married men and women.

Although witnesses indicated that they did not approve of married men committing adultery, they seldom stated directly that the men were behaving improperly as husbands. This may be because they believed that men found it more difficult to control their sexual urges, especially when tempted by a "loose" woman. This did not mean that they approved of what the men did, but indicates that adultery in men, such as John Miller, might have been tolerated somewhat more than in women. On the other hand, witnesses did make statements about how wives were acting improperly.

Agnes Kimberly, for example, testified that Catharine Ducombe of Allegheny County misbehaved as a married woman because she allowed the young men liberties that Agnes thought "Indecent and improper." Other witnesses in this divorce case revealed the lack of privacy in many homes during this time. Mary Hull testified that Catharine and Robert Dawson came to her house and, "went into the bed together" where Mary was lying. She "did not see them as it was dark after they went to bed," but was confident "that Dawson had carnal Knowledge of the Respondent by their conversations and Actions while in bed." The next night, Catharine returned to Hull's house, this time with John Wilkinson. They "came into the same bed with the deponent and then and there to the best of the deponents belief and knowledge the said Wilkinson had carnal knowledge of the Respondent, as he was on her body, and apparently in the Act of Coppulation two or three times in the Course of the night."[54]

Depositions in other cases also recount tales of couples having intercourse with a third person in the bed. The circumstances Mary Hull described occurred in Allegheny County in 1790, but Martha Sill related a similar tale in a Chester County divorce of 1832.

It was July one thousand eight hundred and thirty, at the house of William Sill in Schuylkill township Chester County. I was lying in bed, and Hannah Carpenter in the same bed with me, when John Fowler came to the bed, got into the bed, (the same Hannah Carpenter being entirely undressed) and then and there the said John Fowler had criminal connexion with and carnal knowledge of the body of her the said Hannah Carpenter.[55]

For some reason, the witnesses in these cases never got up, or even screamed, threatened, or kicked the third person out of the bed. Perhaps they enjoyed a vicarious thrill, were afraid, or simply had nowhere else to sleep. Although articles on divorce in New England also mention cases where three people were in a bed, those events were all in the eighteenth century. The evidence in this chapter and subsequent chapters suggests that even in the 1830s, in rural Chester County, at least, families did not live in their own private worlds.

This lack of privacy extended beyond the crowded living quarters of the poor and working classes. The households examined here often included servants and apprentices. Many times they slept in the same room as their employers, or had to pass through their employers' rooms to get to their own. In this way, they were often witnesses to sexual activity taking place. Charles Walters, who lived with and worked for George Alexander in 1799, testified that George lived with a woman named Ann Bauman. Charles "often saw them in bed together, as he slept in the room above them and passed thro' their room when he rose in the morning."[56] Daniel Johnson was an apprentice of Samuel

Dickey's and lived in his house in Chester County. His deposition in the divorce proceedings of Richard Whitting and Elizabeth Whitting reported that one night during the winter of 1829, he was supposed to sit up with Samuel's sick wife for the first part of the night, while Samuel and Elizabeth were to sit up with her the rest of the night. All of them were in the same room of the two-room house. The sick woman was in one bed, and Samuel and Elizabeth were in the other. Johnson sat by the stove, reading a book, when "a noise attracted his attention, he looked round and saw them [Samuel and Elizabeth] in the act of copulation."[57]

Witnesses often indicated that they knew what was going on between a couple by hearing sounds and seeing the couple in bed. At other times, they suspected sexual activity had occurred because the couple was in a room with only one bed, their clothes or the bedclothes were in disarray, or they were seen kissing or fondling. When witnesses described sexual positions, they usually described the "missionary" position, where the man is on top of the woman. Usually the couples were only partially undressed. Nathaniel Hart saw Rachel McMullin "lying on her back and naked from her feet up to her middle, the said George Miller was lying in the bed with her the respondent, and when this deponent entered the room where the bed was he the said George Miller was getting on his knee in the bed." Peter Adams saw Robert Dodd "lying with the said girl on a bed . . . the girl was lying under the said Robert, and [he noticed] that her clothes were up."Sarah Deckers saw Samuel Houston and a woman "lying on the bed, and I saw him get up off from her, with his breeches down." However, witnesses saw Susanna Andreas "committing the act of adultery against a fence with the said Jacob Keister." In addition, some couples apparently indulged in other sexual activities, the warmed and dangled stocking described by Susannah Miller, for instance.[58]

A servant living in a household sometimes became a sexual temptation for husband or wife. When Maria Hyle entered the Philadelphia almshouse in 1801 due to pains in her back and breast and swollen ankles, the docket noted that her husband of twelve years, "took up with their bound Girl in the House by whom he had a Child, and with whom he went-off since the 1 July 1800."[59]

Married men who became involved with their servants did not always run away with them. When a female servant became pregnant by her master, she could be forced to leave or to marry someone else. In one example, the employer even gathered a group together to coerce a shot-gun marriage between the servant he had made pregnant and another man. Susanna Bussard of Northampton Township worked for Jacob Keister and lived with Keister and his wife. When Susanna became pregnant by Keister, Keister told a doctor he met in a tavern that Susanna had been raped and offered him "a Half-Joe if he would use his medical knowledge in obtaining an abortion of the child." The doctor refused. Susanna then swore before a justice of the peace that Abraham Andreas had fathered her child. Susanna's brother, Keister, and others went to Andreas and told him he had to go to the justice. Andreas denied that the child was his, but agreed to go with them. The men stopped at several places and drank large quantities of alcohol. By the time they brought Andreas to the justice he was very drunk, and probably not thinking very clearly. He knew that he could not pay bail, and he was afraid that he would be thrown into prison, therefore, he submitted to the marriage ceremony with Susanna. The couple laid down on a bed together after the ceremony, but in the morning he went back to his brother's and she went back to Keister's house. Witnesses reported that after her marriage, Susanna and Keister were still having an affair, and that Keister's wife had caught them in bed together several times.[60]

Not only servants, but even other family members sometimes came between husband and wife. Edward Williams became interested in his wife's daughter, Eliza. Edward's wife, Sarah, began to drink after she found out that her husband and daughter were intimate. She drank more after he fathered a child by her Eliza. Eventually, Edward and Eliza had a second child, and by that time Sarah was sick as a result of her drinking. According to Edward, it was Eliza who proposed murdering his wife. Edward said he told her that he would run off with her, but Eliza told him, "I don't want to have people say that I took my mother's husband, and run off with him. Says she, just take her life, and then I will go home with you and I can be your housekeeper, and wife too, and Nobody will know but that she died a natural death."

In his confession, Edward revived earlier eighteenth-century views of women as sexual temptresses, and he portrayed himself as the victim of such a one. According to him, Eliza was an evil, lascivious woman who pursued him and plotted the death of her mother. At the same time, she was aware of what society would think of a woman who stole her mother's husband. Nevertheless, the court held Edward accountable for the crime. Edward was convicted of murdering his wife by poison, and he was executed in public on December 31, 1830.[61]

Most extramarital affairs were not so horrible or dramatic, and most probably never became official public events. Yet, with servants or family members living in such proximity, it would have been difficult to keep them secret. As we have seen, however, this did not prevent men or women from having extramarital sexual encounters. When sexual activity took place either between couples living in the same household, or between those who frequently visited each other's residences, it was relatively easy for them to find a place to have relations. Most of the witnesses reported seeing the couples in beds. Other couples met in the woods, in barns, or at friends' houses. Thomas Goodwin, for instance, gave Francis Bourgiois the key to his house on Ninth Street which was empty and to be rented. Goodwin thought Bourgiois was showing the house to friends. When he returned the key, Goodwin asked him if his friends approved of the house. Bourgiois "replied that he approved of the house, for that he had had criminal connection there with a very fine girl of his acquaintance, and with whom he had often before had similar connection."[62]

Others found more unusual places for their assignations. William Burk, after separating from his wife, but prior to their divorce, consorted with a "woman of bad fame." The one time he tried to bring her to the room he shared with a roommate, the roommate threw her out. To this roommate, Burk related, "that he had often carried her into a Burying-ground in Race Street, above Sixth Street, and there had carnal connection with her."[63]

Because of close living quarters, community interaction, and perhaps simply a different sense of privacy than we have today, the men and women examined here often found it difficult to keep their sex lives secret from their families and neighbors. This was true until at least the early nineteenth century in Philadelphia and even later in rural areas. When Samuel Addes told Henry Wilkinson "it was improper and wrong for him to go to such houses [of prostitution] that his wife might hear of it," he was probably speaking the truth.[64]

Living with the gossip of neighbors, however, was not always easy. Cases filed in Chester County reveal that those who were the victims of gossip claimed that their livelihoods suffered and feared that their reputations were ruined by the gossip. Whether guilty or innocent of committing adultery, these people knew that their neighbors considered it wrong. This informal regulation of public morality may not have served to prevent people from committing adultery, but did lead some people to try to clear their names in court.

In one case, Frederick Routhraff, a minister of the gospel, claimed that Edward Emery and Jacob Moyer "contriving and wickedly and maliciously intending to deprive the said Frederick of his good name, character, credit esteem and reputation . . . did say, speak utter and publish these false and approbious words." The document charging Emery with slander then went on to report that Emery had said to people, "that is a devil of a story they have about old Freddy (the said Frederick Routhraff meaning) and Guss's wife." Emery then went on to tell the story of Routhraff at the house of Jacob Guss. Guss's wife told her husband that "the boys want you in the shop." While Guss went down to the shop, Routhraff and Guss's wife continued upstairs, where Routhraff "shagged" her. Routhraff maintained that due to this story, which he declared was false, some of his neighbors had "withdrawn themselves and do every day more and more withdraw themselves from his company and conversation." Because of this he said he had spent considerable amounts of money and great effort to clear his name, and he sought damages of $2,000.[65]

Routhraff understood that during a time when it appeared almost impossible to keep secrets from one's neighbor, a person's reputation was important. Even the older set of traditions that tended to disregard some sexual straying by married men did not condone a man sleeping with his neighbor's wife, while newer ideals stressed sexual restraint for both genders. As a minister, Routhraff was expected to uphold community standards, as well as to live a blameless life himself. As a member of the community, he knew that being able to live with one's neighbors was important both for social purposes and in terms of making a living. Neighbors often supported and comforted one another in times of trouble. In addition, he and they understood that it was not wise to antagonize people who might be possible customers, partners, or employers.

The couples analyzed in this chapter had a variety of sexual problems and experiences. In some cases, sexual tensions caused their marital problems. In other cases, tensions already existing in the marriage—lack of love, drinking problems, the clash of expectation and reality—were expressed sexually. Changing and conflicting ideas about love, sexuality, and marriage, and about how men and women should behave contributed to sexual tensions and problems. Sexual expression is and was an integral part of a marriage. It is not surprising that this sort of intimacy could cause problems for couples.

Yet in the eighteenth and nineteenth centuries, couples could not seek sex counseling as twentieth-century partners can. Even manuals such as *The Married Lady's Companion or Poor Man's Friend,* which gave detailed instruction on such intimate topics as menstruation and childbirth, did not supply any information on sex. When sex was mentioned in manuals, it was usually in the form of warnings about what happened to those who masturbated, or engaged in other "vices." Nevertheless, available records indicate that people did talk of sex with friends and relatives, and occasionally sought advice from doctors and ministers.

In trying to escape from unhappy marriages, both husband and wives found that the images that they presented to others were important in gaining their support. When documenting cases of adultery, the depositions of neighbors were important. Neighbors and household members often witnessed the most intimate behavior of husbands and wives. In smaller households, people shared bedrooms; in larger households, servants observed their employers' behavior. During the nineteenth century, family and community were still closely intertwined in many places. People knew their neighbors and gossiped about them.

In a time when married men and women were expected to behave in particular ways, those who "forsook prudence" to engage in sexual activity outside of marriage often attempted to justify their behavior both to themselves and to others. Despite new ideals of female passionlessness and male self-control, many men and women understood that both genders experienced sexual desire. Yet, a double standard remained. Men and women were both expected to exercise sexual restraint, but women were expected to enforce it. While in Pennsylvania, women were able to divorce husbands who committed adultery; to do so they had to prove that they were blameless and virtuous wives.

CHAPTER 4

"Cruel and Barbarous Treatment": The Forms and Meaning of Spouse Abuse

The women of this land are differently situated than those of any other country. Here, emphatically, whether in the relationship of mother, daughter, sister or wife, woman is man's companion. She is indeed, his 'help meet.' Here, woman's true dignity is asserted and maintained.—Civilly, she is regarded as the most proper object of his protection and while in the old world, the 'lords of creation' may administer to their wives, moderate corporate chastisements, here, where the laws must be administered with *some* regard to the popular will, the husband would be convicted of an assault and battery, who should imitate, the conduct of transatlantic spouses.

"THE WOMEN OF AMERICA," *The American Woman*, 28 SEPTEMBER 1844

In the ideal marriage in the new republic there was no place for spouse abuse. Joined in an affectionate union, the married couples of eighteenth- and early nineteenth-century literature discussed their differences. Husbands explained their arguments with logic and patience, while wives attempted to persuade their husbands by good example and moral certainties, but submitted to their requests if they could not.[1] Of course, in reality marriages did not always work that way, and anger and violence did occur between wife and husband. Both the law and the community recognized that in some cases not even the gentlest and most obedient of wives could sway a cruel husband, and that these wives should receive some comfort and relief. Pennsylvania women and men demonstrated that they understood what it meant to be a model wife or husband; furthermore, they tried to gain sympathy and prove their innocence when their cases of domestic violence came before the public.[2]

The examination of spouse abuse here will include what early Pennsylvanians termed "cruel and barbarous" treatment—that is, both physical violence and the husband's withholding of money and necessities from his wife.[3] Also to be studied here is under what conditions men and women felt that their actions were justified and what effect this had on gender relations in the society of this period. When did men consider it within their rights as husbands to attack their wives, and why did women generally wait until they had suffered brutal assaults to seek legal assistance? Why did so few men report abuse?

During this time in Pennsylvania, women rather than men most often complained of spouse abuse. Although some men reported attacks made on them by their wives, most husbands probably did not report these incidents very often. Legal options, except for pursuing assault and battery charges against their wives, did not exist for mistreated husbands.[4] Also, because men generally held the upper hand in terms of both physical and economic power, it served no purpose for most of them to reveal that they had been attacked by their wives, and only opened them up to ridicule by their peers. This was not true of their wives, however, who though they faced possible repercussions from angered husbands, possessed definite advantages in terms of legal and economic aid and sympathetic support from neighbors and friends if they made their complaints known publicly.[5]

Although we cannot now know what was in the minds of the husbands who abused their wives, we can speculate about their motivations. Were they simply frustrated men who relieved their frustrations on their wives, perhaps as a climax of built-up anger? Were the pressures of finding and keeping work a major source of those frustrations? Did violence result from sexual tensions between husband and wife? Did abuse occur more often among the poor than the rich, or among those in the city rather than the country? Were men who abused their wives mentally ill or alcoholics? To what extent did cultural perceptions about the roles of husbands and wives contribute to their actions? These various possible motivations will be explored here, but it seems safe to assume that in situations of eighteenth- and nineteenth-century spouse abuse, as in twentieth-century cases, episodes of violence or cruelty were often the result of a combination of several of these factors.[6]

Violent behavior is not always part of a habitual pattern of abuse, although it may be harmful and cruel. As the law recognized, murders committed accidentally in the heat of passion are not the same as premeditated murders. For example, in 1733, the *Pennsylvania Gazette* reported that a man had been committed to prison for killing his wife: "'Tis said that upon some Difference he threw a Loaf of Bread at her Head, which occasion'd her Death in a short Time." The court convicted the man of manslaughter rather than murder and sentenced him to be burnt in the hand.[7] It is not likely that the man kept a supply of stale bread close by in order to kill his wife, but he may have habitually expressed his anger at her by throwing objects or otherwise mistreating her. For many men studied here, the violent mistreatment of their wives served as a vent for their frustrations and a display of force in a world in which they had little power.

Although beliefs about marriage were changing during this time and the relationship between husband and wife was supposed to be a loving one, most abused wives and their witnesses felt obliged to prove that women had been severely beaten in order to obtain aid. Most people were starting to believe that any physical attack made by a husband on his wife was unacceptable, but they did not generally consider the husband who gave his wife an occasional slap to be a spouse abuser. And in the continuum of domestic violence, the concept of marital rape did not exist during this time. It undoubtedly did occur, yet sexual violence between husband and wife was never referred to by plaintiffs, defendants, or witnesses in the Pennsylvania cases of this time.[8] Instead, spousal violence in early Pennsylvania generally meant severe beatings or death threats. But marital cruelty also included instances when a husband deprived his wife of necessities. In this way, the Pennsylvania law incorporated a broad definition of what constituted cruel treatment, even though it did not include all forms of marital brutality.[9]

In some cases, the behavior described by these Pennsylvania men and women was cruel but not necessarily violent. Often their pleas for help equated physical abuse and "economic" abuse. In most cases, but not all, the complaints of economic abuse were from wives who lacked food, shelter, clothing, and other necessities. In part, however, the laws and values of their society dictated both their situations and their pleas for help. Husbands occasionally attempted to regain property from vengeful wives, but usually men held power over money and land. Under law, husbands controlled their wives' wages, property, and income if these were not protected by a trust or separate conveyance. Thus, even women whose work contributed a large share of the family's income might find themselves dependent upon their husbands and subject to his whims. For women in happy marriages, there was probably no problem. But for women married to unscrupulous or spiteful husbands, these legal and social constraints could prove severe.

In many instances, wives remained with husbands who abused them because they could not support themselves or their children. In contrast, husbands who were ill treated by their wives were not generally subject to the same financial constraints. In an unusual newspaper advertisement addressed to "Friend Franklin," Richard Leadame noted that his wife "abuses me her Husband so much that I cannot live with her: And I forwarn all persons from Trusting her on my Account, after the Date hereof." [10]

Although Leadame's wife may have physically attacked him (we do not know what form the abuse took), he was able to establish housekeeping elsewhere. His only concern was that his wife not incur debts that he would have to pay. Unlike Leadame, however, most mistreated wives could not simply walk away from their spouses, because their husbands controlled their means of support. Wife abuse during this period must be seen as an extension of gender inequality existing within both the society and within marriage. Laws enacted during the mid-eighteenth century did not provide married women with the right to control their own estates—that would not come until the next century—but did provide at least temporary economic support to wives unable to live with their husbands. [11]

Pennsylvania couples discovered that there were both legal and extralegal means of fighting marital cruelty. Most abused spouses during this time sought help from family, friends, and church officials who helped them during temporary separations and often served as mediators between husband and wife. Only if these "informal regulators"[12] were ineffective in eliminating the cruel behavior, or if the victim lacked family or friends able to help, did an aggrieved husband or wife pursue legal assistance or seek shelter in institutions such as the almshouse. In Pennsylvania, however, the mid-eighteenth century was the beginning of a transition period, where informal regulation was most widely used, but formal regulation was becoming available and was increasingly applied, especially when the informal regulators failed.

As in modern unions, husbands and wives frequently vented the frustrations of everyday life on their spouses. Then, as now, situations of marital abuse usually resulted from a combination of circumstances, among them sexual tensions and jealousies, intoxication, problems with in-laws, and fights over money. In addition, tensions frequently arose from differing expectations about marriage held by husbands and wives, and from conflicts in their perceptions about their roles. In turn, these conflicts became excuses for one spouse to mistreat the other when, for instance, husband or wife fell short of meeting a perceived ideal. The reactions of the abused were motivated as well by their expectations, their desperation, and the knowledge of possible support by family, neighbors, and the law.

Marital cruelty then was only one source of marital problems or tensions. In some cases, these problems arose when wife or husband could no longer live with the vicious treatment from his or her spouse. In other cases, marital cruelty came as a reaction to the problems already existing in the marriage. For the most part, it is impossible to discover cause and effect—did she drink because he beat her, or did he beat her because she drank? Or were both the drinking and the beating individual releases from marital tensions and problems? It is most likely that spouse abuse resulted from a combination of these things, and in almost all the examples studied here, the abuse was only one aspect of a troubled marriage.

The drinking of alcoholic beverages whether done as a release from tensions or simply to be sociable frequently provoked violent behavior. Poor and laboring men in late eighteenth-century Philadelphia often went on drunken binges in attempts to forget their frustrations

Lifting the Mortgage, Frontispiece from the *Pennsylvania Temperance Almanac*, 1837. In the 1830s, temperance became a serious reform movement. Excessive drinking was seen as a threat to the family. This print and the one following are typical of those seen in temperance almanacs of the period. In the first, the drunken husband manages to sign a pledge of sobriety so that he can once again live in harmony with his wife. In the second illustration, the husband is portrayed as an unfortunate victim of evil "rum-sellers." *Both Courtesy of the Chester County Historical Society, West Chester, Pa.*

with their lives, to forge links with their peers, and to prove their manliness.[13] After carousing, some men went home and beat their wives. Drinking was so commonly associated with abusive behavior in husbands and harsh or vile language and lewd behavior in both husbands and wives that examiners in divorce cases regularly asked witnesses if the husband or wife drank habitually. In numerous testimonies, wives and their witnesses reported husbands who squandered away their money on alcohol and beat their wives in drunken rages. For example, Jane Houston, the wife of a grocer, reported in 1805 that her husband frequented "tavern & Lewd houses, & frequently returns home intoxicated with strong liquor & beats and abuses your libellant."[14]

The Rum-Seller's Victim, The Family Christian Almanac, 1848.

Such episodes of drinking and wife-beating were not confined to the poor. Wealthy men faced a different set of pressures in that they often felt compelled not only to earn enough to support a wife and family, but also to reach and maintain the heights achieved by their fathers. Charles Carroll and Harriet Chew Carroll, for example, discussed in Chapter 2, both came from wealthy and prominent families. After a few years of marriage, Charles began to drink more and more, and his wife and children suffered for years as a result. Although Harriet's family and Charles's father, the famous Charles Carroll of

Carrollton, were willing to provide financial and emotional support for Harriet, she continued to live intermittently with Charles for years, enduring his callous disregard for her and their children, as well as his threats, violence, and adulteries. In 1814, J. E. Howard, who was married to Harriet's sister, wrote to her brother, Benjamin Chew, Jr.: "I wish Harriet could be as well satisfied as I am myself that Mr. CC is easily managed with respect to any violence or ill treatment of her or her children. As to his habit of drinking nothing can change that whilst he can get anything to drink." Ultimately, Charles did attack Harriet and the children, and her family convinced her to leave him permanently.[15]

Most women did not have wealthy relatives who could support them when their husbands drank to excess. For them, concerns about money were as pertinent as fears of beatings and alcohol abuse. In their complaints, they expressed their expectations about and disillusionment with their marriages in these terms, since both they and the society around them believed that husbands were supposed to provide financial support for their wives and families. In particular, wives expressed their outrage when money that should have gone to maintain them and their families was thrown away on alcohol, and sometimes on other women. Thus, in addition to accusations of physical mistreatment, these women also condemned their husbands for abusing them economically. Sometimes the squandered money was money the wife had either earned or inherited. How could a woman look up to and obey a husband who depleted their earnings, especially if she had had experience earning, handling, and managing money, and knew that she could do a better job, if only she had the chance?

In a divorce petition filed in 1812, Mary Reilly reported that when she married her husband, Philip, in 1809, she was a widow with several children, but had a "comfortable property" from her previous husband. However, she noted that:

for a considerable time past the said Philip Reilly has become idle and dissipated and frequently addicted to intoxication, having entirely squandered all the property of the Petitioner, which was in his power, and using no means of labor or industry to maintain either himself or your Petitioner and a young child which your Petitioner has had by him. That on the contrary, in his fits of rage and intoxication he has destroyed and injured the furniture &c in the house in which he resides, and treated the whole family with repeated personal violence.[16]

In this petition, Mary Reilly revealed what she thought to be her husband's crimes. He was an alcoholic who would not support his family, including his own child. Moreover, he took advantage of his position as head of the household to dissipate the property that might have supported them, and in his drunken rages, he even destroyed their belongings. Mary provided no reason for her husband's behavior other than his drinking, yet clearly it was not *only* his violence after drinking that bothered her. She was equally annoyed by his idleness and the fact that he squandered the property she had brought to the marriage. Because she may have enjoyed the comparative wealth and freedom she had as a widow and perhaps compared this second marriage to her first, Mary Reilly's motivation to seek her freedom through divorce may have been greater than that of many other abused women who had no alternative experience of how they might be sustained economically.

As Mary Reilly's libel disclosed, even when husbands drank, it was only one source of tensions. Although abused wives sometimes regarded money spent on drink as simply being wasted, they often had real concerns about there being enough money to clothe, feed, and house their families. At issue was both what purchases should be made, and who should decide how money was to be spent. Couples did not always agree on what objects should be purchased for their homes, nor on what type of lifestyles they should pursue. Frequently, these tensions led to physical blows.

In some cases husbands may have been justified in their anger at wives who spent money on objects beyond their incomes, but it is the ones who actually abused their wives as a result of their anger and in an attempt to assert their dominance in the marriage that are of interest here. For instance, John McElwee, a Philadelphia glass merchant, often flew into "great passions" during which he would push and threaten his wife, Rebecca, and throw her out of the house. Apparently one source of tension in this marriage was over how their money was to be spent. He accused her of extravagance because she wanted a new carpet and a shawl "which cost a guinea, because a neighbor had one." At the same time, John was trying to assert his power over his wife. During one argument, he told her that he had raised her "from obscurity," and at another time he stated that he would take her back only if she would eat in the kitchen with the servants—her "proper place." Even after Rebecca received a divorce from bed and board with alimony, the couple continued to squabble over money because John refused to pay the full sum awarded to Rebecca. As he wrote in a letter to her attorney in 1801, he was having enough trouble paying his "legal debts without contributing further to support the the pride Extravagence & letchery of a pair of prostitutes & an old procuress." [17]

McElwee's reference to prostitutes and procuress involved Rebecca, her sister, and her mother. In fact, family members often formed factions and alliances that aided the abusers or the abused. Thomas Cope noted in his diary in June 1802 that he had received a letter from a man who was trying to have his sister-in-law disowned by the Society of Friends.

He says she has charged him falsely with first kicking her out of his house; second that he & his mother, by their improper conduct, were the cause that his wife became crazy; third that when he went out of an evening he locked his wife in her chamber to keep her from young company; & fourth that he had communicated the venerial disease to his wife. [18]

Cope treated what may have been a serious situation rather lightly, calling the man "a blockhead" for giving the accusations so much publicity. Nonetheless, the situation he described, that of a divided family, was common in marriages marked by abuse. For example, a Chester County woman in 1767 described how her husband threatened her with "a couple of hickory rods" after she refused to swear an oath to him that she would never again go to her father's house. In an 1802 example in Bucks County, Catharine Deyly reported that her husband's sons mistreated her. [19]

Spouse abuse also affected families by keeping them in a constant state of fear. The detailed testimony of fifteen year old Elizabeth Brown in her parent's divorce case offers readers a rare and vivid account of what wife-beating could do to family life. Elizabeth was the eldest daughter of Mary Brown and Jacob Brown, a man who was often drunk and violent. Recounting incidents that had occurred over three years before, Elizabeth recalled the time she saw her father attempt to choke her mother. Elizabeth remembered running to a neighbor's to get help. Upon her return, she found her mother, "standing in the other end of the house Crying." Elizabeth noted that she must have seen her father "strike Mother more than a hundred times," and that "towards the last we, the children, got so much afraid of him, when drunk, that we always at such times run away from him."[20]

In addition to alcohol, worries over money, and family problems, sexual tensions provoked violence in some husbands. According to a witness in the divorce of Charlotte and John Brown of Philadelphia, John became jealous when Charlotte "was frequently asked in Company to sing." The witness stated that although Charlotte had a pleasant singing voice, John believed that Charlotte sang to entice the men who were listening. Other men beat their wives when they dared to complain about their husbands' sexual behavior. When Elizabeth Lukins protested in 1781 after her husband brought a woman "of evil Name and Fame" to live in their house, both the husband and the other woman beat her and forced her to leave. This is an extreme example, but lesser flaunting of extramarital sexuality led to similar cycles of violence in response to complaints made by spouses.[21]

Divided families, economic pressures, and sexual tensions did not cause all men to behave violently, but did produce frustrations that some men handled with violence or abuse toward their wives. Certainly alcohol contributed to violent situations by loosening inhibitions in both men and women. Because information on these people is so limited it is impossible to determine whether those who abused their spouses did so from copying behavior observed in parents or other family members, as it has often been proven in the twentieth century.[22] Nevertheless, also important in the instigation of brutal behavior were the perceptions men held about their roles and that of their spouses.

Within these damaged marriages, husbands and wives frequently perceived their roles in quite different ways. In some situations of marital cruelty, husbands believed that it was within their rights as husbands to abuse their wives, whether it was through threats, violent action, or the denial of necessities. Husbands in these relationships often viewed their roles as that of head of the household with the right to "correct" and guide their wives' behavior and conduct, even by physical blows. Although Michael Fisher, a Berks county yeoman, may be an extreme case, he reportedly said about his wife that he believed "beating was necessary to make her a good housekeeper and that she must have more of it."[23] At the same time, evolving societal perceptions of the roles of husbands and wives often influenced how these couples discussed their actions. Some husbands, for instance, attempted to justify their deeds by discrediting their wives. Others, responding to their wives' accusations of brutal behavior, often trivialized their own violence as natural reactions of anger at irritating wives—in other words, wives who went beyond their husbands' expectation of the docile and submissive helpmeet, who, they implied, were abusing them in nonviolent ways.

The very fact that societal norms about marriage were changing in the eighteenth century both allowed some women more freedom of action and gave some wife-beaters an excuse. These men fell back on traditional views to justify their actions by labeling their wives immoral, promiscuous, or derelict in their duties as wives and mothers. Thus, Jacob Burkhart, a Philadelphia County yeoman, explained in 1785 that his wife's "Lewd Conduct and abusive language" provoked him into giving her "One blow with his open hand in such a Manner as to hurt her but very little." Similarly, Andrew McBride noted in 1792 that his "insults" or "indignities" toward her were due to "the violence of her temper and Disposition and by the indifferent and provoking conduct of hir [sic] the said Elizabeth," towards him. Although James Sutter did not exactly blame his wife, he did blame her mother, and denied abusing either of them, except as a result of "a natural warmth of Temper," aroused by the refusal of his mother-in-law to let him enter her house or see his wife or children.[24]

These same men apparently felt compelled to explain that they did not *seriously* injure their wives. They knew well that society imposed limits even though they believed that it was within their rights as husbands to strike their wives when their behavior threatened a man's role as head of household. Wives who sought relief from unfeeling husbands obviously did not agree. Beginning in the eighteenth century, and becoming more frequent after the middle of that century, women left their husbands not only because they feared for their lives, but also because they expected more from their marriages. Although some wives tolerated beatings and neglect from their husbands, others denied that their husbands had the right to "correct" or punish them physically. In doing so, they revealed the influence of these new perceptions about marriage on their own expectations.

Many ill-treated wives complained, as Susanna Brauer did in a 1786 divorce petition, and Charity Barr did in a 1785 newspaper notice, that their husbands were "tyrants," or that a husband who should have been her "best friend" treated her cruelly.[25] Because husbands who denied them food, shelter, or other necessities clearly did not fit the image of ideal husband and father, some wives in this period felt justified in seeking help or in leaving their mates. Women and men often expected different things in marriage. In this era of transition, however, some men fell back on a simplified tradition of right and power to have their way. Thus a time of transition was also probably a time of particular tensions in what was acceptable and what was not.

Because potentially spiteful husbands usually wielded economic power and often, although not always, physical power over their wives, they were more likely to be the ones accused of violence or neglect. Before accusing their husbands publicly, however, mistreated wives had to make some difficult decisions. First, they had to establish what was actually cruel behavior, and how much of it they were willing to accept. Then they had to determine if the risks of taking their husbands to court, deserting them, or taking other actions outweighed the risks of inaction. The decision to leave her husband may have been reached suddenly after his fit of temper, or one that a woman had planned for a while. Either way, once she left their house, she had to decide how she would pursue the matter and how she would live. On the other hand, a wife who filed for divorce had to weigh the pros and cons, perhaps seeking legal advice first before commencing the suit. If she won her suit, she would be legally separated from her husband and he would be ordered to pay alimony to support her and the children. If she did not win her suit, she would be no better off —perhaps much worse—than before she petitioned for divorce. She may have wondered what her husband would do if she made a plea for divorce and lost. Would he take her back? If not, how would she support their children? Would he abuse her even more if she returned to him?

That women were willing to risk economic destitution, perhaps more abuse from angered husbands, and the embarrassment of airing their personal lives in public indicates how desperate they were. It also indicates that many of them knew how to use the legal system, and moreover that they were given some support and encouragement in their endeavors. Court records, for instance, indicate that witnesses who testified that they did not interfere in cases of wife-beating still expressed the belief that it was wrong.

The support and encouragement given to women was part of a gender-conscious perception of spouse abuse that worked both to their advantage and disadvantage. Mary S. Hartman suggests that Victorian women accused of murder in France and England may have escaped severe punishment because of commonly accepted beliefs that respectable women could not be guilty of such crimes of passions and cruelty.[26] This double standard may have been operational in one late eighteenth-century Chester County case. In 1792, the Chester County courts charged Sarah O'Neal with murdering her husband, Constantine (Cundy), by striking him on the left side of his head with an "axe of the value of five shillings." The court determined that there was no case, and she was "discharged by proclamation" of the grand inquest.[27] To some extent in late-eighteenth-century Pennsylvania, abused women fitting the popular image of the virtuous wife were probably more successful in convincing authorities of their blamelessness and their need for relief from cruel husbands (although the courts did not condone murder), while those who did not fit the image were blamed for causing their situations and were not considered worthy of aid. Both women and men were aware of these perceptions and tailored their accusations and defenses to fit.

Yet men were also victims of gender biased perceptions. The divorce law, for example, allowed only women to petition for divorce on cruelty grounds.[28] Nevertheless, in at least two instances, men applied unsuccessfully for divorces citing cruelty from their wives, either out of ignorance or as a challenge to the law.[29] Both public and personal perceptions of manliness also prevented men from acknowledging abuse by their wives. Men of all classes wanted to be considered the head of their households. While jokes and songs about nagging wives were numerous, men did not want to acknowledge that their own wives got the better of them—it was always the wife of some other man.

Although the laws began to reflect these changing ideas and aided men and women in leaving intolerable situations, individuals in early America continued to vary in their responses to marital cruelty. In Pennsylvania, abused wives reacted in various ways ranging from remaining with their husbands, to deserting them, to taking them to court. Throughout this period, many wives tolerated abuse until it became life-threatening, and even then they often returned to cohabit with their husbands after leaving them or pursuing court actions. In part, this was due to situations in which they were financially dependent on their husbands. When they did take action, divorce was only one option. Although a Pennsylvania law passed in 1785 made divorces easier to obtain, most people did not divorce. Divorce proceedings involved months of litigation, and cruelty grounds were difficult to prove. Most people were probably unwilling to take the time and effort to pursue a divorce, instead they left their spouses, perhaps depending on help from friends or family members, found solace in alcohol, sought other legal action, fought back, or relied upon combinations of all of these as solutions to their problems.

Neighbors and relatives were crucial in aiding the victims of marital cruelty. Although in some cases families and friends may have hesitated to step into the middle of a quarrel between wife and husband, in other cases, they rescued the wife from her husband's brutal beatings or economic neglect without considering that they were invading the privacy of a family. These neighbors and loved ones offered emotional solace, financial aid, food, and shelter. They also acted as mediators for the couple. Often when situations became too bad, they offered counsel and advice to the suffering spouse.

Women on the whole usually sought aid first from family members, friends, or neighbors. Harriet Chew Carroll discussed her plight with her brother, sisters, and in-laws in frequent letters and visits. In turn, they gave her comfort and advice throughout the troubled years of her marriage to Charles Carroll. After finally deciding to leave her husband for good in 1816, Harriet wrote to her brother: "I have received your affectionate letter my ever dear Brother and am tenderly sensible of your goodness—Yes, I will come to your protecting arms & find shelter from the fearful conflicts that have assailed me."[30]

On the other hand, Catharine Deyley of Bucks County sought advice at various times from specific members of her community. She asked a church elder and a justice of the peace, among others, to meet with her and her husband, Christian. Each of these neighbors listened to the couple's stories and advised them to mend their differences and live together peacefully. After Catharine contacted them, Christian felt the need to explain his side to his neighbors, but he was conscious of how his wife might have portrayed him. One witness reported that after Catharine left him due to him beating her, Christian said that if she would return and "not repeat old stories about in the Neighbourhood tatling and setting the Neighbours at variance he would use her well and as a husband ought to."[31] These same counselors who advised the couple during their problems served as witnesses on her behalf when Catharine could no longer tolerate Christian's beatings, coldness, and unpleasant manner, and decided to divorce him in 1802.[32]

When their husbands' brutal actions became too much to bear, some women believed that the only solution was to leave. For example, after her husband published a newspaper advertisement stating that she had deserted him without reason, Charity Barr of Bucks County published her own notice declaring that she did have reasons. As was typical of the few wives who responded to their husbands' newspaper advertisements, she noted that his cruel treatment of her had forced her to leave him. In explaining her actions, she proclaimed that she had been beaten and "sometimes almost strangled by him, at other times thrown on the floor and stamped on, [with him] swearing he would murder her." This treatment kept her bedridden for several days. She ended her response with these words: "If such cruel usage, from a man who ought to have been her best friend, be not sufficient cause for leaving him, she leaves the impartial to judge."[33]

Some women were without the wherewithal to leave their husbands to live on their own, and lacked family and friends who could support them, especially if they were sick or injured. The most desperate of these abused wives occasionally sought shelter in the almshouse. Twenty-nine-year-old Bridget Jefferson told the overseers that her husband, William Jefferson, an oysterman, abused her. The entry noted that he "gets drunk, beats & abuses her to such degree that she can not live with him." For some women, the almshouse became a refuge where they recovered from their beatings or neglect.[34]

In extreme cases, women overwhelmed by their difficulties tried to commit suicide, and when rescued were taken to the almshouse. In 1797, Jane Kean, the wife of a bottler, entered the almshouse after trying to drown herself. The overseers noted that she appeared "deranged." Upon examination, she said that "her Husband has severely beaten her & that there from she had become violent."[35] Elizabeth Frazier arrived at the almshouse in 1811 by way of a doctor's carriage after taking a large dose of laudanum. Her husband, John Moffett, was a waiter, but Elizabeth had not been living with him. Not only did she physically separate herself from her husband, she also consciously separated her identity from his by not using his name. As the docket entry noted, "the Ill treatment of her Husband is the reason she calls herself Frazier." Elizabeth may have taken the laudanum simply to relieve her mental or physical pains. On the other hand, tormented by her husband's abuse of her or overwhelmed by the pressure of living on her own, the overdose may have been an attempt at suicide. In either case, the mistreatment she received from her husband led to her collapse.[36]

However, not all poor women were this desperate. Some of them attempted to send their vicious husbands to jail. This they could do by charging their husbands with assault and battery or with disturbing the peace. For instance, although the almshouse docket entry for Ann Mayberry does not provide the details, it states that she sent her husband to prison because he had abused her for a long time. Ann then entered the almshouse after her pregnancy became too advanced and she was unable to work. Esther Vanse's husband was in jail for beating her when she came to the almshouse. The beating she received from him made her incapable of working. After going to the almshouse to recover, she was discharged six weeks later.[37]

Unfortunately for these abused women, neither almshouse nor prison was a permanent solution to marital cruelty. Women who entered the almshouse to escape the brutality of their husbands usually left once their wounds healed, their babies were born, or they had recovered from their illnesses. Likewise, they might be in and out several times over a period of years; men who were sent to the almshouse for intemperance and abusive or disruptive behavior were also only there for a short time. In one example, James Wilson was an alcoholic who abused his family while drunk. His friends asked that he be kept at the almshouse "a few weeks," and they agreed to pay his board while he was there.[38]

The criminal courts did not offer wives much relief. Husbands convicted of assault and battery were typically required to pay a fine ranging from $0.25 to $50. In addition, they usually had to cover the prosecution costs and give security plus one surety bond in the same amount (usually $100) to provide that they would maintain the peace with their wives for a period ranging from a month to one year. Rarely were the abusers imprisoned, other than for nonpayment of fines, unless the assault was made with intent to murder, appeared particularly violent, or was a repeated offense.

The following example from the Philadelphia Court of Quarter Sessions in March 1791 is typical of a sentence given a man convicted of assault and battery on his wife.

Valentine Gosner is ordered to give Security, himself in L30 and one Surety in the like Sum to Keep the Peace and be of good Behavior for Twelve Months particularly towards his Wife Mary Gosner and to stand committed until the order Shall be complied with.[39]

Sentences given in Chester County to husbands convicted of assault and battery on their wives were similar to those meted out in Philadelphia. Marital cruelty was not restricted to the city. Yet whether in the city or in the country, the release of an abusive husband, even under a bond of surety to keep the peace, threatened his wife's safety. Although the violent husbands may have "kept the peace" for the required length of time so as not to forfeit the money put up as security, there was nothing to deter them from beating their wives once the time period was over. Despite increased fines, security, and even short terms of imprisonment, George Beatzel, for example, continued to abuse his wife. Catharine Beatzel was persistent, however; she took him to court six times between 1832 and 1842 for assaulting her.[40]

On the other hand, imprisoning a husband kept him from earning the money to support his wife. For the abused spouse, the decision to risk physical safety to ensure economic survival was a difficult one to make. Financial desperation may have motivated Ann McKissack to ask for the release of her husband, John, from the Chester County "Goal." McKissack had served his sentences for assault and battery on his wife and for contempt of court, but was unable to pay bail. After his wife's plea, the governor pardoned him.[41]

Abused wives understood the reality of their situations. Although in Pennsylvania some wives filed charges of assault and battery against their husbands, others declined realizing that they would not benefit from this action. In 1784, Mary McGowan testified than in her three years of marriage to Capt. John McGowan of the Northern Liberties, she had often been beaten, and that finally, pregnant and with one fifteen-month child, she had been forced to leave him, fearing for her life. She petitioned for a separate maintenance, but requested through her attorney that a bill charging her husband with assault and battery not be sent to the Grand Jury. Mary probably assumed that pressing criminal charges would not help her situation; in addition, if she lost the case, she might have to pay the court costs. A few months later, John deserted Mary, leaving her and their two children without support. The overseers of the Northern Liberties seized John's goods, chattel, and the profits and rents from his lands and tenements to support Mary and the children.[42]

The overseers were authorized to do this under the poor laws of the state, although they were required to obtain a warrant from the court. As long as the husband had some source of income or owned property, obtaining a separate maintenance, rather than, or in addition to having a husband convicted of assault and battery, could be the wife's best solution by separating the couple without eliminating support for her. Sometimes, husbands and wives even made their own separation agreements. Of course, then as now, husbands did not always continue to make support payments; but those who deserted discovered that the overseers could seize their estates to maintain their wives. In these cases, however, the support of the wives was administered through the overseers, and it was done so that the deserted wife would not become a burden to the community.[43]

The courts did not consider separate maintenance to be a long-term solution. Husbands were required to pay their wives the sum determined by the court only so long as the separation continued. Some wives, however, returned to their husbands in between petitions. For example, in 1757, Hannah Pyle of Thornbury Township in Chester County petitioned the court for a separate maintenance, noting that she had been threatened and abused by her husband and his mistress. After apparently reconciling with her husband, she once again left him and asked the court for relief in 1773.[44]

Divorces offered women more advantages than either a separate maintenance or a criminal action, and with the passage of the 1785 act divorce became more obtainable. To some extent, the new accessibility of divorce reflected changes in the public perception of marital cruelty. Before 1785 the state legislature granted divorces submitted as private bills, but there were no statutory grounds for divorce. No men and only one women petitioned for divorce on cruelty grounds prior to the new law.[45] The 1785 act permitted a divorce from bed and board to women who had been forced to leave their husbands due to "cruel and barbarous treatment." Women applying for bed and board divorces were also permitted to petition for alimony. Even so, most women did not seek divorces, and for those who did, it was a last resort.

For example, in 1786, after thirteen years of marriage, Susanna Brauer appealed to the Supreme Court of Pennsylvania for a divorce with alimony from her husband, Jacob. Jacob's threats and beatings had forced Susanna to leave him on previous occasions, but she had returned to him upon the urging of their mutual friends in rural Chester County and upon Jacob's promises to reform. Despite his promises, however, Jacob's behavior grew more violent after this reconciliation. Pronouncing her husband a "tyrant & tormentor," Susanna noted that several times he took "a large club to bed declaring he would beat out her brains." This violence, as well as the need to support their four children, compelled Susanna to petition for a divorce.[46]

Unlike Susanna Brauer, most abused spouses during this time did not initiate divorce proceedings. Nevertheless, between 1785 and 1815, there were 367 divorce cases that came before the Supreme Court of

Pennsylvania under the 1785 act. Of these seventy-five were filed by women on the grounds of cruelty alone. Twenty-seven more petitioned for divorces noting that their husbands had committed adultery, bigamy, or deserted them, besides treating them harshly. Men could not sue for divorce on cruelty grounds under this law.[47]

Although more women filed on the grounds of cruelty alone than for any other reason, the Supreme Court granted only twenty-three pleas out of the seventy-five (31%) citing this complaint. This was the least successful rate of passage. Of all the charges, however, the combination of cruelty and desertion had the most favorable rate of success. The Court permitted divorces for ten of the fourteen women (71%) who petitioned on these grounds.[48]

The law granted only a divorce from bed and board in cruelty cases, but it was still an acknowledgment that women should not be forced to stay in intolerable marriages. The wording of the law, the statements of witnesses, and the few divorces actually granted on cruelty grounds alone suggests that the court granted bed and board divorces only in situations of life-threatening abuse or total deprivation of necessities. Petitioners' chances more than doubled when they indicated that they had been both abused and deserted. The very existence of this clause in the divorce law, however, along with the testimonies of witnesses and the frequency with which articles in magazines and newspapers extolled the fact that in America, unlike England, men were not allowed to beat their wives, indicates that during this era wife-beating was becoming less and less acceptable to the public, not just ignored by it. To some extent the law recognized new ideas about marriage based on love and mutual respect. At the same time, it identified marriage as an economic institution in which it was the husband's duty to support his wife and children. Both of these emphases offered wives in intolerable marriages more hope.

In essence, a divorce from bed and board meant a legal separation that released the parties from marital obligations but did not allow them to remarry. However, the law granted alimony only in bed and board divorces. Alimony was not to exceed one-third of the the husband's annual income or profits from his estate or occupation. Both the divorce and the alimony could be suspended if a reconciliation took place or the husband petitioned "to use her as a good husband ought to do," but if he once again failed in his duty the sentence could be revived and alimony payments in arrears ordered to be paid. The granting of alimony, however, did not always mean that it was paid.

Chester County women who divorced between 1804 and 1850 were much less likely to sue for divorce on cruelty grounds than Pennsylvania women appealing to the Supreme Court between 1785 and 1815. This was not from a lack of ill treatment from their husbands.[49] Rather, these women who were desperate enough to sue for divorce may have believed that it was to their advantage to have a complete separation from their abusive husbands. Also, because divorces on cruelty grounds were not granted very often, it may be that these women chose to petition on other grounds when possible.

One Chester County case may serve as an example. Sarah and Lewis Evans were married in 1801. They lived together until 1811, during which time they had five children, four of whom were living when Sarah filed for divorce in 1811. Sarah accused Lewis of adultery, and witnesses, including a woman by whom he had had a child, supported her claims. With illegitimate children as evidence, adultery was probably an easier charge to prove than cruelty. Nevertheless, if witnesses' claims are to be believed, her husband treated her brutally, and Sarah did bring him to criminal court on charges of assault and battery. Sarah probably knew her husband very well—he did not answer his summons for either the divorce case or the assault and battery case. It was probably to Sarah's advantage to petition for a total divorce, which she received.[50]

Despite the drawbacks of a bed and board divorce, however, it worked to the benefit of some women. For an elderly wife or one who was pregnant, had young children, or was too ill to work, having alimony might be better than having a complete divorce. In addition, if a woman's husband died, a divorce from bed and board would allow the wife to inherit as her husband's widow, which would not be the case in a complete divorce. The law also assumed that the couple might reconcile their differences, and perhaps these abused wives, in a time when to be married was a woman's goal and to reform an errant husband a woman's moral triumph, also still hoped for reconciliations. In spite of what it did not do, in other words, the new law at least improved somewhat the options of a woman trapped in a harmful marriage. Formal provisions for dealing with tensions offered more options than used to be available at the same time that public opinion informally expected more equal interaction between husband and wife.

The ways in which abused wives in early Pennsylvania reacted to the violence and neglect of their husbands depended upon their particular situations. Most relied first upon support from family or friends. Others deserted. Still others, after trying informal actions, used more formal systems of support and regulation by taking their husbands to court or entering the almshouse.

Men and women entering into marriage held preconceived notions of their roles as husbands and wives, based on an awareness of their own gender roles and on acquired societal expectations. They used these notions to justify their own actions and behavior, and to break from or evade their marriages. But how did their families and communities perceive these situations of spouse abuse and how did they react to such problems?

Witnesses to wife-beating responded in different ways. The first problem was when to intercede between husband and wife. In an 1804 deposition, Mary Armbruster testified that she heard her next door neighbor, Catherine France, being beaten by her husband, John France, a carter and drayman in Philadelphia. "Thinking it a pity that no person should go in to help her [she] went in to the house and told the said John France that it was a shame for him to treat his wife so, and if he had no pity upon her, he ought to have a pity on the child she was going to have." France then released his wife and took off after Armbruster with a pair of tongs. In this situation, Mary Armbruster had no doubts that her neighbor was mistreating his wife, nor did she have any doubts that she should come to her aid.[51]

However, in Chester County in 1850, a man beat his wife to death but no one rushed to her aid until it was too late. At first glance this example seems to support the belief that nineteenth-century Americans did not want to interfere in the privacy of the family. On further reading of the depositions in the above case, however, it becomes clear that the neighbors did not at first hurry to help the woman because they they were not on friendly terms with the couple, and not because they considered what was done between husband and wife to be private. Jacob Campbell, the man who beat his wife, had ordered the neighbors to stay away from his house. One neighbor, Margaret Wise, stated that after Jacob Campbell forbade her and her husband from coming on his property, she "never went to his house after that," and Jacob Campbell never spoke to her except to curse at her. Nevertheless, on the occasion of the fatal beating, Margaret Wise did go to help Elizabeth Campbell after Jacob Campbell left the house.[52]

In numerous other cases, neighbors and family members rescued and aided victims of abuse. Yet, individual reactions did vary. Jacob Munshour, a witness for Sarah Evans, described how Lewis first threw stones at her and then struck her repeatedly with his fist. Munshour, "turned away and could not bear to see such carrying on." However, John Lewis, another witness for Sarah, prevented her husband from beating and possibly killing her. He had spent the night at their house, after Lewis Evans insisted. Evans appeared to be angry at his wife, and ordered her to go to bed, giving her a kick. Shortly after this, John Lewis heard Sarah scream from their bedroom, "for God's sake dont kill me, upon hearing of which deponent [John Lewis] jump'd out of his Bed and ran into Libellant's Bedroom, and seized hold of Respondent and pulled him away out of the room."[53]

Family members also helped victims and demonstrated approval of their actions. After she wrote a letter to her father in 1787 describing the treatment she had received from her husband, Elizabeth Black was rescued by her brother and brother-in-law. The two men found her bare-footed and insufficiently clothed for the fall weather and brought her from her country abode to her father's house in Philadelphia. In an 1844 Chester County case, Mary Carter described her daughter's years of trying to live with her abusive husband. Mary repeatedly attempted to talk to the husband, but he ignored her. Because Mary believed that her daughter had done all she could do to reform her husband's behavior without result, she was glad that her daughter finally left her husband, and noting that said, "I could not and would not have lived with such a man for all the world."[54]

In addition to indicating how they responded to seeing marital cruelty, witnesses in divorce cases revealed a knowledge of how to present the victims of abuse to the court. This knowledge included an understanding of public perceptions of wives' and husbands' roles. Whether their words were indicative of how they felt, or whether they were said only to persuade the judge, the witnesses presented mistreated wives as innocent victims, hardworking spouses, and dutiful mothers.

For example, a witness for Charlotte Brown of Philadelphia, testified in 1799 that "she always behaved with propriety & great prudence & sought to promote his [her husband's] happiness." Witnesses for Margaret McCrea of Philadelphia County described her attempts to support herself and her family by keeping a boarding house, despite her husband's violent and disruptive behavior.[55] In a Chester County case in 1845, the mother of the petitioner, Ann Baker, reported that her daughter "would sometimes reply to his [her husband's] abusive language but he was always the aggressor so far as I saw."[56]

In contrast, witnesses typically portrayed the men who abused their wives as lazy, drunken, and violent. Joshua Scott, a Chester County farmer reported in 1832, "that the respondent worked none, but lay about the house intoxicated while the libellant carried wood from the woods on her back for the use of the house." Scott, who lived in the same house as the divorcing couple had numerous opportunities to observe the husband's behavior. He stated that, "the whole conduct of the respondent towards his wife was harsh and cruel in the extreme, such as no husband should hold towards his wife, and such as no wife should be bound to submit to from her husband." Other witnesses in this case called John Taylor "worthless," "drunk," and one said his behavior was "harsh, improper, and unmanly."[57] In similar language expressed nearly thirty years before, witnesses described John France as a lazy man who drank to excess and made his wife support him and their children. William Cummins, for instance, reported that France was an "idle, drunken, abusive man" who did not work because "he had a wife to maintain him."[58]

These witnesses displayed a clear understanding of what it meant to be an ideal husband or an ideal wife. Wives were supposed to submit to their husbands in most matters, but this did not mean that husbands could treat them cruelly. As marriage came increasingly to be based upon love, mutual kindness, and mutual respect, the abuse

of one's spouse flouted community standards. Although the state began to prosecute morals violations less frequently after the Revolution,
neighbors were willing to help the victims of domestic violence, to
intervene in domestic disputes, and to act as witnesses on their behalf,
if the *victim* chose to take the batterer to court.

Pennsylvanians during the late colonial and early national periods
developed their ideas about spouse abuse from the cases they read
about and those they knew about from personal experience, as well as
from the popular perceptions about marriage circulating during this
time in newspapers, magazines, and novels. Newspapers published
accounts of wife-beatings and notices of divorces and separations. In
addition, most people probably knew of women who had been beaten
or otherwise ill treated by their husbands.

In December 3, 1823, Deborah Norris Logan recorded in her diary
an account of a friend who had been abused by her husband. "Poor
Sarah," she wrote, "gave us a dreadful Account of her Sufferings from
her inhuman husband." The woman, who was ill and wasting away,
was on her way to town to sue for a separate maintenance. Although
Deborah Logan clearly sympathized with "poor Sarah," she did not
indicate in any way that she thought her friend's plight or her solution
was unusual.[59]

But a recognition that spouse abuse existed did not mean that people condoned it or believed it a necessary evil. The public perception
of wife abuse was changing in the eighteenth century just as the atti-
tudes about wives and marriage were changing. In popular literature,
for instance, the scolding wife contrasted with the amiable wife, who
obeyed her husband when she could, and changed his behavior with
smiles when she could not.

"Thimble's Wife," a popular late eighteenth-century Philadelphia
song, portrays a scolding wife who remains a terror to her husband
even after her death. It begins with the lines: "Thimble's Wife Lay
Dead. Heigh ho says Thimble/My Dearest Duck's Defunct in Bed,
Death has cabbaged her scolding head." In the following verses,
Thimble is upset that she will be buried with her diamond ring still
on her finger. When the sexton tries to saw off her finger in order to
retrieve the ring, she sits up and scares him away. Finally, Thimble's
wife returns home, but Thimble gleefully declines to let her inside.[60]

Coexisting with this nagging wife was the virtuous wife who used restraint rather than violent passion when dealing with her husband's misdeeds. *The Lady's Magazine* in June 1792 published an essay entitled "On Love." In it, the author declared that in marriage husband and wife should strive to make each other happy, but that it was up to the wife to determine her husband's moods and make him happy. In the event that he was led "into dissipation and debauchery," she should try to change him by her virtuous example rather than by harsh and abusive words. "He will find that the chaste endearments of a virtuous wife, have ten thousand more charms than the meretricious embraces of a harlot." Of course, the wife would be happy, too, the author indicated, because she did not turn her husband away by her behavior.[61]

Of course, images of both the scolding wife and the virtuous wife were stereotypes, but these stereotypes had an effect on the public perception of marital cruelty. For the virtuous wife to be beaten by her husband became unacceptable in the public's perception. Although most believed even "bad" wives should not be treated cruelly, virtuous wives were more likely to gain public sympathy. On the other hand, the examples above indicate that husbands sometimes justified violence toward their wives because they believed them to be nags. Yet husbands who insisted on their innocence had to prove that they, too, fit the image of the proper mate. For them, it meant demonstrating that they had always provided their wives with support and were sober and faithful.

That men and women knew how to use these perceptions in the portrayal of themselves and their friends can be seen in examples from the long and tumultuous marriage of James and Rachel McMullin. In 1804, Rachel made a complaint to the Court of Quarter Sessions that James had thrown her out of the house and refused to support her. However, since the depositions of witnesses stated that James frequently beat and abused Rachel, she may not have wanted to return to him. In February 1805, the Court of Quarter Sessions granted the Directors of the Poor of Chester County a warrant to seize James McMullin's goods in order to support Rachel so that she would not become a burden to the county.[62]

This was not the first time that the couple had experienced marital difficulties, nor was it the first time that the couple's private life had been made public.[63] Over the years, the torments and passions of their marriage had led Rachel and James to friends and to court seeking relief. Meanwhile, their actions provoked neighbors both to accuse and defend them. The documentation of these events reveals possible reasons why James abused Rachel, Rachel's reactions to the abuse, and the interaction of the couple, their community, and the state.

Throughout the years of their marriage and these disruptive episodes, neighbors played a large role in determining James's and Rachel's reputations. To some extent, the gossip of the neighborhood may even have determined the way in which James and Rachel perceived each other. Within their community, rumors spread easily, and interference within homes and families was normal and acceptable behavior for neighbors, tenants, and boarders. At the same time, friends and neighbors were willing to come to the defense of one or the other during their disagreements.

For example, Hannah Hickman, who lived so close to the McMullin's "that a human voice could easily be heard from the one [house] to the other," testified on Rachel's behalf. She noted that she had frequently heard Rachel's cries of distress, including cries of "murder." Several times after hearing these cries, Rachel appeared at Hannah's to tell her that James had abused her. On one occasion, however, Hannah went to the McMullin's when they were quarreling and found Rachel, "spiting blood." Rachel told Hannah that James had knocked out two of her teeth, and Hannah "looked at her mouth & found that two of the said Rachel's teeth were wanting and the gum from whence the [teeth] had been was then bleeding."[64]

Hannah Hickman's deposition is unusual in that it includes her cross-examination by James McMullin. In the course of this inquiry, he asked if Hannah had ever seen Rachel breaking the windows of their house. She acknowledged that she had, but had asked Rachel why she did it. Rachel told her that "Jimmy . . . had turned her out of Doors." James then inquired if Hannah had ever known Rachel to turn "the Boys & Girls" [their children or servants?] out of the house while he was away from home. Hannah answered that she had not. To his question of whether she had frequently seen Rachel drunk,

Deposition of Hannah Hickman, 1806. In this deposition, one of several submitted to the Court of Quarter Sessions in Chester County as part of Rachel McMullin's attempt to receive assistance from the Directors of the Poor, Hannah Hickman describes James McMullin's abuse of Rachel. In one instance, Hannah found her "spiting blood" after James knocked out two of her teeth. *Chester County Archives, West Chester, Pa.*

Hannah responded that she had not. Finally, James asked her if she had ever seen him beat Rachel, to which she replied no.[65]

In her statements, Hannah tried to demonstrate James' repeated cruelty toward Rachel. Moreover, she tried to defend Rachel's character and actions. Meanwhile, James said nothing in his own defense, but tried to prove that Rachel was unworthy of sympathy or aid. He attempted to show that she destroyed property, drank, and was possibly a liar as well. Although all of this might have been true, both Hannah and James recognized that Rachel was more likely to receive assistance if she won the court's sympathy as the innocent victim of James' brutality.

The evidence suggests that James did abuse his wife. According to neighbors he had treated her cruelly in the past, and at this particular time there were several reasons why he may have been angry at her —reasons that had built up over many years. It was likely that Rachel had been unfaithful, and she probably had been drunk many times. She also had made accusations against her husband. Because Rachel had not lived a blameless life James felt that he had the right as her husband to punish her, a justification used by other abusive husbands. His use of violence or even threats of violence can be seen as attempts to control her behavior. There were many reasons why James beat Rachel. But by all accounts he had a violent temper, and Rachel may simply have been the closest target.

Despite the beatings, Rachel apparently did not attempt to leave James in the beginning. It took years of misunderstanding between the couple and perhaps fear that James would leave her destitute before Rachel actually asked the county to grant her support—and then only after James threw her out of the house. Rachel did have other reasons for wanting to leave James, but may have feared living on her own. Besides physically abusing her, James probably committed adultery, and he had attempted to divorce her. Both Rachel and James had reason to hurt each other and end the marriage.

The first documented sign of the couple's troubles came in 1792, eleven years after they were married. James McMullin brought a plea of trespass (essentially an accusation of slander suing for damages) against Robert Wilken and William Hickman. Hickman was a nearby neighbor and the husband of Hannah Hickman, who later testified that James McMullin beat his wife. The case stemmed from an illness McMullin had had. According to his suit, the men were spreading rumors about him around the community, accusing him of being ill with a venereal disease and noting that he "kept a woman known by the name of Betsey Hill [who was his nurse] and Bedded with her . . . and made use of her . . . in a whorish manner."[66]

The men also claimed that McMullin first made his wife sleep on the floor, then turned her out of the house, and finally planned to leave town "in order to defraud his wife . . . of her Right." Furthermore, they believed that his behavior was causing "an uneasiness in the Neighborhood." James, who was a storekeeper and who also sold liquor, claimed that the gossip was hurting his business, as well as injuring his reputation.[67]

Damaging McMullin's reputation was probably Wilken and Hickman's objective. Apparently, both men had had clashes with McMullin prior to the rumors. Hickman had told one witness that he and McMullin had done business together and that McMullin then charged him for goods that he never received. According to another witness, Wilken had accused McMullin of stealing a wagon from him and had obtained a search warrant to look for it. Hannah Hickman had heard Rachel tell Wilken "to beware of Her Husband," because James intended to injure him. Most of the witnesses stated that they had first heard the stories about McMullin having venereal disease and keeping a mistress from either Wilken or Hickman, while two doctors testified that they had treated McMullin for an inflammation of the lungs, not venereal disease.[68]

It is difficult to know how much was truth, and how much was invented for spite. Certainly James had clashed with some of his neighbors and customers. But did he keep a mistress, and force his wife to sleep on the floor? Even more important, did Rachel believe he had been unfaithful, causing her to drink and seek sexual liaisons with other men, and provoking her husband to attack her?

In 1804, James sued for a divorce, accusing his wife of adultery. During the proceedings, the events covered in the trespass case returned to light. Those testifying on his behalf were all neighbors of the McMullin's in Kennet Township or nearby East Marlborough. Although they were summoned by subpoena to appear at court, their accounts may have been colored by family loyalties or attempts to retaliate for what they considered past wrongs. For instance, at least one deponent was a relative, James' brother-in-law, Robert Smith, who was married to James' sister. The Smiths and McMullins were living together at the time of Rachel's alleged adultery. His deposition recounted an episode in which he had seen Rachel leave the bed where she was sleeping with his wife and to go out with Robert Barr, who had been a witness for James in his trespass suit.[69]

The statement given by Barr's widow, Sarah, could easily have been motivated by these old jealousies. Sarah Barr explained that she had known James for thirty years and Rachel for twenty. She then testified to having seen Rachel drunk and sitting on one man's knee, and implied that Rachel had had a sexual encounter with her late husband years before. Others reported seeing Rachel in suggestive situations with various men; however, all these events had occurred many years before, in fact, around the time James was supposedly having an affair with Betsey Hill.[70]

Several of James' witnesses noted that Rachel appeared to be intoxicated when they saw her with the other men. The availability of alcohol from James' store may have made it easy for Rachel to drink. Nathaniel Hart, for instance, stated that he had lived in the same house as the McMullin's seven years before. She appeared to be "somewhat in liquor" when she told him that "she would not live without the use of men because her husband James McMullin did not live without the use of women." A week later, Hart discovered Rachel in bed, naked from the waist down, with a man who also lived in the house. Hart claimed that Rachel was drunk.[71] This image of Rachel as a drunken and lewd woman was an important one if public sympathy was to be against her and for her husband.

Rachel denied the charges. She also dredged up events from years past, accusing James of adultery with three women, one of whom was Betsey Hill. Although her witnesses, also neighbors, did not claim to see James and Betsey Hill in sexual intimacy, they did testify to seeing James in bed with another woman Rachel named in her answer. This woman, Esther Walters, lived near the McMullins and had testified in James' trespass suit. One of the deponents claimed to have discovered them together by looking through the window, and another by peering through a partly opened door. As the divorce case was not continued, either James decided it was hopeless, or the court decided it was, but it seems likely that Rachel's 1804 plea for support on the grounds of James' cruelty was the result. No doubt she feared that he would again file for divorce and win, leaving her destitute, or he might have beaten her after she brought up charges against him during the divorce proceedings.[72]

James and Rachel apparently lived unhappily ever after following Rachel's appeal to the Overseers. Her name does not appear in any records of the poorhouse. In 1814, James wrote his last will and testament leaving Rachel "Fifty three Dollars & one third of a dollar" per year for the rest of her life. However, James stated that his bequest was to be made only if Rachel agreed to renounce all other claims to his estate, and signified her intentions by signing his will. Rachel signed the will, and all of his land went to his brother, Alexander. Other legacies of money and goods went to his brother, sister, and brother-in-law and their children. Whatever practical reasons James McMullin may have had in making his provisions, his will expressed no love or affection for his wife.[73]

The marriage of James and Rachel McMullin was not a happy one. The behavior of both husband and wife contributed to their uncomfortable situation. James was probably guilty of adultery and used physical force against his wife. Rachel, too, might have been unfaithful; she may even have had her affairs to get even with James. Her drinking and promiscuous behavior probably increased the ire of a man who appeared to be easily provoked. In addition, James may have felt justified in striking a wife who did not conform to accepted standards. Thus, abuse did not *cause* the couple's problems, rather it was a component of their disharmonious union, part of a cycle reflecting the existing and troubled state of their marriage.

Yet interaction with their neighbors probably influenced the McMullin's behavior as well. Throughout their married lives, friends and neighbors took sides, serving as comforters and witnesses, and as critics of their reputations. It was to these spectators that James and Rachel tried to defend and justify their actions.

The Will of James McMullin, 1814. James left Rachel "Fifty three Dollars and one third of a dollar" per year, if she renounced all further claims to the estate. *Chester County Archives, West Chester, Pa.*

Several historians have argued that a growing belief in the privacy of the family kept late eighteenth and nineteenth-century people from becoming involved or interfering in the family matters of others. In addition, they have noted that by the time of the Revolution the belief had developed that the state should not be responsible for enforcing morality. As this position evolved, the public began to pay less attention to domestic violence.[74] The McMullin's problems, to the contrary, attracted much attention in their community and involvement from their neighbors.

Other than the passage of the 1785 divorce act, there was little in the way of public reforms against domestic violence during this period. It is also true that the popular literature of the time extolled the belief in family privacy, a belief that was very strong by the 1830s. The example of the McMullins suggests, however, that late eighteenth- and early nineteenth-century Chester County residents were willing both to ignore and to heed the tenets of "the Family Ideal." The McMullins' neighbors might listen at walls and peer in windows and doorways, and they thought nothing of interfering between husband and wife. But they also identified a proper spouse, condemning an errant one, or defending a worthy one in terms of the new beliefs about marriage and family life—at least for the purposes of the courts. In eighteenth- and early nineteenth-century Chester County, and probably Philadelphia and other parts of Pennsylvania as well, the acceptance of new values concerning husband and wife did not necessarily exalt the privacy of the family. Although they did not initiate the prosecution of offenders, members of the community condemned those who flaunted its standards. Thus, their adherence to these beliefs led them to aid battered wives, at least those who were well known to them and whom they considered to have been seriously abused.

The cases discussed in this chapter demonstrate that women and men both understood the necessity of depicting themselves or their neighbors as model wives and husbands. Abusive husbands, however, were more likely to cling to older traditions concerning the degree to which they could beat their wives, while wives who complained were influenced by newer beliefs pertaining to marital love. Because men in eighteenth- and early nineteenth-century Pennsylvania seldom reported beatings by their wives, however, this chapter has focused on wife abuse. It is easy to see these women as victims. Yet, for the most part, the women examined here found ways to fight against their husbands' indifferent and sometimes inhumane behavior. Although some could not cope, others left brutal husbands, usually turning to friends and neighbors as a first step before seeking help from the law. Most women who did leave their husbands were probably desperate. To leave a marriage during this time, especially if burdened with children, or lacking money or a way to make a living, was an act of desperation, and a gamble.

Wives did not easily make the decision to leave a violent husband. Many wives internalized the image of the ideal wife promoted in stories and marriage manuals. In the idealized world these essays promoted, the cheerful and gentle wife could reform the ill-tempered behavior of her brutish husband—and he would be thankful for her guidance. Thus, Harriet Carroll considered it her duty to stay with her drunken husband until her family finally convinced her that he would not change, and Susanna Brauer petitioned for a divorce only after her husband ignored his promises to reform and repeatedly threatened to murder her.

As the colonial period ended and the life of the new republic began, some women left their husbands because they were motivated by expectations of love and companionship in their marriages, as Nancy Cott suggested in her work on divorce in Massachusetts.[75] Yet, the new ideas about marriage promoted in prescriptive literature simultaneously caused other women to give their marriages a second or third chance because they believed that the power of their love could reform their husbands' behavior, and that it was their wifely duty to keep trying until it did. When the strain became intolerable, new intensified societal perceptions that modified laws and institutions in Pennsylvania to some extent now afforded abused wives, especially those perceived as innocent and worthy of help, a limited measure of relief. Thus, the combination of changing expectations, changing opportunities, and desperation prompted early Pennsylvania wives to leave cruel husbands. In taking this step, women consciously portrayed themselves as virtuous wives, but, in doing so, they turned cultural perceptions and restraints to their own advantage.

CHAPTER 5

Runaways: "Wilful and Malicious Desertion"

Charlotte seated on the Sopha behind me was giving me a detailed account of her connections and their place of abode: Her father, she said, Ran away and left her Mother with 9 children!

DIARY OF DEBORAH NORRIS LOGAN, 22 AUGUST 1825

When Hugh Smith placed an advertisement in the 1754 *Pennsylvania Gazette* noting that his wife, Ann, had "elop'd from him," he declared that she lived "in a very disorderly manner." In a 1785 notice, John Hall stated that his wife Ann, had "absconded from his bed and board, and otherwise misbehaved herself," and John Kennard asserted in 1743 that his wife Margaret "does unjustly elope from her said Husband and perhaps may run me in Debt."[1] Philip Schurtz's advertisement placed in 1744 also noted that he would not pay his wife's debts. Anne Elizabeth Schurtz, however, had some foresight. Before eloping with Jacob Frederick Kurtz, she took one hundred pounds with her.[2] In eighteenth-century newspaper advertisements, deserted husbands frequently accused their wives of being immoral or adulterous, of running up debts or stealing the husband's property, and of bringing shame to the husband by their loose behavior. Many times the men declared that their wives had departed without "just cause." Thus, men whose wives left them tended to portray themselves as blameless in the couple's troubles, but condemned their spouses for their lack of obedience and wifely virtues.

Although serving primarily as a legal notice that the husband would not pay his deserted wife's debt, these announcements also stressed that the wife who left her husband was no longer under his protection. In some respects, husbands were exacting economic revenge on their departed wives, but when their wives chose to leave them, these men believed that they were no longer obligated to support them. In order to alert creditors as well, they placed notices in newspapers.

In contrast, by abandoning her husband, a woman lost both her legal rights and her social status. Because American mores did not condone wives leaving their husbands, those who did so were suspect. Despite a new emphasis on mutual affection and partnerships in marriage, most people still expected men to be the head of the household and to support their wives. Therefore, when a woman left her husband, she challenged his position of authority, as well as lost his financial support. The role of a married woman included running the household and raising the children. If she had problems with her husband, she was supposed to gently reform him, if possible, and submit to him, if not. Unless she had been abused, a woman who abandoned her husband could not portray herself as the virtuous and model wife of American expectations.

For men, the situation was somewhat different. A man who deserted his wife did not meet the societal standards of a model husband, but he was still obligated to support her. If he refused to provide for her, his land and goods could be seized. No such provision existed for wives who deserted their husbands. Because they did not legally maintain them, wives could not be prosecuted for nonsupport of their husbands. However, wives who abandoned their mates also relinquished their right to economic upkeep from them, if the courts determined that they had left voluntarily or refused to cohabit with their mates.[3]

Thus the law distinguished between a deserting husband and a deserting wife, placing the burden of financial solvency upon the men. These gender distinctions were based upon the economic aspects of early American marriage. Because the husband was the head of the household and legally controlled the money, the wife, as a feme covert, was dependent upon her husband for financial support. In many instances, this image was an accurate one, as a wife whose husband deserted her was often left in pecuniary difficulties. As a result of claiming her independence from her spouse, a woman took a substantial risk. She could be left in poverty and outside the help a "virtuous" or worthy wife might apply for. Therefore, the consequences of this desperate act also differed by gender.

Gender distinctions also determined the reasons why men and women left their marriages. Both husbands and wives had particular expectations about their own marriages. What part did these hopes play in *causing* a man or woman to desert his or her spouse? And what did the concept of desertion actually mean to eighteenth- and nineteenth-century Pennsylvanians? Were there gender differences and biases in the way the term was applied?

Desertion was the most common means of ending an unhappy marriage in early Pennsylvania. Prior to the divorce law of 1785, a separation of some sort was the only way to leave an unhappy marriage.[4] Although women could apply for separate maintenances from their husbands, and couples could and did draw-up quasi-legal separation agreements, most often a man or a woman simply decided to leave. Desertion could mean moving to the frontier, moving down the street, or moving back to one's parents' house. Even after passage of the law, dissatisfied men and women continued to desert their spouses because it was the easiest method to quit a miserable situation.

On the whole, it was easier for men to leave their wives than it was for women to desert their husbands. From a practical point of view, men could travel more easily than women. Physically, they were unencumbered by the hazards and inconveniences of pregnancy, childbirth, and nursing young children. Socially, it was acceptable for them to travel on their own; it was suspect for a woman. Economically, men had more access to money or employment, making desertion less of a financial risk for them than it was for women.

Many men enlisted in the army to escape a marriage, and others chose to find new homes after heading out to sea. Matthew Kemp, a mariner who commanded an American vessel, left for Virginia, but did not return to his wife after that voyage. A ship captain asserted that he had delivered a letter to Matthew from his uncle, thus proving that Matthew had made the journey safely and was alive. Matthew, however, chose not to reply to the letter. Celeste Kemp received a divorce in 1803. On the other hand, Eleanor Blockwood was one of the many women who went to the almshouse when her husband deserted her and went to sea.[5]

Men had a wider variety of job opportunities available to them than did women. Increasing their employability might be an apprenticeship in a trade or craft and training that most women lacked. Men also traveled as part of their business, and sometimes used these opportunities to leave their marriages. In one instance, Joseph Leonard, a chairmaker in Germantown, told his new bride in 1798 he was going to Wayne County to bring back some rafts of lumber he had bought. He never returned. His wife, Elizabeth, was granted a divorce on grounds of desertion in 1803.[6] Margaret Phillips went to the almshouse in 1812 when her husband deserted her. Because he was a peddlar, he traveled for a living, but chose not to return to his wife after this trip.[7]

In contrast to the men who left their wives while on journeys connected to their businesses, other men, who had been unemployed, deserted their wives while seeking work. Just as it was unremarkable for men to be gone on business trips, so too was it for men to go in search of work and later send for their wives. Sometimes, however, they decided not to ask their wives to join them, and even refused to support them should they come. When Margaret Cooper's husband left her to go to "the Federal City" as a waiter, he "was to have sent for her, and likewise some money." As the 1801 Philadelphia almshouse docket noted, "he has done neither," and since Margaret's sore leg prevented her from working, she was forced to seek assistance there. Eleanor Scott's husband, Joseph, left her in August 1802 to look for work, but by December of that year she still had not heard anything from him. Suffering from "the fever & ague," she, too, was compelled to enter the almshouse in Philadelphia. Similarly, Christiana Sophiadale's husband went to Lancaster to seek employment. Not receiving any word from him, she went to the almshouse in 1804.[8]

Other men left their wives to join the army. For example, Eleanor Murray's husband deserted her in 1810 to enlist in the army, leaving her pregnant and sick. Jacob Goshow also left his wife and infant son in 1810 to join the army. Richard Proctor was a drummer in the army. When he left his wife, Grizel, in late 1801, she was two months pregnant. After struggling for five months to support herself without any assistance from her absent husband, Grizel entered the almshouse. Richard Banesford Proctor was born there June 20, 1802, and died three days later.[9] It is possible that these three men and others like them found the strain of supporting a family as well as their wives too much to handle. The army served as a convenient way to leave those pressures behind and still earn a living for themselves.

Men always had the opportunity to enlist or go to sea, but war gave them additional opportunities to leave their wives. The same unsettled conditions, however, also gave some abandoned wives a chance to operate businesses on their own. Benjamin Davis, for instance, first deserted his wife in 1772 or 1773. He then returned with the British Army in 1777, taking over his wife, Mary's "public house," and forcing her out of the house by his cruel treatment of her. When the British left Philadelphia, Benjamin left with them, and never returned.[10]

The Loyalist Alexander Bartram also left Philadelphia with the British. Jane Bartram, his wife, argued later that she did not share her husband's political allegiance. It is unclear whether Alexander deserted Jane or whether she *chose* not to follow him. Since Americans during this time considered it a wife's duty to follow her husband, Alexander might have accused Jane of deserting him, if it were not for the war. The Revolutionary War gave the Bartrams an opportunity to part, perhaps by mutual design. However, the fact that Jane remained in Philadelphia permitted her later to seek assistance from the victors by claiming her loyalty to the republic over her loyalty to her husband.[11] Thus, war could provide both a means to quit a marriage, and an excuse for avoiding its duties.

Unsettled wartime conditions gave both men and women more opportunity to leave their marriages. For example in 1779, Paul Russel placed the following advertisement in *The Pennsylvania Gazette:*

Whereas Catherine my wife hath eloped from my bed and board without any just cause, on the 18th day of February last, with a Hessian deserter, who goes by the name of Valentine Hertzoor; therefore this is to forewarn all persons from trusting her on my account, as I am determined to pay no debts of her contracting.[12]

Yet, the number of broken marriages in Pennsylvania directly attributable to the Revolutionary War is small. It seems more likely that men and women left their marriages because of new expectations about marriage evolving at this time.[13] The war merely provided openings for some husbands or wives to leave more easily. Although Paul Russel stated that his wife left him without "just cause," it is possible that he was not the loving partner with whom Catherine had anticipated spending her life. The Hessian deserter may have arrived just as she realized how dissatisfied she was with her marriage, giving her a chance to leave it. Similarly, Alexander and Jane Bartram had disagreed regarding their political loyalties. The departure of the British provided Alexander with an opportunity to abandon his wife or allowed Jane an attempt to remain apart from him.

During this time of evolving marital expectations, women and men sometimes found that they could no longer live in a relationship so at odds with their hopes and dreams. The stress of not being able to achieve or maintain what was expected of them as a good husband or wife also contributed to a breakdown in marital relations and the subsequent departure of a spouse. An examination of the reasons why men and women left their partners demonstrates some distinctions in what marriage meant to them, and suggests that the term "desertion" had a gendered meaning to early Pennsylvanians.

An analysis of divorce cases filed on the grounds of desertion reveals both similarities and differences between women and men who left their spouses. Both husbands and wives departed from their spouses in order to have relationships with others. Some left their marriages and soon found new mates. For example, George Staal abandoned his bride after only six months of marriage. When he left in November 1798, Margaret Staal wanted to go with him, but he told her that he would return. After quitting Reading for Pittsburgh, however, he pretended to be a single man, and courted another woman (who when told by a former neighbor that he was married was greatly surprised). George could not be found when his wife initiated divorce proceedings, but it was rumored that he had accepted a commission in the army, was in the "Western territories," and had married a woman from Williamsport, Ohio.[14] Two witnesses in the divorce proceedings stated that George told them he had to marry Margaret. Trapped in a marriage that he did not want, George probably never intended to stay with his wife. Deserting his wife, George cast off his role and responsibilities as a married man as well. That he was soon courting and later wed again suggests, however, that he had rejected Margaret, not the institution of marriage.

Like George Staal, Charlotte Hartman also made a marriage that was apparently doomed from the start. After marrying Tobias Shurtz in April 1785, she moved back to her father's house in December of that year. That she had cohabited with her husband was revealed by Jacob Houck, who noted that he knew they lived as a husband and wife because he slept "in the same Room with them." After Charlotte left Tobias she had a child by another man, Jacob Koup , her father's "hired man." Houk stated that "it is generally reported, [that he] wanted to Marry Her, but the said Francis Hartman would not Suffer it— saying, He would sooner Maintain three more Bastards than the said Jacob Koup should have her."[15] Although impossible to know, it is tempting to speculate that Charlotte had been in love with Jacob before she married Tobias, but that her father did not want her to marry him.

What exactly was her father's role in the couple's marital difficulties? Witnesses report that he had come for Charlotte with a wagon for her household goods when Tobias was away, and that he had maintained her for the past nine years. David Jones described his attempts at mediation, attempts that included Francis Hartman.

He saw the said Defendant and her father That they, all three, sat down on a Trough at the Well—that the Deponent asked the Defendant whether she would live with her Husband again . . . the Said Defendant replied, 'She never would live with him any more—He . . . might go to the Devil and Marry again as quick as He Pleased—She never would hurt the Hair of his Head.'[16]

Since Francis Hartman was willing and able to maintain her illegitimate child, but had forbidden her to remarry, he both assisted Charlotte financially and reinforced her feme covert status and his own position as patriarch. On the other hand, Charlotte had a lover and a child, but did not have to assume the obligations of running her own household and being the perfect wife. Because she had a father amenable to supporting her, Charlotte's desire to leave her husband and perhaps to evade her marital duties was made easier.

Part of Charlotte's wish to leave Tobias may have been because of sexual problems with him. As in most divorces of this time, the records here do not refer directly to sexual tensions between husband and wife. However, if Charlotte was in love (or lust) with another man, her longings or Tobias's jealousy were likely to have hindered intimacy between the couple. Although not uncommon during this period of time, the lack of privacy in their sleeping quarters could also have induced or contributed to sexual complications.

In contrast, one Chester County divorce filed on desertion grounds leaves no doubt that sexual incompatibility was the prime reason the couple did not live together. When Thomas Waters, a blacksmith, filed for divorce in 1839, he reported that "in all respects [he] demeaned himself as a kind and faithful husband." He accused his wife, Sarah, of desertion, noting that "it was the bounden duty of the said Sarah to cohabit with your Petitioner and partake of his bed and board," which she had refused to do.[17]

William W. Elliot, who testified in the divorce case, reported that at the the time of the marriage in December 1835, Sarah lived with his family as a "hired servant." Thomas visited her there and reportedly "cohabited" with her. However, Elliot noted that:

Circumstances of a delicate and disagreeable nature occured between them during this time, and when libellant had the offer of a house and wished to make provision to take her there to live with him she refused to go. [inserted in the deposition, "refused to live with libellant and"] and has ever since continued to live with affirment and libellant had not ever cohabited with her.[18]

Elliot further stated that he knew nothing else "except that her reasons were of a private, personal & indecent character."[19]

Undoubtedly the couple had experienced sexual difficulties. Since Sarah did not reply to her husband's divorce petition and no other papers directly stating her side exist, it is impossible to determine whether Sarah simply disliked making love with her husband, or whether he proposed or attempted something she found shocking or distasteful. What is clear, however, is that her husband considered her refusal to leave her place of residence and move to his house as desertion. The court agreed with him, and granted Thomas a divorce in 1839. By ruling in Thomas's favor, the court promoted the image of the proper wife as one who followed or remained with her husband no matter what problems they had. It further determined that it was her duty to cohabit with her husband no matter how repugnant she found the sex act to be with him.[20] In rejecting Thomas's decision that they should live together, Sarah was found guilty of desertion.

Wives, however, could not charge their husbands with desertion simply for refusing to cohabit with them. When husbands left their wives and refused to support them, then their wives could look for justice in the courts. Yet some men left because they could not provide for their wives. For these men the role of economic provider proved to be too great a burden. Some men abused their wives when they could not meet the image of family breadwinner. Others simply deserted and renounced the burden. In 1794, Anthony Black, for example, "absconded at night with all the property he could take with him and defrauded his Creditors." In 1795, Lawrence Dickinson told a witness that he was leaving Philadelphia because he had stolen some chairs from the store in which he worked and feared prosecution. William Thomson was arrested and sent to jail for debt in Northumberland County. Because his property was seized and sold, his wife and children returned to her father's house in Chester County "to prevent being starved." Upon his release, William visited his wife, Janet, but never offered to support her or the children. He left for the West shortly after that in 1798, taking their oldest son with him. When this son returned, his reports to others implied William was still not steady or responsible. For instance, he noted that his father had taught school for a time, but never set up his own household, and when the son last heard of his father, he was going up the Missouri River.[21] None of these men fit the picture of a financial supporter; instead they left their wives and families to continue their lives elsewhere and perhaps make a new start.

In contrast, William Lawes, by all accounts, tried hard to maintain his wife, Naomi. In her mind, however, it was not enough. When William was on a trip to New York, Naomi sold all his personal property at a public auction. One witness in their divorce suit reported that he told Naomi that William was coming back. Naomi told him that "she didn't care, she was [anxious?] to sell the property & put the money in her pocket and she didn't care what became of him." Other deponents implied that William may have been doing his best to provide for his wife, but that she did not think it was enough. John Craig told the court that William "provides as well for Respondent and his children as other labouring men." Yet William only rented the house in which he and Naomi had lived before the vendue. Thomas Hazard explained that he did not think there was a house William could have had before 1844. William did buy a house in Thornbury Township in 1844, telling his wife that she could return to him. However, she told John Craig that "she left him because she could do better by herself." Naomi continued to live near her husband, but refused to return to him. Although their neighbors considered him a good husband, William Lawes did not meet her expectations, no matter how hard he tried. After cohabitting for twenty-two years, William and Naomi were divorced in 1847.[22]

Sometimes men and women deserted their spouses because they did not believe they were behaving properly as a husband or wife. Yet by abandoning their mates, they flaunted societal standards, as well. In 1841, Mahlon Bruce consulted a lawyer about obtaining a divorce. According to the attorney's testimony, Mahlon wanted the divorce because his sister told him she saw his wife, Catherine, stealing things out of her drawer. When the lawyer informed Mahlon that he could not obtain a divorce on those grounds "and that his wife could make him support her, he told me, he . . . would clear out to the West, and his wife might shift for herself—or words to that effect."[23]

Mahlon did leave his wife. Shortly after their separation, she sued him for nonsupport. By that time, they had had a child. After paying Catherine a small sum of money, he did not contribute any more toward her support. It was rumored that he went to Ohio. Catherine Bruce did not meet Mahlon's expectations as a perfect wife. Perhaps there was also jealousy between her and his sister. Rather than trying to make the marriage work, Mahlon chose to leave his wife. However, by deserting his wife, he neglected his legal and social duty as a husband to provide for her (and their child). Whatever other reasons he had for leaving, his wife could prove him liable for her maintenance in a court of law.[24]

These examples illustrate that both men and women experienced sexual problems and lack of love for their spouses. They also worried about finances, and about meeting the standards set by society and their own spouses about how they should behave. Yet women and men differed in how and when they deserted their mates. Because of economic dependence on their husbands and the need to care for or fear of losing their children, the decision to leave their husbands was particularly difficult for women. Unless they had family or friends who could provide for them, a good job, or a new husband, most women had difficulty keeping themselves above the poverty line, especially if they were sick or had young children to support. Many unhappily married women did not have the independent means that would make leaving their marriages easier. Nevertheless, women did desert their husbands; some left willingly, and others quit in desperation because their husbands were abusive, or unwilling to support them.

Some women abandoned their husbands several times. In some cases, they were unable to support themselves and so returned to their spouses. In 1743, Jonathan Peasley reported that his wife, Dorcas, "hath elop'd from her said husband six Months at a Time about a year and a half ago , and several times Since." He warned readers that he would not pay her debts, noting that she was "intending to run him in Debt, and ruin him."[25] Although no one seems to know why she left, Julian Marshall reported that her mother deserted her father two times before the time mentioned in her father's divorce petition. She said her mother always left without any reason and when she returned was always welcomed "without a Murmur and treated kindly by him."[26]

Mary Rigg's acts of desertion appear to have been prompted by a need to feel wanted. According to one witness, Mary said, "that she would leave libellant and go to her daughters [by a former marriage], as she had more need of help than he [her husband] had." On the other hand, Joseph Jeffries noted of her, "that Respondent is of a restless and discontented and Peevish disposition, and appears not to be satisfied long in any place."[27]

Some husbands also left their wives several times. Although it was generally easier for men to obtain work and support themselves, these men were usually characterized as being drunk and lazy. Because Americans expected wives to take their husbands back, husbands could leave for months, returning when they wanted the security of a home and wife, and they could be fairly certain that they would be taken back.

In other cases, husbands' attempts to abandon their wives were thwarted by the wives following them. Elizabeth Lowry, for example, married her husband, John, in Ireland. He deserted her and left her destitute. She followed him to Cumberland County, Pennsylvania, and lived with him for six days. Then John "under Pretense of taking her to North Carolina decoyed her into Lancaster County . . . where he again deserted her taking with him all the Money your Petitioner had acquired in his absence."[28] Deborah Hutchinson followed her husband from Phoenixville in Chester County to Philadelphia. He left her again, and she moved back to her mother's house. They then lived together in Lancaster County, in Baltimore, and in Delaware County, as he kept deserting her and she kept following him. Finally he went to Richmond, Virginia, in 1836. When he abandoned her there, she returned to her mother because he left her "utterly destitute." He did not return to her, and she filed for divorce.[29] It is not clear why these women continued to pursue men who did not want to be with them. However, an abandoned wife lived in a state of limbo; by finding their husbands and living with them again, these women regained their status. In attempting to reform their husbands and keep their families together, these women were doing what the world around them told them they should do. Yet the laws of this same society permitted them to file for divorce when their attempts proved futile.

Some women and men threatened to leave their spouses before they actually did. Although it was not stated that she left him prior to the time mentioned in the divorce petition, Anna Margaretta Vondersloth must have at least given her husband, Frederick, reason to believe she would. Andrew Grasfer, in whose house the couple lived, explained that he did not know why Anna Margaretta left her husband. Yet he noted that "she had Promised the Libellant in the presence of the Deponent, never to leave her Husband the very night before her departure and seemed they had been in Unity together then." Despite his claims that the couple was in unity, this tantalizing fragment indicates there must have been some disharmony between the pair, and a reason why Anna Margaretta was making a promise before a witness not to leave her husband.[30]

The testimony of witnesses seems to indicate a degree of dissatisfaction among both men and women who actually left their spouses. Nevertheless, men and women tended to view desertion in a slightly different fashion. Women who were deserted often maintained that the desertion left them destitute. They usually mentioned that they had been left without any provisions, that they had children to care for, and that they had to rely upon help from family members or friends.

The destitution these women faced was often genuine. For instance, Rebecca John was left with six children in York County in 1813. When a former neighbor, Isaac Cadwalader, went to York County to bring her back to her father's house in Chester County, he discovered that she was "without any furniture except one skillet and some few articles of bedding, and a small chest, and without any apparent means of subsistence." Cadwalader also reported that Rebecca had never, by his own admission, given her husband a reason to leave her, and that after deserting Rebecca, David John received a large inheritance from his father's estate, "which from common report has been squandered." It seems clear that Rebecca John was in dire straits, but according to this witness, she was also the innocent victim of a callous husband who took her away from her family and neighbors and then abandanoned her.[31]

Unlike Rebecca John and many of the women discussed here, some women did not have friends and family to sustain them after their husbands deserted them. Without the means to support themselves, and perhaps being ill or pregnant, these women were forced to seek assistance from the poorhouse officials, either through outrelief or by actually entering the almshouse.[32] Families already living on the margin suffered drastically when the primary breadwinner left.

Mary Derborough, for instance, complained in 1804 that her husband, Daniel, "neglects and Refuses support and maintain [sic] her and five small children." She was sick and unable to work, and she was "suffering from want of Medical aid and that she and her Children are perishing for want of food." The court ordered the Constable of E. Whiteland Township to take her and her two small children to the poorhouse (presumably the older ones could be bound out). Then the court ordered the Directors of the Poor to seize Daniel Derborough's real and personal property. All of his personal estate was to be sold and three quarters of the rents and profits from his land were to go to support his wife and children.[33]

Men's complaints about desertion, however, were different from women's. As they could not collect support payments from them, they did not protest that the departure of their wives left them destitute. Instead, as illustrated earlier, they charged their wives with taking their belongings or accused them of running up debts that the husband had to pay.

In addition to economic worries, deserted husbands could be left with the unaccustomed task of childcare. Even a man who occasionally rocked the baby's cradle or amused his children for an hour was unlikely to be used to the day to day care of children. For Thomas Matson, this responsibility proved to be too great a burden. According to the brief entry in the Philadelphia Almshouse's Daily Occurrence Docket, Matson was a twenty-eight-year-old Philadelphia resident. He was brought to the almshouse because "his wife has absconded & left him with three children to support, which is supposed to be the cause of his derangement."[34]

Valentine Clemons, on the other hand, solved his problem by putting his children out to board, "at his own expense," after his wife deserted him. Valentine was a cordwainer, and a hardworking man, according to his employer and co-workers. His wife took in boarders, but her misconduct with them caused him to lose business. She threatened to "go into Irish Town, and become a common whore," if he turned the lodgers out, so he left. In his absence, she sold his goods and furniture. After nine months, however, he returned, and wanted to live with his wife and children. She refused at first, but according to Valentine's employer, then remembered there were items of his she had not yet sold. She agreed to his return, but shortly afterwards she deserted him again, after robbing him "of his bed-clothes, and other articles." Valentine was then left to care for their four children. The court granted his request for a divorce in 1791.[35]

Where women argued that their husbands neglected their duty in supporting them, men complained of their wives' "disobedience" toward them. James Patterson, for example, accused his wife, Jane, of "wilful and malicious desertion" after she refused to leave Miflin County. James' divorce petition states that "after the Increase of his Family aforesaid and conceiving it expedient and promotive of his Happiness to remove and dispose of his property in the said County of Miflin in order to settle elsewhere," he sold his plantation and bought a tract of land in Westmoreland County. Jane declared that she would not move. Nowhere does James mention that he discussed the move with his wife or asked her what she desired. Perhaps she did not feel like leaving her home and starting again in a new place. Although James was the one leaving the area, Jane was the one accused of desertion. He assumed his wife would go along with his wishes.[36]

Husbands who charged their wives with desertion were often looking back to an older tradition of patriarchy. Although these men believed it was their duty to support their spouses, they also expected to make the decisions about how and where the couple would live. On the other hand, women who deserted often sought a mutual partnership in their marriages. Both men and women, however, emphasized the financial responsibilities of the husband when seeking legal separations. By placing an advertisement in a newspaper or by applying for a divorce, a husband signaled his intentions or desire not to support his wife. Women in their pleas for aid or for divorce established that their husbands had neglected their duty to provide for them.

What then did desertion mean to men and women of early Pennsylvania? Both the divorce act and poor laws depicted desertion in economic terms. These laws made husbands liable for supporting their wives, and permitted almshouse officials to seize and sell property to support the wife and children. Husbands who could be found were also required to pay for the maintenance of their wives and children so long as the couple was living apart.

Divorce also served as an economic remedy by aiding deserted wives recover their feme sole status. If a husband left his wife, she was placed in a sort of economic limbo. In contrast, a divorced woman was free and clear to make contracts on her own, take over the family business, and even marry again. Thus, by permitting her to divorce, she became less of a burden on the community. The revision of the divorce law in 1815 changed the period of "wilful and malicious" desertion from four years to two years, reflecting both the precarious economics of the nineteenth century and the growing reluctance of Pennsylvanians to support able-bodied citizens.[37]

Men, too, benefited by divorce. In winning a divorce from his wife, a man was no longer responsible for her debts and did not need her signature to sell their property and goods. He also could remarry, finding a new woman (one he did not have to pay) to take care of the house and any children living with him.

Thus, Pennsylvania laws reduced desertion to an economic equation. It was not defined in terms of distance. A deserting spouse could live down the street, rather than disappearing "west." It also made no difference as to how long the couple had been married before the desertion occcurred. For instance, when Peter Brown deserted his wife, Jane, the day of their wedding, she applied for and received a divorce three years later.[38] Yet the petitions for aid and divorce do reveal gender differences. A man could accuse his wife of desertion if she simply refused to share his bed and board. Abandoned wives, however, could not appeal for assistance unless their husbands also refused to maintain them. Women's requests carefully established that they had not received any monetary support, and that they had had *no contact* with their husbands for a specific period of time, for instance, more than two or four years if they were applying for a divorce.

Both men and women defined the desertion of their spouses in terms of husbands' and wives' roles. For instance, Susanah Sheifly noted in her divorce petition that by his frequent drinking her husband, George, "hath rendered himself incapable of managing and taking care of his said Family as a husband ought to do," but that she was a "poor Woman and endeavors by honest labour and Industry to earn bread and clothing for herself and children." In another case, witnesses for Anthony Felix Weibert declared that despite his case of gonorrhea and his frequent absences from home, he was a man of "great Chastity," "a Man of Worth & Honor," and "a very domestick Man & very well calculated for Domestic Happines." In contrast, they reported that his wife, Altathea was "lewd" and an "infamous woman."[39] Finally, in a Chester County divorce suit, William Early stated that Jacob Hoofman was an "Indulgent Husband a good provid[er]; and . . . a sober Orderly Industrious Man, nor has he ever heard Libellant give Respondant an Angry or a Cross Hand."[40]

Desertion, then, had a different meaning both to husbands and wives and for husbands and wives. It was easier for men to leave their wives, but women did desert. Changing expectations contributed to both men and women leaving. Men may have expected more submissive wives, while women who left were often seeking more independence or looking for a spouse who met their expectations as a perfect husband.

Desertion, however, could be only an imperfect solution to marital difficulties. A man who abandoned his wife was still liable for her support, and could be put in jail for non-support unless he moved to another state or to the frontier. When a woman deserted, she lost the status of wife and the economic maintenance of the husband she held under coverture. In addition, leaving one's husband could also mean having to make the difficult decision to leave one's children. For some women, the physical restraints of pregnancy prevented them from leaving their husbands. Legal restrictions as a feme covert and social restrictions requiring women to stay in their own "sphere" prevented still others from leaving, and hindered their abilities to provide for themselves and their children. Both men and women remained legally tied to their deserted spouses. Neither could lawfully remarry unless the bonds were broken by death or by divorce.

CHAPTER 6

For a Maintenance: The Economics of Marital Discord

My little old man and I fell out;
I'll tell you what 'twas all about,
I had money and he had none,
And that's the way the noise begun.

TRADITIONAL NURSERY RHYME

Divorce did not always settle tensions between married couples. In fact, sometimes it caused new stresses or increased old ones. Martha Tiffin, for instance, received a divorce from bed and board from her husband, James, in December 1802. The following September, the court determined the alimony. From the beginning, James fought against paying it. He said he was in debt, and blamed Martha for it, declaring that "aspersions she threw on his character" caused his business as a hat vender to decline. Yet the men who examined his books asserted that they were kept "in the deranged state [in which] they were found on purpose to cause him to appear as poor as possible." James believed that Martha was well provided for without his alimony payments, and noted that she owned quite a bit of property across the Delaware: three large brick houses, a four-acre garden, and forty-seven acres of land, "some of which is good meadow." In addition, she possessed two turnpike shares and some funded debts of the United States, for which he had granted her power of attorney.

Notwithstanding James' assertions, the court ruled against him. According to the ensuing alimony agreement, James was to put the New Jersey property "in complete tenantable Repair," and deliver the title deeds to Martha, releasing all his rights to the property to the "Trustees for her use in fee." Martha was also awarded the turnpike shares, a gold watch that had belonged to her before the marriage, and three hundred dollars per year. If payments were delayed three weeks or more, an attachment could be issued without applying to the court. This settlement was in lieu of all dower claims. Furthermore, she had to relinquish the title to their house on Second Street, in Philadelphia.[1]

Apparently, the couple cohabited again in 1806, but shortly thereafter separated. James was deeply in debt. According to Henry Ward, who lived with them, Martha offered to lend James some money, providing Ward would agree to advance some money, too. Ward declined because the debts were too large. Martha either left James because of this situation, or she left after his house and furniture were sold to Ward, who then ordered her out of the house. She went to New Jersey, and shortly thereafter James left on a trading voyage.[2]

In 1807, Martha obtained an attachment for the alimony James owed her from the last time she left him. According to her testimony, the amount due was $325. His attorney contested Martha's claim to alimony, and asked that the attachment be quashed. The court ruled in James' favor, stating that Martha lost her right to the alimony when she returned and cohabited with James, and setting a precedent for later cases.[3]

Although the Tiffins possessed more wealth and property than many Philadelphians of their time, they were not alone in their squabbles over money and possessions. Then, as now, financial problems and disagreements were a major source of marital tension. Both rich and poor couples fought over money. In some cases, these controversies were simply for the basic necessities of life—food, clothing, and shelter. In other cases, arguments occurred over which partner would get more of their belongings. Embittered husbands and wives frequently continued to bicker over money after a divorce or settlement was awarded.

In a marriage, as in society as a whole, the person with money frequently has power over those without it. Disputes over money were therefore sometimes contests to maintain or establish dominance over one's spouse. Under Pennsylvania law, husbands controlled the family property. Due to these legal constraints, as well as the social ones limiting paying work for women, it is not surprising that women more often than men were left in a precarious financial situation after the breakup of their marriages. After separating temporarily or permanently from their spouses, some women did receive financial support from them. Others, as Martha Tiffin's experience indicates, found it more difficult to collect money from their husbands. In many cases, court decrees did not solve spouses economic disputes, and in some instances legal decisions led to still further differences between husband and wife.

The economic situation of each marriage varied. Couples who disagreed over finances at one period of their life together could be more harmonious at another period. Although in theory, husbands provided for their wives and families, in actual practice, both husbands and wives often contributed to the family economy, and either could suffer if the other left. A woman who had relied upon her husband to support her had to find a way to cope if he left her. The man who depended on his wife to do the laundry, the cooking, and care for the children had to adjust if his wife left him. Similarly, the inheritance of money by husband or wife could upset the status quo of a marriage, causing new temptations and new tensions. Thus, in some instances it was actually the possession of money by one partner that caused troubles in a marriage.

Nevertheless, enduring the pain of an already troubled marriage with all of its emotional upheavals also involved coping with its attendant economic worries. It is not surprising that marital discord brought about economic changes in the lives of the individuals involved, although degrees of financial distress varied. Where some experienced a loss from not being able to collect the rents from a disputed property, others could not afford the meanest food and shelter. The question then is not did some unhappily married individuals suffer financial distress during and after their marriages, but rather how did they cope when they did? To what extent did they suffer? Were the options and strategies different for men and women? What circumstances allowed them to carry on?

The handling of money matters depended upon the particulars of the marriage. Involvement in a discordant marriage sometimes left husbands and wives stranded in a marital limbo in which their spouses could be living apart from them, but nearby; living fifty miles away, or even living somewhere in bigamous second marriages. In addition, the day-to-day conditions of a troubled marriage could change—a runaway spouse might return; an abusive spouse might reform. Unless the couple divorced, or one of them died, their marital bonds were not dissolved. Unsettled and uncertain marital situations made it difficult for husbands and wives to receive pecuniary relief from local officials, who had to be sure of such things as the petitioner's legal residence, and whether he or she had a valid reason for aid. Nevertheless, if a man deserted his wife, leaving her without any means of support, or a woman became an alcoholic incapable of caring for the household and children, the spouse had to cope with the situation in some way.

Part of married women's economic problems arose from coverture. Under the system of common law inherited from England, a married woman was a feme covert. A feme sole, or single woman, could enter into legal agreements, own property, and bequeath her possessions, but a wedded woman could not do this without special legal arrangements. In some cases arrangements were made prior to the wedding for the woman to retain a separate estate. It is probable that these prenuptial agreements were fairly common among the wealthy and those who had some knowledge of law and finance. Until the Revolutionary period, however, the courts of equity would enforce the arrangement only if it were in the form of a trust. In these cases, a third party acted in the name of the woman.[4] By the end of the eighteenth century, the courts no longer required trustees for prenuptial separate estates, but did make them mandatory for the creation of postnuptial settlements, and they could be created only with the consent of the husband. Without a separate estate, a married woman could not sell, transfer, or give away (even in a will) real or personal property.[5]

The law, therefore, contributed to the economic dependency of wives upon their husbands. The experience of Elizabeth Clandennin illustrates the patterns of power and dependency in many troubled marriages and the complications that could occur over a woman's inheritance. In February 1779, Elizabeth married John Clandennin. At the time of their marriage, she possessed a "Personal Estate belonging to the Estate of her late Husband William Woodward to the amount of near four hundred Pounds, which came into the hands of the said John Clendinnin." The couple lived "in a House called the Robinhood Tavern, the Property of her said late husband."[6]

The marriage did not proceed smoothly. In a December 1780 petition to the Philadelphia Court of Quarter Sessions, Elizabeth noted that ten weeks before, her husband's violence toward her had forced her to leave their house at night and seek shelter "in the House of a Friend." When she tried to return to their house a few days later, her husband refused to let her inside. Only ten months into the marriage, Elizabeth asked the court to force John to defray the costs she had incurred since they had lived apart, to pay her a weekly allowance, and "to deliver up the wearing Apparrel of the Petitioner."[7]

The court ordered John to pay Elizabeth seventy-five pounds per week Pennsylvania currency. John paid one week and then asked Elizabeth to return to him. She agreed to the reconciliation, "but it soon became evident that that the said John was actuated more by the desire of evading the payment of the weekly allowance aforesaid than by any affectionate motive." John continued to abuse her, and Elizabeth again moved out of the house in August 1785. In April 1786, she filed for a divorce from bed and board, and asked for alimony, noting that she was without "any means of livelihood or support."[8] Unfortunately for Elizabeth, it appears that her attempts to collect alimony were not any more successful once she was divorced. The divorce papers include an attachment for contempt against John, noting that he was to pay her twenty shillings a month.[9]

Whatever their reasons for marrying, Elizabeth and John had certain expectations for their lives together. However, their actual married life did not match their dreams. In marrying John, Elizabeth not only surrendered the money and property she had inherited from her previous husband, but she relinquished her personal independence as well. As a widow, Elizabeth was used to making decisions about her life and that of her children, and about the day-to-day running of the inn. Perhaps she saw in John a partner who would share her beliefs and desires. On the other hand, John, clinging to traditional forms of patriarchal power, insisted that his word was final and that he had the right to the house, property, and to the physical correction of his wife. No doubt the birth of a child the year after they were married increased the tensions of the household and further increased Elizabeth's dependency role. Not only had she lost control of her income, property, and belongings, but she had a young baby and three children by her previous husband to support. Resentment or desperation drove her out of the house and led her to petition the court.

The law of Pennsylvania required John to provide for his wife and child. As legal head of the household, it was his obligation and his duty. Therefore legislation made it possible for women such as Elizabeth Clandennin to petition the court for redress when their husbands refused to maintain them. Yet the very act of marriage denied women the opportunity to provide for themselves and kept them dependent upon their husbands.

Even when they were left money by others, married women, as Elizabeth Clandennin' experience illustrates, did not necessarily have control of it. The passage of the 1832 Act Relating to Orphans' Courts was a significant step for married women in that it forced husbands to post security before the sum of money their wives inherited would be paid. However, the inherited money was then paid to the husband, the security ensuring that after his death the money would go to the widow or her heirs. If the husband were unable or unwilling to post security, trustees would be appointed, although the interest went to the husband, unless he desired it "to be settled for the separate use of the wife." Wives might also make a declaration before the judge— without their husbands present—to forego having their husbands post the bond.[10]

Although this law gave women some security, and assured them some protection in their widowhood, its effect during marriage was limited. In an ideal marriage, of course, it did not matter. Husbands and wives would make joint decisions on how money would be spent, and husbands would not want to leave their wives and families destitute. But many marriages were not ideal. Despite changing expectations about what marital relationships should be like and new laws assisting married women, husbands frequently sustained power over their wives by maintaining economic control, or threatened them when they could not have that control.

The right of husbands to control their wives' inheritances prompted careful friends and relatives to make special arrangements for their benefit. For example, after Peter Constantine made a will leaving his personal estate and three thousand dollars "to be invested in public stock for her own benefit" to Elizabeth Crozer, now wife of John Boddy, he attached a letter to James Mazurie, the man he named his executor. In it he noted that "the motives of my two donations to Betsy Boddy are defeated by her husbands right to get hold of the one altogether and the interest of the other and as my Intentions never were to favour a Spendthrift and a bad husband I annull those two donations and make them over to you."[11] Constantine then requested Mazurie to let Betsy Boddy have whatever she needed from his estate, and to pay her sums of money from the sale of the remainder as she needed it. He was also to "help her along with part of the Three Thouseand dollars if she needs it," whether she was living with her husband or apart from him.[12]

Both before and after the passage of new laws, some men abused their wives in order to gain control of their estates. For example, Johanna Delany was admitted to the Philadelphia Almshouse in 1797. Her husband was a mariner who had not lived with her for several years. Upon returning from his last voyage, he demanded that she make her property of two or three houses over to him. When she refused, he "ill used" her, forcing her to flee to the almshouse. (She was also described as being venereal, perhaps making her unable to work.)[13]

Sometimes these abused wives were widows who had remarried, as Elizabeth Clendennin did. In a 1767 example, Sophia Conner's husband, Edward, took control of her inheritance, then advertised in the *Pennsylvania Gazette* that he would not be responsible for her debts. Sophia replied to his advertisement with one of her own. In it, she

explained that Edward had spent all of what her former husband had
left to her and their children, leaving her destitute:

of all manner of Substance, then I was obliged to shift for myself, and when
some Christian People bestowed their Charity upon me, he would spend it;
and now he took from me all Things of any Value, for he would not have
had a Stitch of Clothes to his Back, if he had not taken a Suit of Clothes that
was sent to my Son from London for a present.[14]

In an 1847 Chester County divorce case, Priscilla Place's mother
noted that John Place expected Priscilla to inherit a sizeable estate
from her previous husband. When it turned out to be much smaller
than he expected, "from that time his conduct towards my daughter
changed." Several witnesses reported seeing John Place ill treat his
wife, quarrel with her, and refuse to provide her with necessities,
even during the birth of their child. Samuel Williams, who was the
guardian of Priscilla's child by her first husband, wanted to pay the
support money for the child directly to Priscilla. Williams was advised
by his attorney to pay Place instead, who threatened to sue him if he
did not. Later, when Williams wanted to pay part of his debt to Place
for thrashing his wheat directly to Priscilla, Place refused and threatened again to sue Williams if he did not pay him. Finally, Priscilla
was forced to leave him, and John left the area shortly afterward,
reportedly marrying a woman in Pottsville.[15]

However slight the laws and legal arrangements were in some cases,
they were intended to protect married women. But sometimes these
arrangements caused trouble within a marriage. John Place expected
that his wife's inheritance would be much larger than it was. When
his expectations were not realized, he used his legal right as her husband to control what she did have and attempted to control her as
well.

Issac Hoopes was also disappointed when he learned he would not
gain control of his wife's 1829 inheritance. Sidney Marsh, a witness
in the divorce case of Issac and Hannah Hoopes, testified that "the
primary cause of Hannah Hoopes leaving the Libellant Isaac Hoopes
arose in the will of her mother Mrs. Jones: she the said Mrs. Jones
left the property intended for her daughter Hannah Hoopes in trust;
this was one cause of dissension." Upon Hannah's death, the trustees,
Hannah's brothers, or their executors were to pay the legacy to her

children. Because the money was in the form of a trust, Issac could not touch it. Apparently, Issac believed he should manage the money, the fact that his wife had her own income upset him. On the other hand, the conditions of Rebecca Jones' bequest gave Hannah some independence (subject to any restraints put on her by the trustees). Having an inheritance that her husband could not control may have given Hannah an incentive to leave him as well.[16] Thus, legal guidelines established some protection for married women, but the expectations men and women had about their marriages and their roles, and concerns over who would control money and property, sometimes led to marital tensions when expectations were not met or conditions in the marriage changed.

Even when women married for love, they usually expected that their husbands would be able to support them. However, some women and men admitted to marrying their spouses for money. Catharine Ducombe of Allegheny County allegedly told an acquaintance that she only married her husband, "for the sake of a good living." Edward Blaney, who habitually ill treated his wife, told his mother-in-law that "he would never have married, if he thought his wife could not support him."[17]

Although some men married for money, most did not expect their wives to support them. Increasingly, popular literature through the end of the eighteenth and nineteenth centuries portrayed men's role as that of the breadwinner outside of the home, and women's role as nurturer within it. Home was a serene environment to which men returned after their day's work, and which women ran smoothly and with dedication. This idealistic picture defined the boundaries for model men and women's lives. On the other hand, this ideal was not achieved by many. The lower sorts knew that all family members, except the youngest or the infirm, had to help to support the family. Farm families also understood that husbands and wives both assisted in maintaining the farm. "Middling" respectable women helped to make ends meet by taking in lodgers or running small businesses, even if they had husbands who worked. Yet some men and women took seriously the domestic ideal permeating the literature of the time, and were more distressed when the realities of their lives clashed with their expectations.

Whatever their expectations, most married women depended upon their husbands at least to some degree for economic support. Since husbands could legally control their income, property, and financial affairs, wives frequently suffered during periods of marital upset. Money problems could occur several times within one marriage, as couples broke up housekeeping together and then reconciled.

Hannah Pyle, for instance, first applied to the Chester County Court of Quarter Sessions for relief in 1757 after noting that her husband, William, had beaten her, and that he and his mistress had threatened to kill her. She lived with her brother after leaving her husband, but feared that she would be left in poverty, although she had brought "a Considerable Estate" to her marriage. William had refused to grant her a maintenance, despite her appeals. The court ordered him to pay her the considerable sum of three shillings per week in quarterly payments plus give her "one side saddle, one feather Bed, six of his best Chairs, one Iron pot, one tea table, half a dozen of Pewter plates and one dish, and that what part of the said William Pyle's household goods the said Hannah hath got into her possession." If William sold his land and plantation, he was to secure one hundred thirty pounds, from which she would be paid the interest during the separation. This type of provision was not always entered in court dockets, but the sentiment that it was the husband's duty to provide for his wife was consistent with other cases of the time. As with other separation agreements, the weekly payment was to cease upon a reconciliation or upon Hannah's death.[18]

Apparently, Hannah and William reconciled. Then in 1773, Hannah once again petitioned the court, noting that she and her husband had been living apart for about nine months, and that he would neither support her, nor allow her to live with him. Due to age and "bodily weakness" she could not earn her living, and again asked for a maintenance. The court ordered William to "pay into the Hands of Robert Mendenhall" five shillings per week for Hannah's maintenance.[19]

In November 1775, Hannah once again made a plea to the court. This time it was for an additional allowance and for some of her goods. Although she acknowledged the alimony awarded to her "about Nine Months past," she noted that she was "Oblig'd to wander from house to House for a Living, & sometimes Dificult to get a House to put my head in which to me, now in the Decline of Life seems hard." She asked for a larger allowance from her husband, as well as "a Bed & Bedding, & Goods to furnish a Room, & my saddle & bridle," believing that if she could obtain this she would not be such a burden to her friends and neighbors.[20]

Whether the couple reunited again is unknown. Hannah outlived her husband, and he remembered her in his will. There was no sign of affection in the document, but he left her the sum of twenty pounds a year, the use of a house during the rest of her life, and some household furnishings including, "Six of the best Cheares with all my Pewter." This bequest, he stated, was "In Lieu and full Satisfaction & Barr of her Dower, of and in all the Lands and Tenements which I shall Die Seised of." After leaving legacies to various friends and relatives, William divided the remainder of his estate equally between his one living brother and the children of his two dead brothers.[21]

In this example, which is typical of others, the law provided some protection to the injured wife because of the expectation that it was the husband's obligation to provide for her. Yet, the same law that made this protection possible and declared that the wife was to inherit a third of her husband's estate, denied her the right to earn wages and own property in her own name without special arrangements or her husband's permission. Thus, many women such as Hannah Pyle suffered economic hardship when their husbands abandoned them, or forced them to leave. Many others stayed with abusive husbands or periodically attempted reconciliations not only because they loved their husbands and believed conditions would get better, but because they could not afford to leave.

New laws aided women whose husbands deserted them or refused to support them. In some instances, they also posed constraints on them. Under eighteenth-century poor laws, for example, women could petition for support after their husbands deserted them. Unfortunately, the woman could not petition the court directly. Instead, an overseer of the poor had to make the actual appeal to the court, and the court proceedings that followed could take months.

Under the 1771 Act for the Relief of the Poor, the Overseers of the Poor were allowed to seize the goods and chattels and receive the rents of the fugitive husband or wife, in order to support his spouse or her children. First the overseers of the district obtained a warrant from two magistrates of the district. Then the court of Quarter Sessions confirmed the procedure and allowed the overseers to sell such goods and chattels "as the court shall think fit," in order to support the deserted spouse or children. If there was no estate, then the court ordered the deserting man or woman to pay a sum of money to maintain the spouse or children who had been abandoned, or go to jail until the sum was paid. Of course, this assumes the recalcitrant husband or wife could be found.[22] Later laws continued to make the husband liable for his wife's support.

In one 1781 example, the Overseers of the Poor for the district of Southwark seized the goods and chattels of Christopher Lamb "to the Value of five hundred Pounds Specie lawful Money of Pennsylvania," and received the rents and profits of his lands and tenements to the value of thirty pounds. Among the goods seized and sold were a walnut tea table, a dining table, five Windsor chairs, a pair of bedsteads, a feather bed, bedding, a quilting frame, a delph bowl [sic], a pewter plate, a map, and various other household goods, such as dishes, a salt cellar, a ladle, and a keg. In addition, the overseers took possession of Lamb's lot in Southwark with its two tenements worth thirty-six pounds per year. The money obtained from the sale of the goods plus the rents went to support his wife, Mary, so that she would not be a burden on the district.

Yet, it was up to the court, with help from the overseers, to decide on how the estate should be administered. Under the law, Mary could not even make out the complaint against her husband. Instead, she had to contact the overseers of the poor to bring the suit, and then await the sometimes lengthy court proceedings. Because she no longer had a husband to provide for her, Mary lost the economically (if not emotionally) comfortable situation she had enjoyed with him. Consequently, in addition to surrendering her home, Mary lost her belongings. One can only wonder how she felt about losing the use of her possessions some of which, such as the Delft bowl and Windsor chairs, gave her some status and comfort, and some of which, such as the bedding and quilting frame, may have been of practical use to her.[23]

Perhaps because the property had belonged to her before her marriage, Sarah Thomson of Ashton Township, in Chester County, was more fortunate than Mary Lamb. Sarah joined with her husband, James, in selling the land she had owned before their wedding. But after this sale, James "through inattention & other Proceedings" ran into debts forcing the sale of all his personal property. He then deserted Sarah, and went "to some distant part on the frontier." With large debts still outstanding, Sarah feared the plantation in Thornbury and Ashton would also be sold. She also expected that James would acquire even more debts. Describing herself in a petition to the court as being in poor health with two young children, one likely to become a cripple, she asked that alimony or a separate maintenance be granted from the remainder of her fortune. The court granted her three-eighths part of the forge, which she had owned before her marriage, the house in which she was residing, the stable, a garden and orchard, the drawwell, some meadowland, and some woodland. All this and any profits accrued were for her use, "according to her will & Discretion Free and Seperate from the said James Thomson and all other Persons whatsoever during the natural Life of her the said Sarah."[24]

Still, in most cases in Pennsylvania, the rights of creditors came before those of wives, at least until the passage of the 1848 act to secure the rights of married women. Before that time, even after the guardians of the poor—by court order—seized the real estate of a deserting husband, creditors who had a prior claim could recover the property for their own use. This meant that property owned or inherited by married women could be used to pay debts contracted by their husbands, unless protected by a separate trust.[25]

Nevertheless, in some instances, the courts served as a means to bring legal action against husbands who deserted their wives, even when there was no formal separation or divorce. One curious 1826 case demonstrates the degree to which women believed that they could go before the court and expect to be granted relief. In December 1826, the Philadelphia Court of Quarter Sessions ordered John Enew to pay three dollars per week to support his wife and children. This allowance was reduced in February 1827. In March 1827, Jane Enew petitioned the court, "claiming to be the lawful wife of the Defendant and alleging that the woman to whom the Court had granted support is not his wife." She asked that the court consider annulling the decision. On motion of John Enew's attorney, the court declined.[26]

Yet the laws that were designed to protect wives with the expectation that husbands would support them could work to the detriment of husbands. Alexander Rutherford's property in Delaware was attached to pay the debts of his wife's former husband. Although Agnes deserted Alexander, when he was called away from home on business she gained access to the house and made off with much of his personal property. He feared that whenever he was away, Agnes, as his wife, would be able to enter the house and take whatever she wanted, which prompted him to ask for a divorce.[27]

On the other hand, James Cahill attributed his bankrupt state directly to the divorce settlement obtained by his wife, Pricilla. Pricilla brought sixty-four acres of land to the marriage, "the occupancy of which he enjoyed untill . . . the said Pricilla obtained . . . a divorce from the bonds of matrimony with him, thereby leaving him in a destitute situation." James explained in an insolvency petition that he had acquired most of his debts during coverture, that they were almost all for the use of his family, and that he expected "on the strength of his life estate to be able to pay them." He pleaded that the " said divorce has rendered him altogether unable to pay his debts." The court dismissed James Cahill's insolvency petition. Apparently the court weighed as evidence against him the fact that he was a chronic drinker, and that, prior to the divorce, when drunk he beat and abused his wife so badly that at times she made excuses to leave the house in order to run away. Obviously he was not maintaining his wife and managing her estate properly during the term of their marriage as a proper husband would have done.[28]

Although men generally had an advantage in terms of being able to earn money, they, too, could face monetary difficulties if their spouses deserted them. George Beck's wife, Mary, left him several times and ran up debts. In a newspaper advertisement, he stated, "I am reduced to follow a circumstance in life, that I am become unable to pay any more debts." When John Rubbel of Lancaster County reported that he would not pay the debts his eloped wife, Christiana, accrued, he mentioned also that she had left five young children at home.[29]

In other instances, men took over the care of households when their wives became incapacitated through abuse of alcohol. When the men could no longer cope with the situation, one option was to put their wives in the almshouse, sometimes agreeing to pay a sum of money for board. (Women occasionally did this with drunk or incapacitated husbands, too.) The conditions of the almshouse meant this was a fairly drastic solution. Either these people were unable to handle their spouses, who perhaps needed full time care, or they wanted to be well rid of them.

In one 1802 example, Nelly Lyons was admitted to the almshouse after her husband stated that he could not keep her sober, "and when Drunk she neglects her Two Children."[30] In another example of 1805, Elizabeth Snell, the twenty-three-year-old English-born wife of Captain James Snell, was admitted to the almshouse in Philadelphia. The Captain was "a Man of esteem'd reputation." Due to the "abandoned conduct" of his wife, he was "obliged to break up house-keeping, she being in a state of Intoxication the whole of her time."[31]

Despite these examples, women more often than men faced the brunt of the economic problems generated by troubled marriages. Some were fortunate enough to have help from family members or friends. Others, as we have seen, had trusts established in their own names. But in spite of coverture, and the social restraints of going outside their "sphere," many of them worked. Some women managed well and were astute "Men of Business." For others, however, employment amounted to low paying, low status, or even demeaning jobs.[32]

The divorce petitions of women forced to support themselves and their children and the depositions of their witnesses occasionally provide glimpses of the types and variety of work women could do. For instance, Mary Trenchard and her husband, James, lived apart from each other. Although James, who was an engraver, was supposed to give Mary a sum of money to pay her rent, he often did not. Mary tried to earn her living by "penciling chintz" and calico. She worked for a calico printer in Kensington, but he did not employ her during the slow winter months. Despite the fact that Mary also took in sewing, she was often in want because she was frequently sick and unable to work. Sewing for others was not especially lucrative, in any case;

the work often involved spending long hours doing close work in poor light, but most women could turn to it if necessary as respectable work. Catharine Griscom, for instance, supported her two children by needlework, although her father paid her rent, and Ann Taylor "would work at her sewing all night to obtain sufficient money to buy bread for her family."[33]

Other wives supported themselves and their families by teaching or running small businesses or taverns. Because her drunk and abusive husband refused to provide for her, Elizabeth Martin kept a school, assisted by her sister-in-law. Mary Burk, whose licentious husband abandoned her, maintained herself and her child by teaching at the "Girl's free school at the University."[34] Ann Carson and Jane Bartram both ran shops after being deserted by their husbands.[35] In the 1730s, Catherine Pattison petitioned the court in Chester County for a tavern license after her husband had been gone for less than a week. Apparently the tavern was already in operation, as she asked for the license for another year. She indicated that she was destitute, and that this was the only way in which she could make a living. Mary Henderson kept "a public house" in the 1790s to provide for herself and her drunken husband, Alexander. He was a shoemaker, but did not work at his trade. These are just a few examples that appeared in public records after marriages broke up, but no doubt many other women ran family businesses or more informal drinking establishments.[36]

Prostitution was another means by which wives attempted to provide for themselves. Mary Bangs, for example left her husband for another man. She allegedly told a witness testifying in her husband's divorce suit that "she was obliged to see a Gentleman, and have intercourse with him, in order to get money to support herself and the said Duffield." On the other hand, Rachel Brooks, by her account, was deserted by her husband. He lived with her for four years, giving her four children, who all died, plus a case of venereal disease. A year after he abandoned her, she left her home in Maryland, and "came to Philada. where being much exposed to temptation, was Seduced & led astray, & by her evil courses during the short space of 9 weeks was compelled to take shelter in the alms house much diseased." From there, a visiting committee from the Magdalen Society, a charitable group that sought to reform prostitutes, placed her in their own asylum. After fifteen months, she gave "proof of her stability," and was released to a pious family in the country.[37]

In some instances, however, the presence of husbands made it even more difficult for their wives to support themselves. For example, Margaret McCrea kept a boarding house. Although William McCrea refused to maintain her, he thwarted her attempts at providing for them herself by using the existence of the boarders to provoke fights with her. On one occasion, he became angry and said that they ate before he did and that he had to eat their leavings. Due to his behavior, the lodgers finally left.[38]

Some women supported themselves even when their husbands were not drunk or abusive, but simply could not or would not provide for their wives and families. In the divorce case of Elizabeth and Daniel Hare, a witness for Elizabeth Hare testified that "the parties lived together upon peaceable and good terms, but that the said Daniel was not steady to his business being of a speculative disposition and a searcher for the Philosopher's Stone." Daniel eventually deserted Elizabeth, leaving her with two children and pregnant with a third. Although both she and witnesses claim he left her without any support, she stated that in the twelve years he had been gone, she supported the children by her own labor, bringing them up "in such a Manner as was suitable to their situation in Life."[39] Elizabeth Hare managed to obtain her divorce because her husband had deserted her, but clearly she was able to support herself. By obtaining a divorce, however, she could keep Daniel from claiming all she had earned.

Other women, abandoned or abused by their husbands, were too sick to work. For these women, "poor and destitute of friends," the almshouse was the only alternative. Rhodah Coombes was "violently afflicted with a pain in her head to such a degree, that she has lost the sight of one of her eyes, [and was] entirely incapable of contributing towards a living by her work." Susannah Curtis, whose husband left her two years before, entered the almshouse, "progressing fast in a consumption." Ann Wilges suffered with a "fever and ague," and Mary McMicken had "a sore leg and [was] not able to work for her living." After the English-born Elizabeth Fenimore's second husband deserted her, she supported herself by working as a maid. Only thirty-two

Almshouse in Spruce Street, 1799. This was a place where desperate people usually came as a last resort. Husbands and wives were separated, and often even young children were taken from their mothers and bound out as apprentices. The prison-like atmosphere of this structure can be seen here—the brick walls were intended to keep the "inmates" on the premises. *Courtesy of the Historical Society of Pennsylvania.*

years old, she had to enter the almshouse because she was almost blind, and "incapable of doing housework."[40]

Pregnancy prevented other women from supporting themselves. Eleanor Winterscale entered the almshouse "far advanced in her pregnancy and near lying-in." Sarah Robinson's husband sailed off in a sloop bound for Charleston, South Carolina, "but took care not to provide for her, or that she should receive any part of his wages during his absence." Sarah, left "near her time of Lying in, and no way of providing for herself," procured an order to be admitted to the almshouse.[41]

The women who entered the almshouse as a result of reduced circumstances occasioned by their marital problems were never wealthy.

While some of them had lived comfortably until their husbands left them, or until they themselves could not earn a living, others were on the bottom rungs of the economic ladder prior to their marital troubles. Often, these were black women and immigrants, and always they were unable to work due to ill health or pregnancy. One such was Sarah Fettis who had only come from Ireland eighteen months before her admission to the almshouse, and who was left pregnant and deserted by her husband after only six months of marriage.[42]

Many poor men and women were frequently in and out of the almshouse, leaving when they were cured of illnesses, had had their babies, or the weather had cleared. For most women, and men, the almshouse was a last resort. Those who were not forced by circumstances to be there did not enter. Those who did usually tried to leave as soon as possible. A few women, however, chose to remain in the oppressive and demeaning atmosphere of the almshouse rather than leave with husbands who could not support them. The wife of Thomas Archer, "the Noted Drunken infamous Tinker," refused to leave the almshouse with him "knowing that he had no Place to take them to nor any Kind of Provision made for them." Surely this woman was desperate, or feared life with her husband even more than she feared the almshouse.[43]

Yet other women found it impossible to support both themselves and their children. When Elizabeth Dean, an ex-slave, did not receive any money from her seafaring husband, Abner, she had to put her sick son, Charles, in the almshouse. She could not care for the two year old, as the necessary care "prevents her going to work." Similarly, Rebeccah Daugherty could not care for her seventeen month old, who was very ill. Rebeccah herself was only seventeen; she had been married for two years, but her pedlar husband deserted her after their first year of marriage, and "she [was] not of ability to support herself and at the same time take care of her Infant."[44] After Andrew Campbell beat his wife and turned her out of the house, she became a housemaid to "Lawyer Ervin." Unable to support herself and her daughter, Ann, she placed Ann in the almshouse. In the meantime, Andrew Cambell deserted them both.[45]

These women put their offspring in the almshouse as a last resort. Those who had family members, or even other children, could probably rely on them to care for the babies. Older boys and girls were bound out as servants and apprentices. But for women without family, friends, or money to hire caretakers, the almshouse was the only place to leave their young children. Thus the economic deprivation brought about by the separation of husband and wife often separated mothers and their children as well.

In contrast to those left destitute and forced to seek shelter in the almshouse, there were others who were fortunate enough to have the support of family and friends. The experience of Harriet Chew Carroll provides an example of how important a family's support could be. Harriet's family gave her both financial and emotional assistance, as her marriage slowly disintegrated.

In 1814, Charles Carroll of Carrollton, "the old Gentleman," made arrangements for money to be paid to his daughter-in-law, Harriet Chew Carroll for her support in Philadelphia. In a letter to her brother, Benjamin Chew, Jr., he wrote:

I fear it will be necessary to make Ph.[iladelphia] her permanent residence unless a great & unexpected reformation of my unhappy son should take place. Harriet is well acquainted with my plan for the support of herself & daughters in the event of such a contingency, which I forsaw must sooner or later happen on my son's relapsing into his former habits.[46]

Harriet, nevertheless, did return to her husband, Charles, and their Maryland home, Homewood, in 1815. By then, however, Charles's drinking was not the only problem. Harriet convinced herself at first that stories about Charles and other women were false. But when the old Gentleman produced a bill for seventy dollars indicating a hack had been hired for women, she had to believe the stories were true. Nevertheless, she still tried to remain with Charles. By 1816, Charles, however, had become violent, and Harriet, finally fearing for the lives of her children and herself, fled to her brother's "protecting arms," saying, "I may hither to have appeared willing to suffer misery while I had a hope of saving him from destruction, the time is now past."[47]

Although there were a few years of emotional anguish for Harriet, when Charles made allegations that she had turned him into an alcoholic, and the couple fought for influence over the children, Harriet's family comforted her and took her side. Her father-in-law provided financial support for her and her children. She had a well-furnished house in Philadelphia; her son went to college. The will of Harriet's father also provided her with an income. The money was held in trust, and managed by her brother, Ben, and brother-in-law, Col. Howard. Harriet remained in Philadelphia with her family close around her, outliving her husband by many years.

Arrangements for Harriet Carroll's support were made for her by members of her family. Most women were not as wealthy as Harriet Carroll, but because of coverture, for wives at all economic levels the help of family members was often crucial when a marriage broke up. As the examples in this chapter demonstrate, even a woman who obtained a divorce and regained her feme sole status sometimes found that she had lost her property to her ex-husband, or discovered that he would not pay the alimony ordered by the court.

Some family members tried to assure that their married female relatives would be provided for by making arrangements in wills. Jane Paxton left money in trust for her mother, Mary Henry, "Provided She Continues to live Seperate and Apart from her Husband Samuel Henry." The money was to cease when Mary cohabited with Henry, indicating that Jane was concerned about her mother and wanted to make sure she had some financial support while separated from her husband. Robert Moore left his daughter Susannah Hill eighty dollars "to be paid to her in six yearly payments after the decease of my wife," in case her husband, James, "dies, deserts or leaves her." Robert apparently felt the need to protect his daughter, but trusted his widow to care for her after his death. He also may have feared that if he left the money to Susannah before the death of his wife, her husband would gain control of it, and thus leave his widow without support.[48]

For many married men and women, family members provided much needed help. In times of trouble, both men and women frequently moved to their parents' home. In less serious situations, they sought solace and advice from mothers, fathers, brothers, and sisters. For others, however, friends and neighbors lent much needed financial and emotional support—and more. A neighbor of Ann Taylor rescued her from her garret window when she fled there after her husband threatened her life. In addition, Taylor credited her neighbors with saving her children and herself from starvation, as her husband provided her with no food, clothing, or fuel.[49] When Elizabeth Shrock's husband deserted her, leaving her and her children destitute, she went to live with the Widow Caves. This widow had taken in Elizabeth and her family on previous occasions when Samuel Shrock refused to provide for them.[50]

Friends and neighbors helped unhappily married or deserted men, too. The wife of Valentine Clemons' employer, for example, asked him to eat with them. Because she knew his wife's reputation as a "bad Woman," she assumed he had not been eating well. Valentine acknowledged that he had not eaten dinner for ten days because "his wife squandered everything he brought into his house, and made no provision for the family."[51]

In numerous cases of marital discord, family, friends, and neighbors rallied around the afflicted individual, lending emotional and financial support and assistance. The bonds of womanhood linking mother to daughter, sister to sister, friend to friend; the bonds of family linking parent to child; and the bonds of community linking neighbor to neighbor were often tightly knit, and able to intervene when the bonds of marriage frayed. For women especially, these support networks were crucial. Often they were the key to survival without a husband. For those who were sick, disabled, or "poor and destitute of friends," however, the almshouse many times remained the only solution.

How individuals confronted the financial upsets involved in marital discord depended on several factors: whether they had access to assets free from the control of their spouse, whether they were male or female, whether or not they had family and friends willing and able to help, and whether their age and health allowed them to work. These factors could change throughout an individual's life cycle. An injury or a serious illness, for instance, could make a formerly self-supporting person unable to work.

Just as degrees of financial distress varied, so did the ways in which individuals handled their situations. Husbands and wives often faced distinctly different situations. Poor women, and those left unprotected by inheritances, family, and friends, experienced the worst financial distress, and sometimes destitution, after the breakup of their marriages. Although men sometimes experienced an economic decline as a result of marital difficulties, they were not for the most part dependent on their spouses for financial support. On the other hand, women, due to legal constraints and social customs and conditions, did tend to rely on their husbands for an economic maintenance. Nevertheless, both men who expected to support their wives and could not, and women who expected to be supported and were not failed to achieve the idealized roles of husband or wife that their society expected of them and for which many of them had hoped.

Conclusion:
Unraveling the Bonds

If marriage can be compared to a woven fabric, then this work is a study of how that cloth was woven in eighteenth- and early nineteenth-century Pennsylvania and what conditions made it unravel. This examination of marital discord reveals a picture of discontentment caused both by evolving societal expectations and by distinctions between how husbands and wives viewed marriage. Changes in American society between the mid-eighteenth and early nineteenth centuries promoted and spread a view of marriage as "companionate," where husband and wife were loving partners who shared in making important decisions. The older tradition of marriage as a patriarchal institution continued, however, both within the laws and as a part of individual beliefs. The encumbrances of coverture, for instance, kept married women second-class citizens, legally dependent upon their husbands for economic support.

Within troubled marriages, men and women often had disparate beliefs about their roles. When either spouse felt unable to conform to his or her presumed part, it caused problems within the marriage. Similarly, tensions arose when a wife or husband believed that his or her spouse did not meet the accepted norms. Conflicts ensued in some cases when husbands retained their patriarchal viewpoints while their wives embraced newer companionate forms of marriage, and in other instances emerged when husbands failed to take charge as the master of the house. Thus, it was not only the development of new expectations, but also gender distinctions regarding the new ways of looking at marriage that caused marital discord during this time.

Men and women were therefore torn between the conflicting mores of their society. How could women be morally superior and yet so dependent? How could men be partners and still be "head" of the household? Although these conflicts have yet to be resolved even in the twentieth century, they were particularly acute in this period of rapid transition. With the world changing all around them, some individuals embraced new standards, while others kept hold of the old in an attempt to recreate a past ideal, no matter how false, when husbands held tight control over their wives and families, and their mates submitted without question.

At the same time, many of the problems they faced or created in their marriages existed in earlier periods and also exist today. Some of them had sexual problems or drank too much, others had spouses who abused them. Affected by changing economic conditions, as well as by restrictions placed upon them by their assigned roles as husbands or wives, many couples fought over money, arguing over who was going to control it, or how much support a wife deserved from her husband.

Despite the problems that some couples faced, most men and women expected to marry. Even those who faced problems in their own marriages generally believed that the married state was the most favorable condition for the majority of people. For example, Ann Carson wrote at one point, "I did not indeed, place so high an estimation on the marriage state as the generality of women do; the example I had seen of the conduct of husbands, disgusted me." Yet, on the next page of her memoirs, she went on to state that "I ever regarded marriage as a wise and proper regulation to enable society to hold an authority over the conduct of both sexes."[1] Ann was perhaps more cynical or honest in her assessment of marriage than most people are, but even she regarded it as the best and proper status for the greatest number of individuals. Indeed, when she married Capt. Carson, she noted that her "pride was gratified by being the bride of a United States' officer, and my sense of right satisfied by my obedience to my parents in becoming his wife."[2]

Men and women solved their marital problems in various ways, ranging from desertion to divorce. Most couples who separated did so without the aid of lawyers and courts. New laws, however, made it easier to obtain divorces and legal separations in Pennsylvania. Women profited most from these laws because a divorce allowed them to resume their feme sole status or to obtain alimony from their husbands. Nevertheless, even the relatively liberal 1785 divorce law and its subsequent early nineteenth-century revisions required one partner to be the guilty party, and thus placed spouses in adversarial roles.

In order to influence the court, both husbands and wives tried to prove that they met the standards expected of them. Men said that they were good providers, that they never hit their wives (too hard), and that they welcomed back wives who had temporarily left them. They complained that their wives were lewd, disobedient, and disloyal.

In contrast, women portrayed their husbands as lazy men who did not support them, or as men lacking the proper affection a husband should have for his wife. In their own defense, these women emphasized that they were acting appropriately as wives, taking the drastic step of leaving their husbands only when forced to do so by constant physical abuse or economic deprivation. Even some women guilty of adultery demonstrated their awareness of new standards in marriage and tried to justify their behavior by claiming that if their husbands had shown them more affection they would not have strayed.

Despite scholars claims that in the nineteenth century the family became more private and isolated from the world, the cases represented here reveal a world where friends and neighbors knew and talked about the couples' problems and assisted those in need.[3] Members of the community often served as mediators or helped to draw up informal separation agreements. They aided women who were being abused by violent husbands, and they provided financial relief to those left destitute by absconding or lazy ones. Their depositions in divorce and separate maintenance cases were crucial, providing proof for the libellant, or justification for the defendant.

Marriage remained the ideal. And perhaps because of that the pressures to succeed in it became more extreme. Scholars examining divorce in the late nineteenth and early twentieth centuries suggest that increased expectations about marriage during that time led to a rise in marital tensions.[4] In the eighteenth and early nineteenth centuries, new beliefs regarding marriage were evolving. But it was not only the changing marital ideals, the transitions from patriarchal to companionate relationships, that caused problems, but also the differing ways in which husbands and wives perceived what marriage was and how it should be. In the period studied here, distinct gender differences caused husbands and wives to view marriage differently. In fact, men and women *entered* marriage with these gender-based views about what marriage should be.

For example, Thomas Cope was a Quaker merchant born in 1768. He was influenced by Revolutionary ideals of freedom and his diary reflects admiration and respect for his wives and for other women. He loved both his first and second wives. Nevertheless, he believed women should marry, and that once married, they should serve their mates' every need and desire. It was a wife's *duty* to make her husband happy and content. In 1800 he wrote:

The love of independence is inherent in the human mind & the thraldom, mental & corporeal, in which women have been held for ages, is derogatory to justice & humanity. But before a woman indulges that practice of freedom so eloquently insisted on by Mary Wollstonecraft & by herself so proudly maintained, she should be certain that her charms will insure her the unalterable attachment of her husband, or she will find it a dangerous experiment. A woman in society must be either a mistress or a wife . . . when she bursts asunder the shackles of implicit obedience to her husband, she should by a contented & studied line of conduct endeavour to make his home his chief delight & to hold his affections riveted to her person by an easy, cheerful, attentive & rational system of behaviour.[5]

Grace Growden Galloway also held contradictory views about marriage. In some ways she remained very much a believer in the old ideals. For instance, she expected her husband to take care of her, and she valued her position as Joseph Galloway's wife. However, she did not love him.

Yet she was unhappy when he made business and personal arrangements without consulting her, revealing that she did expect to be a partner, at least as far as major decision-making went. At one point she wrote:

> never get Tyed to a Man
> for when once you are yoked
> Tis all a Mere Joke
> of seeing you freedom again.[6]

By the mid-nineteenth century, women were able to gain more freedom after marriage. In addition to the laws on divorce, legislation passed in the 1830s and 1840s gave married women some control over their money and property.[7] More important, perhaps, women became used to stepping outside of, or at least extending their roles as wives and mothers, as they became involved in the religious and reform movements of the nineteenth century.[8] As men and women reevaluated marriages and their roles within it, new designs developed for the marital fabric. In turn, these patterns created strains and tears in some marriages, and the woven bonds became both easier and more likely to break.

Notes

Introduction: The "Open Question" of Marriage

1. Among native-born Philadelphia women, only 4.2% never married, according to Susan E. Klepp, "Philadelphia in Transition: A Demographic History of the City and Its Occupational Groups, 1720–1830" (Ph.D. diss., University of Pennsylvania, 1980), 50. Similarly, Robert Gough found that only 3% of Philadelphian elites never married in his "Towards a Theory of Class and Social Conflict: A Social History of Wealthy Philadelphians, 1775 and 1800" (Ph.D diss., University of Pennsylvania, 1977), 328. For Andover, Massachusetts, the figures are comparable with only 7.4% of third-generation women and 3.6% of fourth-generation men not marrying. Philip J. Greven, *Four Generations: Population, Land, and Family in Colonial Andover, Massachusetts* (Ithaca: Cornell University Press, 1970), 121, 207. In contrast, 23.5% of Pennsylvania and New Jersey Quaker women born after 1786 may not have married, as Robert Wells discusses in "Quaker Marriage Patterns in a Colonial Perspective," in *A Heritage of Her Own: Toward a New Social History of American Women,* ed. Nancy F. Cott and Elizabeth H. Pleck (New York: Simon and Schuster, 1979), 90–91, 94–96.

2. Linda K. Kerber, *Women of the Republic: Intellect and Ideology in Revolutionary America* (Chapel Hill: University of North Carolina Press, 1980), Chap. 9; Jan Lewis, "The Republican Wife: Virtue and Seduction in the Early Republic," *William and Mary Quarterly 44* (October 1987), 689, 709. Nineteenth-century Americans did not emphasize the word virtue, but it was expected that wives would provide a favorable influence on their families and guide the moral education of their children.

3. *Pennsylvania Gazette,* 11 May 1732; Daily Occurrence Dockets, 29 July 1814, Guardians of the Poor, Philadelphia City Archives (PCA).

4. Among these studies are Nancy F. Cott's pathbreaking studies of di-

vorce in early Massachusetts, "Divorce and the Changing Status of Women in Eighteenth-Century Massachusetts," *WMQ* 33 (October 1976), 586–614 and "Eighteenth-Century Family and Social Life Revealed in Massachusetts Divorce Records," *Journal of Social History* 10 (Fall 1976), 20–43; Thomas R. Meehan, "'Not Made Out of Levity': Evolution of Divorce in Early Pennsylvania," *Pennsylvania Magazine of History and Biography* 92 (October 1968), 441–464; Kerber, *Women of the Republic*, esp. Chap. 6; Lyle Koehler, *A Search for Power: The 'Weaker Sex' in Seventeenth-Century New England* (Urbana: University of Illinois Press, 1980). Robert L. Griswold examines divorce in late nineteenth-century California, *Family and Divorce in California, 1850–1890: Victorian Illusions and Everyday Realities* (Albany: State University of New York Press, 1982).

5. Jan Lewis, "The Republican Wife," 700–703, 711–712; Mary P. Ryan, *Womanhood in America: From Colonial Times to the Present* (New York: Franklin Watts, 1983), 88–89, 125–134, 146.

6. Ryan, *Womanhood in America*, 115–119.

Chapter 1: Dissolving Matrimonial Bonds

1. Elizabeth Sutter v. James Sutter, 1794, Petition of Elizabeth Sutter, Divorce Papers, 1785–1815, Division of Archives and Manuscripts, Records of the Supreme Court, Eastern District, Pennsylvania Historical and Museum Commission (PHMC). Hereafter cited as Supreme Court Divorces. Dates refer to the date the petition was filed, unless otherwise indicated. For more information, see Select Bibliography.

2. Ibid., Notice, September 1794; Motion and Rule, April 1795.

3. Ibid., Answer of James Sutter, April 1795.

4. George Elliott Howard, *A History of Matrimonial Institutions* (Chicago: The University of Chicago Press, 1904; rpt., New York: Humanities Press, 1964), II, 102–109; Marylynn Salmon, *Women and the Law of Property in Early America* (Chapel Hill: The University of North Carolina Press, 1986), 60.

5. John Milton, "Doctrine and Discipline of Divorce," *Prose Works*, III, 241, 251–258; and "Colasterion," III, 423–433, cited in Howard, II, 87.

6. Nancy Cott, "Divorce and the Changing Status of Women," *William and Mary Quarterly*, 33 (October 1976), 587–589.

7. Linda Kerber, *Women of the Republic: Intellect and Ideology in Revolutionary America* (Chapel Hill: University of North Carolina, 1980), Chap. 6, esp. 159–162; Suzanne Lebsock, *The Free Women of Petersburg: Status and Culture in a Southern Town, 1784–1860* (New York: W. W. Norton, 1984), 68–70.

8. "Act of 1700: An Act for the Preventing of Clandestine Marriages," in *Digest of the Laws of Pennsylvania, 1700–1846*, ed. George M. Straub (Philadelphia, Thomas Davis, 1847), 794–795; Thomas R. Meehan, " 'Not Made Out of Levity': Evolution of Divorce in Early Pennsylvania," *The Pennsylvania Magazine of History and Biography*, 92 (October 1968), 442–443; *The Statutes at*

Large of Pennsylvania from 1682 to 1801, 2nd series (Harrisburg, 1896), II, 8, 180, 161–162, 178–179, 182–183.

9. See D. Kelley Weisberg, " 'Under Greet Temptation Heer,' Women and Divorce in Puritan Massachusetts," *Feminist Studies*, 2 (Summer-Fall 1975), 183–193, who sees early Massachusetts divorces as a means of controlling social order and eliminating economic burdens from the towns.

10. But the laws could work to the disadvantage of husbands; see John Goggin, below.

11. This case is discussed in detail in Chap. 3.

12. Meehan, 443–445.

13. *Votes of the Assembly*, 23 January 1766, 5840–5841.

14. *Pennsylvania Archives*, Eighth Series (1935), VII, 6309–6310; *Statutes at Large*, of Pennsylvania from 1682–1801 (Harrisburg, 1896–1908), VII, 163–165.

15. Prior to her conviction, however, Elizabeth Keemle had accused her husband of turning her out of the house and of not supporting her. Philadelphia Mayor's Court Docket, July 1769, Historical Society of Pennsylvania (HSP).

16. This edict lasted in Canada until 1867. William Renwick Riddell, "Legislative Divorce in Colonial Pennsylvania," *PMHB* 58 (1933), 175–180; *Minutes of the Provincial Council*, X, 104–105; *Statutes at Large*, VIII, 243–245.

17. See Chaps. 4 and 5 for more on this.

18. William Thompson allegedly tried to get rid of his wife, Jane, by selling her in Kentucky. Thompson v. Thompson, 1803, Petition of Jane Thompson, Supreme Court Divorces (PHMC). It is unclear if Thompson was following the English folk custom of wife selling, but the attempt was obviously against Jane's will.

19. Meehan, 446–450, *Statutes at Large*, XI, 174–175; X, 267–269.

20. Meehan, 450.

21. Jay Fliegelman, *Prodigals and Pilgrims: The American Revolution Against Patriarchal Authority, 1750–1800* (New York: Cambridge University Press, 1982), 126.

22. Ibid., 124; *The Pennsylvania Magazine*, I (June 1775), 264.

23. "An Essay on Marriage or the Lawfulness of Divorce" (Philadelphia, 1788), rpt. in *The Colonial American Family: Collected Essays*, ed. David and Sheila M. Rothman (New York: Arno Press, 1972), 3.

24. Fliegelman, *Prodigals and Pilgrims*, esp. Chap. 4.

25. Lebsock, *Free Women of Petersburg*, 16–18; Kerber, *Women of the Republic*, 72; Cott, "Divorce," 592–594, 613–614; Michael Grossberg, *Governing the Hearth: Law and the Family in Nineteenth-Century America* (Chapel Hill: University of North Carolina Press, 1985), 19–20.

26. See Chap. 2 for more on marital expectations.

27. Kerber, Chap. 6; Meehan, "Evolution of Divorce," 452–453.

28. Meehan, "Evolution of Divorce," 455.

29. Ibid., 453, #42; "An Act Concerning Divorces and Alimony," Sect. I, *Statutes of at Large*, XII, 94.

30. Ibid., 97.

31. Grossberg, 20–21.

32. See Commonwealth v. Addicks, 5 Binney 520.

33. Page v. Page, 1801, Petition of Eve Page, Supreme Court Divorces, PHMC.

34. "An Act Concerning Divorce," *Statutes at Large*, XII, 98.

35. Ibid., 95–96.

36. Robert Whitehill to George Bryan, 1789, Bryan Papers, HSP. My thanks to Joseph Foster for this reference.

37. Commonwealth v. Addicks, 5 Binney 520 and Commonwealth v. Addicks and Lee, 2 S. & R. 174, cited in Harold M. Stureon, *The Pennsylvania Law and Procedure in Divorce*, 3rd ed., revised by Richard Henry Klein (Philadelphia: George T. Bisel Co., 1937), 830–831, 847.

38. "Act of 26th February 1817," *Digest of the Laws of Pennsylvania*, 314–318.

39. Massachusetts apparently had a much stricter interpretation of what constituted cruelty than did Pennsylvania. Robert L. Griswold, "The Evolution of the Doctrine of Mental Cruelty in Victorian American Divorce, 1790–1900," *Journal of Social History* 20 (Fall 1986), 128–130.

40. I have crossed-checked the divorce papers with the separate decrees existing for the years 1785–1800 and 1801–1805 because court papers do not always indicate if a divorce was granted or not.

41. For more on spouse abuse, see Chap. 4.

42. McArthur v. McArthur, 1789, Petition of Alexander McArthur, Supreme Court Divorces, PHMC.

43. See Chap. 5 for more on desertion.

44. Nancy Cott suggests that women found it difficult to obtain divorces on adultery-exclusive grounds in Massachusetts until after the Revolution. Due to the changes in divorce practices in Pennsylvania, it is impossible to make comparisons. Cott, "Divorce," 599–604.

45. Wright v. Wright, Petition filed 1788; Quarter Sessions Court of Dauphin County, May 1788 attached, Supreme Court Divorces, PHMC.

46. Pemble v. Pemble, 1803, Deposition of Francis Lyon, Supreme Court Divorces, PHMC; "An Act Concerning Divorces, *Statutes at Large*, XII, 96."

47. Kyle v. Kyle, 1800, Answer of Elizabeth Kyle, Supreme Court Divorces, PHMC.

48. Shearer v. Shearer, 1790, Petition of William Shearer, Supreme Court Divorces, PHMC.

49. Crawford v. Crawford, 1802, Answer of Respondent and Libel of Ann Crawford, 1802, Supreme Court Divorces, PHMC.

50. Thompson v. Thompson, 1803, Supreme Court Divorces, PHMC.

51. Ibid.

52. Miller v. Miller, 1793, Answer of Defendant; Corvaisier v. Corvaisier, 1795, Answer of Bartholomew Corvaisier; Engleman v. Engleman, 1794, Supreme Court Divorces, PHMC.

53. John Lesher v. Margaret Lesher, 1786, Answer of Margaret 1787; Margaret Lesher v. John Lesher, Petition 1787, Supreme Court Divorces, PHMC.

54. These occupational categories are based partly upon those used by Lisa Wilson Waciega in "A 'Man of Business': The Widow of Means in Southeastern Pennsylvania, 1750–1850," *WMQ*, XLIV (January 1987), 50.

55. "A Supplement to the Act, entitled 'An Act concerning Divorces and Alimony,' " *Laws of the Commonwealth of Pennsylvania* (Philadelphia: 1810), IV, 182–183.

56. 1 "Act of 13th March, 1815," and "Act of 26th February 1817," *Digest of the Laws of Pennsylvania*, 314–318.

57. Court of Common Pleas, Columbia County, Pa., Vol. I, 1814–1823 and Vol. II, 1824–1836, Microfilm, HSP.

58. Kerber, *Women of the Republic*, Chap. 6; Elaine Tyler May, *Great Expectations: Marriage and Divorce in Post-Victorian America* (Chicago: University of Chicago Press, 1980); Robert L. Griswold, *Family and Divorce in California, 1850–1890: Victorian Illusions and Everyday Realities* (Albany: State University of New York Press, 1982). Griswold suggests that women left their marriages more often than men by means of desertion.

59. Nancy Cott noted that cases that came before the Massachusetts Assembly citing cruelty were primarily from women in urban areas. She suggests that these petitioners may have been more "sophisticated" or that they may have been less willing to put up with abuse from their husbands than their rural counterparts. This does not seem to be the case in Pennsylvania since Chester County women did take their husbands to court on assault and battery charges, even if they did not divorce them. Cott, "Divorce," 609. For more on spouse abuse in Pennsylvania, see Chap. 4 here.

60. The above figures are based upon the primary grounds given by the plaintiff.

61. In 1830, the Pennsylvania Legislative Committee on the judiciary system studied the divorces granted by legislature. They concluded that the court was the appropriate venue for divorce applications, although they acknowledged that there would be some cases, "which although not within the law, would be good causes of divorce depending upon their own peculiar circumstances." The committee's suggestion was to have all divorce petitions directed to the legislature reviewed by a committee with the sole purpose of determining if the application could be heard in court or not. This would relieve the legislature of unnecessary work, and it would eliminate the fear that hearings would be held without sufficient notification of both husband and wife. *The Register of Pennsylvania. Devoted to the Preservations of Facts and Documents, Useful Information Respecting the State of Pennsylvania*, ed. by Samuel

Hazard, Vol. V. (January to July 1830). My thanks to Lucy Simler for bringing this citation to my attention.

62. "An Act Dissolving the Marriage of Thomas Adkinson and Rebecca, His Wife," *The Statutes at Large* (1805), XVII, 929–930.

63. "An Act to Dissolve Thomas Dewess and Mary His Wife," in *Laws of the Commonwealth of Pennsylvania* (1804), VI, 493; "An Act to Dissolve David Carmack and Mary Carmack," *Laws of Pennsylvania* (1809–1810), 82–83.

64. Ibid. (1805–1806), 326–327; (1810–1811), 12.

65. *Statutes* (1802), XVIII, 530–531; *Laws of Pennsylvania* (1807–1808), 146–147; (1808–1809), 161–162, (1809–1810), 194–195.

Chapter 2: Weaving the Bonds

1. Cited in *America's Families: A Documentary History*, ed. Donald M. Scott and Bernard Wishy (New York: Harper and Row, 1982), 64.

2. Harriet Chew Carroll to Benjamin Chew, Jr., 25 November 1801, Chew Family Papers, Historical Society of Pennsylvania (HSP).

3. "A Curious Sermon on Marriage," *The Ladies Magazine* I (August 1792), 108.

4. Catherine Chew to Elizabeth Chew, 18 June 1804; J. E. Howard to Benjamin Chew, Jr., 19 May 1813; Harriet Chew Carroll to Benjamin Chew, Jr., 17 June 1816, Chew Family Papers, HSP. Harriet never obtained a divorce. She moved back to Philadelphia and was provided for by her father-in-law. For more on this, see Chap. 6.

5. Harriet Chew Carroll to Benjamin Chew, Jr., 15 November 1813, Chew Family Papers, HSP. Here she is referring to being resigned to her unhappy marriage rather than to being resigned to leaving her husband.

6. Phyllis Rose, *Parallel Lives: Five Victorian Marriages* (London: The Hogarth Press, 1984), 6–7. On the two marriages, see Jessie Bernard, *The Future of Marriage*, 2nd ed. (New Haven: Yale University Press, 1982), Chap. 1.

7. My use of the term "gender" has been influenced by a recent article by Joan W. Scott, "Gender: A Useful Category of Historical Analysis," *The American Historical Review* 91 (December 1986), 1053–1075, esp. 1067. According to her definition, "gender is a constitutive element of social relationships based on differences between the sexes, and gender is a primary way of signifying relationships of power." Recent sociological studies also suggest that women and men view themselves and their worlds differently. See, for example, Carol Gilligan, *In a Different Voice: Psychological Theory and Women's Development* (Cambridge: Harvard University Press, 1982). One historian who finds evidence of a women's culture in their private writings is Carroll Smith-Rosenberg. See "Hearing Women's Words: A Feminist Reconstruction of History," and "The Female World of Love and Ritual: Relations Between Women in Nineteenth-Century America," both in her *Disorderly Conduct: Vi-*

sions of Gender in Victorian America (New York: Alfred A. Knopf, 1985), 11–52; 53–76.

8. Companionate marriage is a term used by several historians. For example, Suzanne Lebsock, *The Free Women of Petersburg: Status and Culture in a Southern Town, 1784–1860* (New York: W. W. Norton, 1984), 17–18, 28–35; Carl N. Degler refers to "marriage between companions" in *At Odds: Women and the Family in America from the Revolution to the Present* (New York: Oxford University Press, 1980), 297.

9. I am chiefly concerned here with how the clash between economic realities and companionate ideals affected expectations about marriage and the roles of wives and husbands. Although her focus differs from mine, Suzanne Lebsock also noted women in Petersburg, Va., who had problems adjusting to the realities of married life. *The Free Women of Petersburg*, Chap. 2.

10. Christine Stansell addresses this point in her study of working women in New York City. *City of Women: Sex and Class in New York, 1789–1860* (New York: Alfred A. Knopf, 1986), 77–80. For another example, see the Lloyds, below.

11. The classic work on the cult of domesticity and separate spheres is Barbara Welter, "The Cult of True Womanhood: 1820–1860," *American Quarterly* 18 (Summer 1966), 151–174. Lisa Wilson Waciega offers a rebuttal in "A 'Man of Business': The Widow of Means in Southeastern Pennsylvania, 1750–1850," *The William and Mary Quarterly* 44 (January 1987), 40–64. Also see Linda K. Kerber, "Separate Spheres, Female Worlds, Women's Place: The Rhetoric of Women's History," *The Journal of American History* 75 (June 1988), 9–39, which provides a thoughtful review of the literature on separate spheres and questions the use of the term.

12. See Stansell, *City of Women*, esp. 11–18, 77–78; she also discusses the involvement of children in the family wage economy, 50–54. Laurel Thatcher Ulrich notes that northern New England farm women were often busy with chores and duties outside of their homes, but some also worked as midwives, engaged in trade, or assisted their husbands in business. *Good Wives: Image and Reality in the Lives of Women in Northern New England, 1650–1750* (New York: Oxford University Press, 1982), esp. 45–50. Among middling women in the Brandywine Valley, participation in the butter trade was used to increase productivity, according to Joan M. Jensen, *Loosening the Bonds: Mid-Atlantic Farm Women, 1750–1850* (New Haven: Yale University Press, 1986), Chap. 5.

13. Waciega, "Man of Business," 51.

14. Kerber, "Separate Spheres," 37.

15. On middle-class male culture see Edward Anthony Rotundo, "Body and Soul: Changing Ideals of American Middle-Class Manhood, 1770–1920," *Journal of Social History* 16 (Summer 1983), 23–38, and "Manhood in America: The Northern Middle-Class, 1770–1920" (Ph.D. diss., Brandeis University, 1982).

16. Barry Levy, "The Birth of the 'Modern Family' in Early America: Quaker and Anglican Families in the Delaware Valley, Pennsylvania, 1681–1750," in *Friends and Neighbors: Group Life in America's First Plural Society*, ed. Michael Zuckerman (Philadelphia: Temple University Press, 1982), 32–33.

17. Eliza Cope Harrison, ed., *Philadelphia Merchant: The Diary of Thomas P. Cope, 1800–1851* (South Bend, IN: Gateway Editions, 1978), 292–293.

18. See Chap. 1 for more on divorce. Men's petitions never refer to wives as tyrants, but do question their wives' obedience. Women's reflections of themselves as political beings can be seen in their petitions for government compensation after the war. For a Pennsylvania example, see Wayne Bodle, "Jane Bartram's 'Application': Her Struggle for Survival, Stability, and Self-Determination in Revolutionary and Post-Revolutionary Pennsylvania," Paper presented to the final conference of the Transformation of Philadelphia Project, Philadelphia Center for Early American Studies, 15–18 May 1988, forthcoming in *The Pennsylvania Magazine of History and Biography* (April 1991). For other examples, see Kerber, *Women of the Republic*, 91–94, 98–99.

19. On marriage as a republican contract see Jan Lewis, "The Republican Wife: Virtue and Seduction in the Early Republic," *WMQ* 44 (October 1987), 708–710; and Jay Fliegelman, *Prodigals and Pilgrims: The American Revolution Against Patriarchal Authority, 1750–1800* (Cambridge: Cambridge University Press, 1982), Chap. 5.

20. Seale v. Seale, 1792, Libel of Mary Seale, Divorce Papers, 1786–1815, Division of Archives and Manuscript, Records of the Supreme Court, Eastern District, Pennsylvania Historical and Museum Commission, Harrisburg, PA (PHMC). All further references to divorces granted by the Supreme Court of Pennsylvania will be cited as Supreme Court Divorces. Dates given are the dates the petitions were filed unless otherwise noted.

21. Ethel Armes, ed., *Nancy Shippen, Her Journal Book* (Philadelphia: J. B. Lippincott, 1935), 145.

22. Ibid., 101.

23. Ibid., 129, 273, 286–289. Linda Kerber, *Women of the Republic*, 183. In New York, Henry was the legal guardian of the child. In order to have obtained a divorce in Pennsylvania, Nancy would have had to establish residency there, permitting Henry to take the child to the South, which he had threatened to do. Divorce laws are discussed in Chap. 1.

24. Ellen K. Rothman, *Hands and Hearts: A History of Courtship in America* (New York: Basic Books, 1984.), 26–30. Fliegelman, *Prodigals and Pilgrims*, Chap. 5, esp. 130–137.

25. Rebecca Shoemaker to Anna Rawle, 16 April 1783, Shoemaker Papers, HSP.

26. Robert Parker to his sisters, Parker Family File, Chester County Historical Society (CCHS). Courtesy of the Chester County Historical Society, West Chester, PA.

27. Herman R. Lantz et al., "Pre-industrial Patterns in the Colonial Family in America: A Content Analysis of Colonial Magazines," *American Sociological Review* 33 (June 1968), 413–426.

28. Fliegelman analyzes the "best-sellers of 1775," *Prodigals and Pilgrims,* Chap. 2; Kerber discusses what eighteenth-century women read in *Women of the Republic,* Chap. 8. On the growth of literacy see Kenneth A. Lockridge, *Literacy in Colonial New England: An Enquiry into the Social Context of Literacy in the Early Modern West* (New York, 1974).

29. Linda Kerber first coined the term "Republican Mothers" in "The Republican Mother: Women and the Enlightenment—An American Perspective," *American Quarterly,* 28 (1976), 187–205 and then in *Women of the Republic.* In her view, the early republic developed the notion that a mother could guide and raise virtuous and patriotic children. Jan Lewis, on the other hand, believes the new republic advanced the notion of "Republican Wives" rather than mothers, Jan Lewis, "Republican Wife," 690.

30. *Pennsylvania Gazette,* 26 February 1754.

31. *The Royal Magazine* I (February 1774), 68.

32. *The Pennsylvania Magazine* I (June 1775), 265; *The Lady's Magazine* I (July 1792), 60–62; (October 1792), 242.

33. For two examples of prescriptive literature offering this viewpoint, see William A. Alcott, *The Young Man's Guide* (Boston: Perkins and Marvin, 1836) and his *The Young Wife or Duties of Women in the Marriage Relation* (Boston: George W. Light, 1837; repr., New York: Arno Press, 1972).

34. Ruth H. Bloch, "The Gendered Meanings of Virtue in Revolutionary America," *Signs* 13 (Autumn 1987), 47–52.

35. For more on women, religion, and reform, see Mary P. Ryan, *Cradle of the Middle Class: The Family in Oneida County, New York, 1790–1865* (Cambridge: Cambridge University Press, 1981), 77–104.

36. Reverend Nicholas Collin, "Remarkable Occurrences," July 1800, August 1800, Marriage Records of Gloria Dei Church, HSP. Hereafter cited as "Occurrences." Jean R. Soderlund estimates that black men and women made up 8 to 10 percent of Philadelphia's population by the mid-eighteenth century, *Quakers and Slavery: A Divided Spirit* (Princeton: Princeton University Press, 1985), 81, #52; also her "Black Women in Colonial Philadelphia," *PMHB* 107 (January 1983), 61. Billy G. Smith states that the free black population of Philadelphia increased from approximately 1,000 in 1783 to 6,083 by the end of the century, *The 'Lower Sort': Philadelphia's Laboring People, 1750–1800* (Ithaca: Cornell University Press, 1990), 193.

37. Collin, "Occurrences," July 1800, HSP.

38. Daily Occurrence Dockets, 18 November 1793, Guardians of the Poor, PCA.

39. Philadelphia Monthly Meeting (Arch Street), 29 /10M/1700; Collins, "Occurrences," March 1813, HSP.

40. Charlotte Wilcocks McCall, Diary, 5 October 1842, HSP; Daily Occurrence Dockets, 12 June 1801, Guardians of the Poor, PCA; *The Lady's Magazine* I (August 1792), 110.

41. Collins, "Occurrences," January 1809, HSP.

42. Carver v. Carver, 1801, Deposition of John Cooper, Supreme Court Divorces, PMHC; Wrightstown Monthly Meeting, 9/3/1799, 2/4/1800, 4/7/1800.

43. Charles Carroll to Charles Carroll, Jr. 22 June 1800; Charles Carroll, Jr. to Benjamin Chew, 16 July 1800, Chew Family Papers, HSP.

44. For more on the economic condition of married women see Chap. 6.

45. "An Act for the Relief of the Poor," *The Statutes at Large of Pennsylvania from 1682 to 1801* (Harrisburg, 1896–1908), VII, 93–94.

46. The Pennsylvania divorce law, passed in 1785, expressed in republican language the belief that men and women should have the freedom to divorce. However, it maintained a patriarchal outlook in various features, including the bed and board divorces with alimony, available only to women, and the requirement that female petitioners submit their petition through a "next friend," *Statutes at Large*, XII, 94–99. See Chap. 1 for more on divorce.

47. Marriage Articles executed by Charles Carroll of Carrollton, Charles Carroll, Jr. and Harriet Chew, 28 June 1800, Chew Family Papers, HSP.

48. Agreement between George Roe and Hester Bizard, 1763, CCHS.

49. Marylynn Salmon, "Equality or Submission? Feme Covert Status in Early Pennsylvania," in *Women of America*, ed. Carol Ruth Berkin and Mary Beth Norton (Boston: Houghton Mifflin Co., 1979), 98–99.

50. George Roe, "Agreement," CCHS.

51. Billy G. Smith discusses the problems that the laboring poor in Philadelphia had in making ends meet, "The Material Lives of Laboring Philadelphians, 1750 to 1800," WMQ 38 (April 1981), 180, 188, 201. For more on the working poor of the early to mid-nineteenth century, see Priscilla Ferguson Clement, *Welfare and the Poor in the Nineteenth-Century City, Philadelphia, 1800–1854* (Rutherford: Fairleigh Dickinson Press, 1985), 31–34. Lebsock suggests that separate estates became more common for women in antebellum Petersburg, Va., because their husbands saw this as a way of maintaining economic security, *Free Women of Petersburg*, Chap. 3.

52. Philadelphia Monthly Meeting 29/1st month/1695, 29/11M/96, 27/11M/98–99, 24/12M/98. Pennsylvanians of this time followed the Old Style Calender in which March was the first month of the new year.

53. Albert Cook Myers, ed., *Hannah Logan's Courtship* (Philadelphia: Ferris and Leach, 1904), 145.

54. Ibid., 45–46, 173, 183, 195, 216–218.

55. Jean R. Soderlund, "Women's Authority in Pennsylvania and New Jersey Quaker Meetings, 1680–1760," WMQ 44 (October 1987), 722–749, 729.

56. Anna Rawle to Rebecca Shoemaker, 20 July 1783, Shoemaker Papers, HSP.

57. Harriet Manigualt Wilcocks Diary, 6 June 1816; Charlotte Wilcocks McCall Diary, 5 October 1842, HSP.

58. For more on this see, Smith-Rosenberg, "The Female World."

59. Rotundo, "Manhood in America," 282–286; Stansell, *City of Women*, 80, 89–91.

60. Rothman, *Hands and Hearts*, 70–84.

61. See Chap. 1 for more on divorce.

62. *Pennsylvania Gazette*, 23 November 1749, 26 February 1754, 30 April 1767; Henderson v. Henderson, 1798, Supreme Court Divorces, PMHC.

63. Feeley v. Feeley, 1802, Deposition of Thomas Harley, Supreme Court Divorces, PMHC; Carpenter v. Carpenter, 1830, #5, Common Pleas Papers, Chester County Archives (CCA).

64. Sarah Lloyd v. Benjamin Lloyd, 1801, Deposition of Catherine Page, Supreme Court Divorces, PMHC.

65. See, for example, "An Act Relating to Orphans' Court," 29 March 1832, *Laws of the General Assembly of the State of Pennsylvania* (Harrisburg, 1832), 190–213, sect. 48. Also see Salmon, "Equality or Submission," 99–101.

66. *Pennsylvania Gazette*, 19–26 January 1730/31.

67. Kerber, *Women of the Republic*, Chap. 4.

68. Raymond C. Werner, ed., "Diary of Grace Growden Galloway," *PMHB* 55 (1931), 87–88, and 58 (1934), 152–189, esp. 177; Kerber, *Women of the Republic*, 75–76.

69. Werner, "Diary of Grace Growden Galloway," 34, 57, 59–60, 63–64.

70. Blaney v. Blaney, Deposition of Sarah Durang, 1797, Supreme Court Divorces, PMHC. Thomas Minor left his wife only five shillings because she had abandoned him several times to his "great grief and loss." Will of Thomas Minor, #2789, 1773, CCA.

71. There is no record of the divorce being granted. See Chap. 1 for divorce statistics. Badger v. Badger, 1806, Petition of Bela Badger and Answer of Respondant, Supreme Court Divorces, PMHC.

72. Ibid.

73. Journal Letter, Anna Rawle Clifford to Rebecca Shoemaker, 9–18 October 1783, Shoemaker Papers, HSP.

74. Lee Virginia Chambers-Schiller, *Liberty, A Better Husband: Single Women in America: The Generations of 1780–1840* (New Haven: Yale University Press, 1984), 17–19, 40–41.

75. Guemeteau v. Guemeteau, 1805, Deposition of Joseph Matica, Supreme Court Divorces, PMHC.

76. Carver v. Carver, 1801, Deposition of James De Larcy, Supreme Court Divorces, PMHC.

77. Graves v. Graves, November 1844, #34, CP Papers, CCA.

78. Carver v. Carver, 1801, Deposition of Joel Carver, PMHC; Graves v. Graves, 1844, CCA.

79. Sidney George Fisher to Elizabeth Ingersoll, 21 August 1850, Sidney George Fisher Collection, HSP.

80. "Fragment," *The Lady's Magazine* I (October 1792), 242.

81. Armes, *Nancy Shippen*, 297–301.

82. William Stern Randall, *A Little Revenge: Benjamin Franklin and His Son* (Boston: Little, Brown, 1984), 106–107; 138–139. Simon Gratz, "Some Material for a Biography of Mrs. Elizabeth Ferguson, nee Graeme,"*PMHB* 39 (1915), 261–267. Claude-Anne Lopez and Eugenia W. Herbert, *The Private Franklin: The Man and His Family* (New York: W. W. Norton, 1975), 68–69

83. Lopez and Hebert, *The Private Franklin*, 97–98.

84. Gartz, "Mrs. Elizabeth Ferguson," 39: 258.

85. Gratz, "Mrs. Elizabeth Ferguson," 41: 387.

86. Gratz, 39: 260.

87. This, of course, was only the beginning of changes that continue even today.

Chapter 3: *"If We Forsook Prudence"*

1. Cited in Susan Koppleman, ed., *The Other Woman: Stories of Two Women and a Man* (Old Westbury, NY: The Feminist Press, 1984).

2. Collady v. Collady, 1806, Deposition of William Wonderly, Divorce Papers, 1786–1815, Division of Archives and Manuscripts, Records of the the Supreme Court, Eastern District, Pennsylvania Historical and Museum Commission (PHMC), hereafter cited as Supreme Court Divorces. The date indicates the date the libel was filed.

3. Impotence and adultery/bigamy are the only sexual problems I have found between married couples in my sources, including both divorce papers and quarter sessions records, probably because they were both traditionally grounds for ending marriages. Sexual dysfunctions, such as premature ejaculation and pain during intercourse, are not mentioned. The cases of incest and rape that I have found I would place in the category of violence or child abuse, while the few prosecuted cases of bestiality involved single men. I have found no mention of homosexual encounters or group sex. This does not mean that there was not any, but only that those involved did not refer to it, or were not prosecuted.

4. Collady v. Collady, Deposition of William Wonderly, 1806, Supreme Court Divorces, PHMC.

5. Ibid., Deposition of Sophia Hight.

6. Ibid.

7. Ibid., Deposition of John C. Otto.

8. Ibid., Petition of Sophia Collady.

9. Masters and Johnson would probably diagnose Jacob as having sec-

ondary impotence because he had had successful coital encounters prior to marriage with Sophia. Typically, secondary impotence involves an episode after previous successful encounters. The initial failure might be due to fatigue, alcohol consumption, or distraction, but after it occurs, the individual begins to become apprehensive. This then leads to a pattern of impotence. William H. Masters and Virginia E. Johnson, *Human Sexual Inadequacy* (Boston: Little, Brown and Co., 1970), 157 and Chap. 6. More recent research indicates that some diseases, medications, and physical conditions may also cause impotence, but that it is often a combination of both the psychological and the physical that causes men to have episodes of erectile dysfunction. Current treatment usually includes physical and psychological evaluations. See Arnold Melman, M.D., "Evaluation and Management of Erectile Dysfunction," *Surgical Clinics of North America* 68 (October 1988), 965–981; Alma Dell Smith, Ph.D., "Psychologic Factors in the Multidisciplinary Evaluation and Treatment of Erectile Dysfunction," *Urologic Clinics of North America* 15 (February 1988), 41–51. I am indebted to Gwenne Baile, C.N.M., for these references.

10. "An Act Concerning Divorces and Alimony," *The Statutes at Large of Pennsylvania from 1682–1801* (Harrisburg, 1896–1901), XII, 94.

11. The surviving papers of divorces cases do not always indicate if the divorce was granted.

12. Neither provide much detail. For example, Leah and Francis Gallacher of Lancaster cohabited almost eleven years without consummating their marriage. The few papers of the case do not indicate why Leah finally initiated divorce proceedings. Gallacher v. Gallacher, 1802, Supreme Court Divorces, PHMC.

13. Robert Griswold discusses one such case in his article, "Sexual Cruelty and the Case for Divorce in Victorian America," *Signs* 11 (Spring 1986), 529–541. In addition, some men and women probably deserted in order to escape their sexual problems. Although the record of their desertion might appear, their record of the sexual problems does not.

14. Petition of Anna Maria Boehm, 1728/29, Philadelphia and Montgomery Counties Folder, Box 6, 144E, Historical Society of Pennsylvania (HSP). See also Martin Duberman, "Male Impotence in Colonial Pennsylvania," *Signs* 4 (Winter 1978), 395–401, for a transcription of these papers.

15. Ibid.

16. The discussion of new ideas on married love is more fully developed in Chap. 2.

17. M. Clark, *The Memoirs of the Celebrated and Beautiful Mrs. Ann Carson*, 2nd ed. (Philadelphia, 1838), 59.

18. Ibid., 87–88. Ann later married again after Carson had been gone for four years, and she had received reports of his death. Carson returned to "reclaim" his wife, her second husband shot him, and Ann was arrested for bigamy. Carson died from his wounds a few days later. In a rather blatant

example of male belief in dominance over women and this relationship to female dependence, Ann's second husband kidnapped her and forced her to marry him, over her protests. Ann submitted, however, and learned to love this man after he demonstrated he was a good husband and father.

19. Daniel Scott Smith invented the term "domestic feminism" to describe what he sees as nineteenth-century women's increased power within the family, a power obtained by gaining control over sex and reproduction. Daniel Scott Smith, "Family Limitation, Sexual Control, and Domestic Feminism in Victorian America," *A Heritage of Her Own: Toward a New Social History of American Women*, ed. Nancy F. Cott and ELizabeth H. Pleck (New York: Simon and Schuster, 1979), 222–245. Carl N. Degler argues that nineteenth-century reformers believed that the overindulged sexual appetites of husbands injured their wives. Thus, their aim often was to limit sexual encounters between spouses in order to improve the position of women within marriage. Carl N. Degler, *At Odds: Women and the Family in America from the Revolution to the Present* (New York: Oxford University Press, 1980), 271.

20. Smith, "Family Limitation," 233–236; Degler, *At Odds*, 274–276. On ideals of manhood, see Edward Anthony Rotundo, "Body and Soul: Changing Ideals of American Middle-Class Manhood, 1770–1920," *Journal of Social History* 16 (Summer 1983), 23–38, and his dissertation, "Manhood in America: The Northern Middle Class, 1770–1920" (Ph.D. diss., Brandeis University, 1982).

21. Nancy F. Cott, "Passionlessness: An Interpretation of Victorian Sexual Ideology, 1790–1850," in Cott and Pleck, *A Heritage of Her Own*, 162–181. Cott notes that although the literature expressed sympathy for seduced women, in reality they were often ostracized, while the men escaped punishment, 170. Also see Christine Stansell, *City of Women: Sex and Class in New York, 1787–1860* (New York: Alfred A. Knopf, 1986), 24–28.

22. Ellen K. Rothman, *Hands and Hearts: A History of Courtship in America* (New York: Basic Books, 1984), 44–55.

23. Clark, 107.

24. Minutes of the Board of Managers of the Magdalen Society, Vol. I, 1800–1810, 3 May 1808, 108–109, HSP.

25. See Chap. 1 on divorce.

26. Will of Jacob Barr, City of Philadelphia Laborer, proved 27 March 1775, HSP. My thanks to Susan Mackiewicz for this reference.

27. Both Ann Carson's husbands, for example, seemed to feel that they owned her. Also see, Stansell, *City of Women*, 29.

28. Du Rocher v. Du Rocher, 1800, Supreme Court Divorces, PHMC; Lightwood v. Lightwood, 1797, Depositions of Mary Holt, John Falmer, Supreme Court Divorces, PHMC.

29. Wilkinson v. Wilkinson, 1810, Depositions of Samuel Addes, Peter A. Brown, Divorce Papers, Chester County Court of Common Pleas, Chester County Archives (CCA).

30. Burk v. Burk, 1797, Deposition of Griffith Jones, 1797, Supreme Court Divorces, PHMC.

31. Thomas v. Thomas, 1801, Deposition of Louisa Faut; Gore v. Gore, 1787, Deposition of John Cannon; Brown v. Brown, 1802, all Supreme Court Divorces, PHMC.

32. Thomas v. Thomas, 1801, Supreme Court Divorces, PHMC.

33. Venereal diseases were usually referred to as simply one disease, not syphilis, gonorrhea, etc. It is possible that what was sometimes diagnosed as venereal disease may not have been. In women, especially, the "venereal disease" might have been some other type of vaginal infection.

34. Steenburg v. Steenburg, 1812, Deposition of Isaac Cathrall, Supreme Court Divorces, PHMC.

35. Col. J. E. Howard to Benjamin Chew, Jr., 2 June 1816, Chew Family Papers, HSP.

36. Houston v. Houston, 1805; Irwin v. Irwin, 1795, Deposition of Thomas Evans, both cases Supreme Court Divorces, PHMC. Abuse in the Houston case is discussed in Chap. 4.

37. McMullin v. McMullin, 1804, CP Papers, CCA; Steenburg v. Steenburg, 1812, Supreme Court Divorces, PHMC. See Stansell, *City of Women*, esp. 27 and 97, about the misinterpretations of women being on the street alone, and the harassment they encountered.

38. Jones v. Jones, 1804, Deposition of Mary Evans, Samuel Townsend, CP Papers, CCA.

39. Murray v. Murray, 1797, Deposition of Hannah Shank, Supreme Court Divorces, PHMC.

40. For a discussion of married women's economic status under the law see Marylynn Salmon, "Equality or Submission? Feme Covert Status in Early Pennsylvania," in *Women of America*, ed. Carol Ruth Berkin and Mary Beth Norton (Boston: Houghton Mifflin, 1979), 92–113, and "The Married Women's Property Act of 1848," *Laws of the General Assembly of the State of Pennsylvania* (Harrisburg, PA, 1848), 536–538. For more on this subject in the context of marital breakups, see Chap. 6.

41. Shriner v. Shriner, 1794, Supreme Court Divorces, PHMC.

42. Whitting v. Whitting, 1831, CP Papers, CCA; Quarter Sessions Docket, November 1824, CCA.

43. Miller v. Miller, 1811, CP Papers, CCA.

44. Ibid., Answer of Susanna Miller.

45. Ibid., Martha Brown's Deposition.

46. Ibid., Ann Cornag's deposition.

47. Ibid., Elizabeth Hannum's deposition.

48. Ibid., Joseph Estworthy's deposition.

49. Ibid.

50. Ibid., Susanna Pennington's deposition.

51. Ibid.

52. Ibid.

53. G. S. Rowe, "Women's Crime and Criminal Administration in Pennsylvania, 1763–1790," *PMHB* 109 (July 1985), 353, 36.

54. Irwin v. Irwin, 1795, Depositions of Agnes Kimberly and Mary Hull, Supreme Court Divorces, PHMC.

55. Carpenter v. Carpenter, 1830, Deposition of Martha Sill, # 5, CP Papers, CCA.

56. Alexander v. Alexander, 1800, Deposition of Charles Walters, Supreme Court Divorces, PHMC.

57. Whitting v. Whitting, 1831, Deposition of Daniel Johnson, CP Papers, CCA.

58. McMullin v. McMullin, 1804, Deposition of Nathaniel Hart, CP Papers, CCA; Dodd v. Dodd, 1800, Deposition of Peter Adams, Supreme Court Divorces, PHMC; Houston v. Houston, 1805, Deposition of Sarah Deckers, Supreme Court Divorces, PHMC; Andreas v. Andreas, 1799, Deposition of Jacob Andreas, Supreme Court Divorces, PHMC.

59. Daily Occurrence Docket, 25 July 1801, Guardians of the Poor, Philadelphia City Archives (PCA).

60. Andreas v. Andreas, 1799, Depositions of Jacob Andreas, James Taylor, and Jacob Penningher, Supreme Court Divorces, PHMC.

61. *Report of the Trial of Edward Williams for the Murder of His Wife*, and clipping of his confession, Edward Williams Envelope, Chester County Historical Society (CCHS), courtesy of the Chester County Historical Society, West Chester, PA; Quarter Sessions Papers, November 1830, CCA, Smith Futhey and Gilbert Cope, *The History of Chester County, Pennsylvania, with Genealogical and Biographical Sketches* (Philadelphia: Louis H. Everts, 1881), 409.

62. Bourgiois v. Bourgiois, 1805, Deposition of Thomas Goodwin, Supreme Court Divorces, PHMC.

63. Burk v. Burk, 1797, Deposition of Ephrain Dare, Supreme Court Divorces, PHMC.

64. Wilkinson v. Wilkinson, 1810, Deposition of Samuel Addes, CP Papers, CCA.

65. Common Pleas Papers, August 1839, #68, #69, CCA

Chapter 4: "Cruel and Barbarous Treatment"

1. See, for example, "Female Advice," *The Royal American Magazine* I (April 1774), 151; "On Matrimonial Obedience," *The Lady's Magazine* I (July 1792), 66; "On Love," *The Lady's Magazine I* (June 1792), 35; William Alcott, *The Young Man's Guide* (Boston: Perkins and Marvin, 1836), 263.

2. Sources for this chapter include, but are not limited to, Pennsylvania Supreme Court Divorce papers (1785–1815), Records of the Supreme Court, Eastern District, Pennsylvania Historical and Museum Commission (PHMC); Chester County Divorces (1804–1845), Common Pleas Papers, Chester County

Archives (CCA); Philadelphia Quarter Sessions Dockets (1753–1830), Historical Society of Pennsylvania (HSP) and Philadelphia City Archives (PCA); Daily Occurrence Dockets (1785–1815), Guardians of the Poor, PCA; and Chester County Quarter Sessions Dockets and Papers (1730–1840), CCA. Philadelphia Court records are incomplete. A few docket books and most of the papers are missing. Sometimes in both Philadelphia and Chester County it is impossible to determine the relationship of the abuser and the abused from court dockets. I have used only those that I have been able to determine are husbands and wives.

3. The 1785 divorce act states "that if any husband shall maliciously, [either] abandon his family or turn his wife out of doors, or by cruel and barbarous treatment endanger her life or offer such indignities to her person as to render her condition intolerable or life burdensome, and thereby force her to withdraw from his house and family," the Supreme Court would grant a divorce from bed and board with alimony upon the wife's complaint and with "due proof." "An Act Concerning Divorces and Alimony," *The Statutes at Large of Pennsylvania from 1682–1801* (Harrisburg, 1896–1908), XII, 98. As will be demonstrated here, "indignities" encompassed both physical and economic neglect.

4. For one of the few such examples, see Commonwealth v. Mary Foy, Assault and Battery on Micheal Foy, December 1806, Philadelphia Q.S. Docket, PCA. Mary Foy was convicted and ordered to pay a fine of six dollars. There are no further details provided in the docket, but Mary did file for a separate maintenance that same month.

5. Under the 1785 divorce law, only women could obtain a divorce from bed and board with alimony on the grounds of "cruel and barbarous treatment." Child abuse also existed and probably contributed to marital tensions, but seldom appeared in records of marital discord during this period. Typically, in divorce cases, separate maintenance petitions, and newspaper notices, husbands seldom referred to their children except to say that their wives did not take proper care of them, while wives mentioned their children only to illustrate that they had to care for them without financial support from their husbands.

6. For twentieth-century cases of spouse abuse see Murray A. Straus, "Wife-Beating: How Common and Why?" in *The Social Causes of Husband-Wife Violence*, ed. Murray A. Straus and Gerald T. Hotaling (Minneapolis: University of Minnesota Press, 1980), 23–36.

7. *Pennsylvania Gazette*, 21–28 June; 21–28 September 1733.

8. Examples, such as that of Susanna Brauer whose husband took a club to beat her with in bed, and other cases in which husbands complained that their wives did not cohabit with them might actually be instances of sexual violence and problems. For more on mental and sexual cruelty see Robert L. Griswold "The Evolution of the Doctrine of Mental Cruelty in Victorian American Divorce, 1790–1900," *Journal of Social History* 20 (Fall 1986), 127–

148, and "Sexual Cruelty and the Case of Divorce in Victorian America," *Signs* 11 (Spring 1986), 529–541.

9. Griswold, "Doctrine of Mental Cruelty," 128, notes that in 1790, Sir William Scott (Lord Stowell) "delivered what became in American courts the leading decision on the subject of matrimonial cruelty." Stowell's interpretation was very strict, stating that cruelty had to include physical violence or the "reasonable apprehension" of physical abuse. However, the wording of the divorce law in Pennsylvania prompted wives to claim destitution and abuse without necessarily providing details of physical mistreatment.

10. *Pennsylvania Gazette*, 17 March 1742/3.

11. See, for example, "The Married Woman's Property Act of 1848," *Laws of the General Assembly of the State of Pennsylvania* (Harrisburg, PA, 1848), 536–538. Twentieth-century abused wives also face problems of low self-esteem and no job skills.

12. This is the term Elizabeth Pleck used in "Wife Beating in Nineteenth-Century America," *Victimology* 4 (1979), 62–74.

13. Christine Stansell, *City of Women: Sex and Class in New York, 1789–1860* (New York: Alfred A. Knopf, 1986), 80. There was a great increase in drunkenness in the postrevolutionary period, and the years between 1790 and 1830 were "probably the heaviest drinking era in the nation's history," according to Mark Edward Lender and James Kirby Martin in, *Drinking in America* (New York: The Free Press, 1982), 38–40, 46.

14. Houston v. Houston, 1805, Petition of Jane Houston, Supreme Court Divorces, PHMC. No similar claims were made by husbands against their wives in divorce records. Some men who placed their spouses in the almshouse, did, however, accuse them of drunkenness and violent behavior. This violence was not necessarily directed toward the husbands. See, for example, Admission of Peggy McGrotto, Daily Occurrence Docket, 4 December 1810, Guardians of the Poor, PCA.

15. Col. J. E. Howard to Benjamin Chew, Jr., 16 June 1815, Chew Family Papers, HSP.

16. Reilly v. Reilly, 1812, Libel of Mary Reilly, Supreme Court Divorces, PHMC.

17. McElwee v. McElwee, 1800, Deposition of John Way, Letter from John McElwee to Moses Levy, Esq., 2 December 1801, Supreme Court Divorces, PHMC.

18. Eliza Cope Harrison, ed. *Philadelphia Merchant: The Diary of Thomas P. Cope, 1800–1851* (South Bend, IN: Gateway Editions, 1978), 126–127.

19. Pennsylvania Gazette, 27 August 1767; Deyly v. Deyly, 1802, Petition of Catherine Deyley, Deposition of William Kern, Esq., Supreme Court Divorces, PHMC.

20. Brown v. Brown, November 1844, #8, CP Papers, CCA.

21. Brown v. Brown, Deposition of Mary Leo, September 1799, Supreme

Court Divorces, PHMC; Philadelphia Court of Quarter Sessions, Docket, March 1781, HSP.

22. For example, see twentieth-century patterns noted by Straus, "Wife-beating," 34–35.

23. Fisher v. Fisher, 1790, Deposition of [illegible] Miller, Supreme Court Divorces, PHMC.

24. Burkhart v. Burkhart, Answer of Respondant, 1785; McBride v. McBride, Plea and Answer of Andrew McBride, 1792; Sutter v. Sutter, Answer, 1795, all Supreme Court Divorces, PHMC.

25. Brauer v. Brauer, 1786, Supreme Court Divorces, PHMC; *Pennsylvania Gazette*, 9 August 1785.

26. Mary S. Hartman, *Victorian Murderesses* (New York: Schocken Books, 1977).

27. Chester County Court of Quarter Sessions, Docket D, February 1793, and Court of Oyer and Terminer, February 1793, CCA.

28. See "An Act Concerning Divorces and Alimony," *The Statutes at Large*, XII, 94.

29. See McArthur v. McArthur, 1789, Supreme Court Divorces, PHMC; Heslet v. Heslet, Columbia County Court Records, 1821, HSP.

30. Harriet Chew Carroll to Benjamin Chew, Jr., 17 June 1816, Correspondence and General Papers of Benjamin Chew, Jr., Chew Family Papers, HSP.

31. Deyly v. Deyly, 1803, Deposition of Joseph Fry, Supreme Court Divorces, PHMC.

32. Ibid., Depositions of Jacob Stener, Peter Kern, and William Kern, Esq. The case was dismissed.

33. *Pennsylvania Gazette*, 10 August 1785.

34. Daily Occurrence Docket, 23 August 1800, Guardians of the Poor, PCA.

35. Ibid., 23 May 1797.

36. Ibid., 18 April 1811.

37. Ibid., 15 June 1803, 11 April 1803, 31 May 1803.

38. Ibid., 20 June 1809. For a history of the Philadelphia almshouse and its inmates, see Priscilla Ferguson Clement, *Welfare and the Poor in the Nineteenth-Century City: Philadelphia, 1800–1854* (Rutherford, NJ: Fairleigh Dickinson University Press, 1985).

39. Philadelphia Q.S. Docket, March 1791, PCA.

40. Chester County Q.S. Docket K, July 1832, August 1835; Docket M, February 1837, February 1839, February 1840, February 1842, CCA.

41. Chester County Q.S. Docket F, August 1808, July 1809; Indictments, August 1808, CCA.

42. Philadelphia Q.S. Docket, March 1784, September 1784, HSP.

43. For more on desertion and warrants of seizure, see Chap. 4.

44. Chester County Q.S. Docket, November 1757, Docket B, August 1773; Indictments, August 1773, CCA.

45. Thomas R. Meehan, " 'Not Made Out of Levity': Evolution of Divorce in Early Pennsylvania," *The Pennsylvania Magazine of History and Biography* 92 (October 1968), 448.

46. Brauer v. Brauer, 1786, Supreme Court Divorces, PHMC.

47. "An Act Concerning Divorces and Alimony," 98. For more on divorce see Chap. 5.

48. Ibid. The Supreme Court granted a greater percent of women's petitions citing the grounds of desertion and adultery than of cruelty alone. See Chap. 5.

49. After 1804, men and women were permitted to divorce through their county Court of Common Pleas. See "A Supplement to the act, entitled, 'An Act Concerning Divorces and Alimony,' " *Laws of the Commonwealth*, IV, 182.

50. Evans v. Evans, 1811, CP Papers, CCA.

51. France v. France, 1804, Deposition of Mary Armbruster, Supreme Court Divorces, PHMC.

52. Campbell clipping, 13 April 1850, Campbell Family Envelope, Chester County Historical Society (CCHS).

53. Evans v. Evans, Deposition of John Lewis, CCA

54. Black v. Black, 1791, Deposition of Jacob Graff, Supreme Court Divorces, PHMC; Brown v. Brown, 1844, #8, # 9, Deposition of Mary Carter, CP Papers, CCA.

55. Brown v. Brown, 1799, Deposition of Mary Leo; McCrea v. McCrea, 1798, Depositions of Thomas Humphrey Cushing and Leniah Anderson, Supreme Court Divorces, PHMC.

56. Baker v. Baker, 1845, #3, Deposition of Rachel McClean, CP Papers, CCA.

57. Taylor v. Taylor, 1832, Deposition of Joshua Scott; also depositions of Benjamin Reese, Thomas Woodward, Lewis W. Williams, and Samuel Worth, CP Papers, CCA.

58. France v. France, 1806, Deposition of William Cummins; also depositions of Henry and Mary Armbruster, Supreme Court Divorces, PHMC.

59. Deborah Norris Logan Diaries, 3 December 1823, HSP.

60. I am indebted to Ric Northrup for bringing this song to my attention. The husband, Thimble, represents the stereotypical abused husband—a tailor. *Elizabeth and Eliza Henry Songbooks* (1795), HSP.

61. "On Love," *The Lady's Magazine* I (June 1792), 32.

62. The Directors of the Poor and the House of Employment of Chester County v. James McMullin, Deposition of Hannah Hickman, October 1805, Quarter Sessions Records Related to the Directors of the Poor, CCA. McMullin is variously spelled McMullin, McMullen, or McMullan in court documents. I have chosen to use McMullin in all the references, as that spelling

appears most often. For poor laws, see "An Act for the Relief of the Poor," *Statutes at Large*, VII, 93.

63. For information on the public nature of Pennsylvania courts see G. S. Rowe, "The Role of Courthouses in the Lives of 18th Century Women," *The Western Pennsylvania Historical Magazine* 68 (January 1985), 5–23.

64. Directors v. James McMullin, July 1806, Q.S. Records Related to the Directors of the Poor, CCA. Christine Stansell notes that shouting "murder" was often a signal for a woman's New York City neighbors to come to her aid. Stansell, *City of Women*, 81.

65. Ibid.

66. James McMullin v. Wilkin and Hickman, ADI file 1792 and 1794, CCA.

67. Ibid.

68. Ibid.

69. McMullin v. McMullin, 1804, Deposition of Robert Smith, CP Papers, CCA.

70. Ibid., Deposition of Sarah Barr. Also see depositions of Nathaniel Hart and John Hicklin.

71. Ibid., Deposition of Nathaniel Hart.

72. Ibid., Answer of Rachel McMullin.

73. Will of James McMullin, #6070, CCA.

74. Elizabeth Pleck argues that "the single most consistent barrier to reform against domestic violence has been the Family Ideal—that is, unrelated but nonetheless distinct ideas about family privacy, conjugal and parental rights, and family stability." In addition, she argues that "isolated incidents of community regulation were remnants of a much more extensive form of social policing that ended with the demise of the Puritan experiment." See *Domestic Tyranny: The Making of American Social Policy against Family Violence from Colonial Times to the Present* (New York: Oxford University Press, 1987), 7, 33. Similarly, Myra Glenn argues that the 1830s and 1840s campaigns against corporal punishment did not include campaigns against wife-beating because Americans believed interfering between husband and wife intruded upon the privacy of the home. Focusing on reforms, reformers, and the public perception of wife-abuse, Glenn's thesis is not supported by the individual cases studied here. *Campaigns Against Corporal Punishment: Prisoners, Sailors, Women and Children in Antebellum America* (Albany: State University of New York Press, 1984).

75. Nancy F. Cott, "Divorce and the Changing Status of Women in Eighteenth-Century Massachusetts," *William and Mary Quarterly* 33 (October 1976), 613–614.

Chapter 5: Runaways

1. *Pennsylvania Gazette*, 10 October 1754; 20 July 1785; 28 April 1743.

2. Ibid., 13 September 1744.

3. See "An Act for the Relief of the Poor," *Statutes at Large of Pennsylvania from 1682 to 1801 (Harrisburg, 1896–1908)*, VIII, 93. A wife could choose to bring her husband to court for nonsupport, claiming she had been forced to leave him, or she could challenge a husband's divorce suit. The court would have to determine who was telling the truth.

4. Divorce is discussed in Chap. 1. Prior to the 1785 divorce act, divorce was possible through the legislature only, resulting in very few divorces.

5. Kemp v. Kemp, 1802, Libel of Celeste Kemp, Deposition of Augustin Guigue, Divorce Papers, 1786–1815, Division of Archives and Manuscripts, Records of the Supreme Court, Eastern District, Pennsylvania Historical and Museum Commission (PHMC). Hereafter, Supreme Court Divorces. Under the 1785 divorce law, a spouse must have been gone for four years or more before the abandoned wife or husband could file for divorce on desertion grounds. Daily Occurrence Dockets, 9 May 1810, Guardians of the Poor, Philadelphia City Archives (PCA).

6. Leonard v. Leonard, 1802, Petition of Elizabeth Leonard, Depositions of William Juston, Jr. and Susanna Juston, Supreme Court Divorces, PHMC.

7. Daily Occurrence Dockets, 8 April 1812, Guardians of the Poor, PCA.

8. Daily Occurrence Dockets, 3 January 1801; 18 December 1802; 16 January 1804, Guardians of the Poor, PCA.

9. Ibid., 21 March 1810; 29 March 1810; 3 April 1802; 20 June 1802; 23 June 1802.

10. Davis v. Davis, 1799, Libel of Mary Davis, Deposition of Peter Smith and Rebecca Fance, Supreme Court Divorces, PHMC.

11. See Wayne Bodle, "Jane Bartram's 'Application': Her Struggle for Survival, Stability, and Self-Determination in Revolutionary and Post-Revolutionary Pennsylvania," Paper presented to the Transformation of Philadelphia Project, Philadelphia Center for Early American Studies (May 1988), esp. 18–19, *Pennsylvania Magazine of History and Biography*, forthcoming (April 1991). On the Revolutionary loyalties of married women see Linda K. Kerber, *Women of the Republic: Intellect & Ideology in Revolutionary America* (Chapel Hill: University of North Carolina Press, 1980), Chap. 4.

12. *Pennsylvania Gazette*, 26 May 1779.

13. Both Nancy Cott and Linda Kerber report that there were few divorce cases in Massachusetts and Connecticut directly attributed to the war. Nancy F. Cott, "Divorce and the Changing Status of Women in Eighteenth-Century Massachusetts," *William and Mary Quarterly* 33 (October 1976), 592–593; Kerber, *Women of the Republic*, 174. Because Pennsylvania, unlike Massachusetts and Connecticut, did not grant judicial divorces until 1785, it is impossible to compare before and after statistics.

14. Staal v. Staal, 1803, Depositions (1805) of John Hiener, George Replier, Andrew Kepner, Henry Betz, Peter Shoemaker, James Bell, and Frederick Weitzel, Supreme Court Divorces, PHMC.

15. Shurtz v. Shurtz, 1794, Deposition of Jacob Houck, Supreme Court Divorces, PHMC.

16. Ibid. Deposition of David Jones.

17. Waters v. Waters, 1839, Petition of Thomas Waters, Divorces Papers, Chester County Court of Common Pleas Papers, # 34, Chester County Archives (CCA).

18. Ibid. Deposition of William W. Elliot.

19. Ibid.

20. Sexual cruelty was not grounds for divorce. For a discussion on this topic, see Robert Griswold, "Sexual Cruelty and the Case for Divorce in Victorian America," *Signs* 11 (Spring 1986), 529–541.

21. Black v. Black, 1802, Petition of Mary Black, Deposition of Abraham Langhrage, Supreme Court Divorces; Dickinson v. Dickinson, 1801, Libel of Phoebe Dickinson, Deposition of Sarah Wright, Supreme Court Divorces, PHMC; Thomson v. Thomson, 1813, Libel of Janet Thomson, Deposition of Samuel Thomson, CP Papers, CCA.

22. Lawes v. Lawes, 1846, Petition of William Lawes, Depositions of John Craig, Thomas Hazard, Thomas Huston, Perry Johnson, Solomon Hazard, #38, CP Papers, CCA.

23. Catherine Bruce v. Mahlon Bruce, 1844, Deposition of U.V. Pennypacker, # 41, CP Papers, CCA.

24. Ibid., Depositions of William Graham, Isaac Derrickson.

25. *Pennsylvania Gazette*, 25 August 1743.

26. Jacob Hoofman v. Margaret Hoofman, 1813, Deposition of Julian Marshall, 1813, CP Papers, CCA.

27. Rigg v. Rigg, 1842, Depositions of Mary Ellen Creswell and Joseph Jeffries, CP Papers, #29, CCA.

28. Lowry v. Lowry, 1792, Petition of Elizabeth Lowry, Supreme Court Divorces, PHMC.

29. Hutchinson v. Hutchinson, 1840, Deposition of James C. Allen, CP Papers, #53, CP Papers, CCA.

30. Vondersloth v. Vondersloth, Libel, 1791, Deposition of Andrew Grasfer, Supreme Court Divorces, PHMC.

31. She received a divorce in 1824. John v. John, Petition of Rebecca John, 1823, Deposition of Isaac Cadwalader, CP Papers, CCA.

32. Priscilla Ferguson Clement, *Welfare and the Poor in the Nineteenth-Century City, Philadelphia, 1800–1854* (Rutherford: Fairleigh Dickinson University Press, 1985), esp. Chap. 3. The economics of marital discord are discussed further here in Chap. 6.

33. Quarter Sessions Records Related to the Directors of the Poor, 4 September 1804, CCA.

34. Daily Occurrence Docket, 9 December 1809, Guardians of the Poor, PCA.

35. Clemons v. Clemons, 1791, Libel of Valentine Clemons and deposition of George Frilker, Supreme Court Divorces, PHMC.

36. Patterson v. Patterson, 1797, Libel of James Patterson, Supreme Court Divorces, PHMC. Also see Badger v. Badger, 1806, Supreme Court Divorces, PHMC, discussed in Chap. 2.

37. Clement, *Welfare and the Poor*, 50–54, 64–66.

38. Brown v. Brown, 1837, Petition of Jane Brown, CP Papers, CCA.

39. Sheifly v. Sheifly, 1800, Petition of Susannah Sheifly; Weibert v. Weibert, 1787, Petition of Anthony Felix Weibert, Depositions of John R.B. Rogers, John Shea, and Peter Peres, Supreme Court Divorces, PHMC.

40. Hoofman v. Hoofman, 1813, Deposition of William Early, CP Papers, CCA.

Chapter 6: For a Maintenance

1. Tiffen v. Tiffen, 1802, Answer of James Tiffin, Report of James Tiffin's Accounts, 1803, Divorce Papers, 1786–1815, Records of the Supreme Court, Eastern District, Pennsylvania Historical and Museum Commission (PHMC).

2. Ibid., Deposition of Henry Ward, Attachment filed 25 March 1807.

3. Tiffin v. Tiffin; 2 Binney 202 (1809).

4. For more on common law and courts of equity, see Marylynn Salmon, "Equality or Submission? Feme Covert Status in Early Pennsylvania," in *Women of America*, ed. Carol Ruth Berkin and Mary Beth Norton (Boston: Houghton Mifflin, 1979), 92–113, esp. 99–101.

5. Salmon, 98–105. On p. 100, Salmon notes, "The courts were consistently more conservative in handling settlements entered into after marriage, enforcing them according to the letter of the law, because they were philosophically opposed to independent legal actions by married women."

6. "The Petition of Elizabeth Clendinnin, Wife of John Clendinnin of Philadelphia County, Innholder," Philadelphia Quarter Sessions Docket, December 1780, Philadelphia City Archives (PCA). Their name is spelled Clandennin in the divorce papers.

7. Ibid.

8. Elizabeth Clandennin v. John Clandennin, 1786, Petition of Elizabeth Clandennin, Supreme Court Divorces, PHMC.

9. Ibid., Attachment for Contempt.

10. "An Act Relating to Orphans' Courts," *Laws of the General Assembly of the State of Pennsylvania* (Harrisburg, 1832), 190–213, sect. 48.

11. Will of Peter Constantine, 24 January 1816, #9, Bk. 5, Historical Society of Pennsylvania (HSP).

12. Ibid.

13. Daily Occurrence Docket, 16 March 1797, Guardians of the Poor, PCA.

14. *Pennsylvania Gazette*, 26 February, 1767.

15. Place v. Place, 1847, Depositions of Martha Lewis Green and Samuel Williams, Esq., #27, Chester County Common Pleas Papers, Chester County Archives (CCA).

16. Hoopes v. Hoopes, 1841, Deposition of Sidney Marsh, CP Papers, CCA; Will of Rebecca Jones, 12 October 1829, #8416, CCA.

17. Ducombe v. Ducombe, 1800, Deposition of Agnes Kimberly; Blaney v. Blaney, 1798, Deposition of Sarah Durang, both Supreme Court Divorces, PHMC.

18. Chester County Quarter Sessions Docket, November 1757, CCA.

19. Chester County Q.S. Papers, August 1773, and Docket "B," August 1773, CCA.

20. Chester County Indictments, November 1775, CCA.

21. Will of William Pyle, 12 January 1789, #3992, CCA.

22. "An Act for the Relief of the Poor," *Laws of the Commonwealth of Pennsylvania* (Philadelphia, 1810), I, 344–345.

23. Philadelphia Q.S. Docket, March 1781, HSP.

24. Chester County Q.S. Docket "C," February 1784, CCA.

25. Thomas v. McCready, 5 S. and R. 387 (1819).

26. Philadelphia Q.S. Docket, December 1826; March 1827, PCA.

27. Rutherford v. Rutherford, 1788, Libel of Alexander Rutherford, Supreme Court Divorces, PHMC.

28. The Petition of James Cahill, December 1833, Insolvent #17, CCA; Cahill v. Cahill, 1832, Petition of Pricilla Cahill; Depositions of Eliza Cormick, Elizabeth Haugings, Joseph Hampton, and William Fullerton, May 1833, CP Papers, CCA.

29. *Pennsylvania Gazette*, 5 November, 1767; 22–29 November, 1733.

30. Daily Occurrence Docket, 1 June 1805, Guardians of the Poor, PCA.

31. Ibid., 18 June 1802.

32. Lisa Wilson Waciega argues that middle-class Philadelphia and Chester County women understood finances and often ran or helped to run family business, both during their husbands' lives and after their deaths. See, "A 'Man of Business': The Widow of Means in Southeastern Pennsylvania, 1750–1850," *William and Mary Quarterly* 44 (January 1987), 40–64.

33. Trenchard v. Trenchard, Depositions taken 1795, see John Meare, Hannah Summers, Sophia Fisher, and John Hewson, Supreme Court Divorces, PHMC; Griscom v. Griscom, 1797, Deposition of Mary Krider, Supreme Court Divorces, PHMC; Taylor v. Taylor, 1832, Deposition of Joshua Scott, CP Papers, CCA.

34. Martin v. Martin, 1805, Deposition of Elizabeth Martin (sister of Mib-

som); Burke v. Burk, 1798, Deposition of Alexander Ramsay, both Supreme Court Divorces, PHMC.

35. On Ann Carson, see M. Clarke, ed., *The Memoirs of the Celebrated and Beautiful Mrs. Ann Carson . . . Whose Life Terminated in Philadelphia Prison*, 2nd ed. (Philadelphia, 1838); For more on Jane Bartram, see Wayne Bodle, "Jane Bartram's 'Application': Her Struggle for Survival, Stability, and Self-Determination in Revolutionary and Post-Revolutionary Pennsylvania," Paper presented to the Transformation of Philadelphia Project, Philadelphia Center for Early American Studies, May 1988, *Pennsylvania Magazine of History and Biography*, forthcoming (April 1991).

36. Petition of Catherine Pattison, #125, Tavern Papers, II, 1729–1736, CCA; Henderson v. Henderson, 1795, Depositions of Hester Fister, Sarah Nelson, and William Barry, Supreme Court Divorces, PHMC.

37. Bangs v. Bangs, 1807, Deposition of Lear Tucker, Supreme Court Divorces, PHMC; Minutes of the Magdalen Society, 7 June 1808, II, 110–11, HSP.

38. McCrea v. McCrea, first libel filed 1796, see 1798 depositions of Leniah Anderson and Thomas Humphrey Cushing, Supreme Court Divorces, PHMC.

39. Hare v. Hare, 2 July 1789, Deposition of William Thomas, Supreme Court Divorces, PHMC.

40. Daily Occurrence Dockets, 13 August 1801; 3 September 1800; 9 December 1802; 5 May 1801; 12 November 1803; 19 October 1801, Guardians of the Poor, PCA.

41. Ibid., 5 March 1799; 15 April 1802.

42. Ibid., 6 November 1802.

43. Ibid., 28 December 1789.

44. Ibid., 15 June 1802, 9 July 1801.

45. Ibid., 30 December 1802.

46. Charles Carroll of Carrollton to Benjamin Chew, Jr., 17 June 1814, Carroll Correspondence, 1800–1814, m.d., HSP.

47. Col. Howard to Benjamin Chew, Jr. 2 June 1816; Harriet Chew Carroll to Benjamin Chew, Jr., 17 June 1816, Benjamin Chew, Jr. Correspondence, HSP.

48. Will of Jane Paxton, #225, 30 November 1772, HSP; Will of Robert Moore, 7 December 1816, CCA.

49. Taylor v. Taylor, 1832, Petition of Ann Taylor, CP Papers, CCA.

50. Shrock v. Shrock, 1805, Deposition of Elizabeth Caves, Supreme Court Divorces, PHMC.

51. Clemons v. Clemons, 1791, Deposition of George Frilker, Supreme Court Divorces, PHMC.

Conclusion: Unraveling the Bonds

1. M. Clarke, ed., *The Memoirs of the Celebrated and Beautiful Mrs. Ann Carson . . . Whose Life Terminated in Philadelphia Prison*, 2nd ed. (Philadelphia, 1838), 125, 126.

2. Ibid., 40. However, for more on the growing number of antebellum women who chose not to marry, see Lee Virginia Chambers-Schiller, *Liberty, A Better Husband: Single Women in America: The Generation of 1780–1840* (New Haven: Yale University Press, 1984).

3. For arguments on the privacy of the family in this context see Elizabeth Pleck, *Domestic Tyranny: The Making of American Social Policy Against Family Violence from Colonial Times to the Present* (New York: Oxford University Press, 1987), and Myra Glenn, *Campaigns Against Corporal Punishment: Prisoners, Sailors, Women, and Children in Antebellum America* (Albany: State University of New York Press, 1984), discussed further here in Chap. 4.

4. See Robert L. Griswold, *Family and Divorce in California, 1850–1890: Victorian Illusions and Everyday Realities* (Albany: State University of New York Press, 1982); Elaine Tyler May, *Great Expectations: Marriage and Divorce in Post-Victorian America* (Chicago: University of Chicago Press, 1980), and William L. O'Neill, *Divorce in the Progressive Era* (New Haven: Yale University Press), 1967.

5. Eliza Cope Harrison, ed., Philadelphia Merchant: *The Diary of Thomas P. Cope* (South Bend, IN: Gateway Editions, 1978), 46–47.

6. From Grace Growden Galloway, "Dear Polly Attend," quoted in Mary Beth Norton, *Liberty's Daughters: The Revolutionary Experience of American Women, 1750–1800* (Boston: Little, Brown, 1980), 47. See Chap. 2 here for more on Grace Galloway.

7. See Chap. 6 for a discussion of these laws.

8. Mary P. Ryan, *Cradle of the Middle-Class: The Family in Oneida County, New York, 1790–1865* (Cambridge: Cambridge University Press, 1981), 83–98, and Chap. 5; also Ryan, *Womanhood in America: From Colonial Times to the Present*, 3rd ed. (New York: Franklin Watts, 1983), 125–134. Carroll Smith-Rosenberg, "Beauty, the Beast, and the Militant Woman: A Case Study in Sex Roles and Social Stress in Jacksonian America," in *Disorderly Conduct: Visions of Gender in Victorian America* (New York: Oxford University Press, 1985), 109–128, examines this development in greater detail by focusing on a single group, the New York Female Moral Reform Society.

Select Bibliography

Manuscript Sources

CHESTER COUNTY ARCHIVES

Chester County Court of Common Pleas. Divorce Papers, 1804–1840, and Continuance Dockets.
Cases are filed by year. Missing years, 1808–1809, 1814–1815, 1818–1819. Some entries lack petitions and/or depositions of witnesses, and some suits do not indicate the final decision of the court. The continuance dockets do not generally include much detail, but do usually indicate if divorces were granted. There are also cases in the dockets that do not appear among the papers.

Chester County Court of Quarter Sessions. Dockets and Papers (Indictments).
Entries do not always indicate marital status nor relationship of plaintiff and defendant.

Chester County Quarter Sessions Records Related to the Directors of the Poor.
These include warrants granted by the court to the Directors to seize the goods and property of men who deserted their wives or who forced them to flee. Some records include the depositions of witnesses.

Chester County Wills.

CHESTER COUNTY HISTORICAL SOCIETY

Campbell Family Papers.

Parker Family Papers.

George Roe and Hester Bizard Marriage Agreement.

HISTORICAL SOCIETY OF PENNSYLVANIA

Bryan, George. Papers.

Chew Family Papers.

Columbia County (PA) Court of Common Pleas.
Includes divorce petitions and decrees for suits granted, 1814–1846. Does not include depositions of witnesses.

De Tilly-Bingham. Letters.

Fisher, Sidney George. Letters.

Galloway, Grace Growden. Diary.

Gloria Dei Church. Marriage Records.

Logan, Deborah Norris. Diaries.

Magdalen Society. Papers.

McCall, Charlotte Manigualt. Diary.

Manigault, Harriet. Diaries.

Philadelphia Court of Quarter Sessions. Docket, Dec. 1780–1785.

Philadelphia Wills.

Shoemaker, Rebecca and Anna and Margaret Rawle. Letters and Diaries.

Supreme Court of Pennsylvania. Decrees of Divorce.
Petitions, decrees, and some additional court papers for divorces that were granted between 1785–1799. Does not include depositions of witnesses. Divorces that were not approved do not appear here.

CITY ARCHIVES OF PHILADELPHIA

Guardians of the Poor.
Most helpful were the Daily Occurrence Dockets. In general, the eighteenth-century volumes provided more detailed entries. Marital status was not always indicated.

Philadelphia Court of Quarter Sessions. Dockets.
Some years are missing or are incomplete. Marital status can not always be determined from the entries. Many of the entries simply list the accused's name and the charge, but applications by women for separate maintenences are often more detailed.

PENNSYLVANIA HISTORICAL AND MUSEUM COMMISSION

Divorce Papers, 1786–1815. Records of the Supreme Court (Eastern District).
These papers, on microfilm, are arranged alphabetically by the last names of the couples. Some of the cases are incomplete. Others included petitions, depositions, and

General Motions and Divorce Docket. Records of the Supreme Court (Eastern District).
Consists of petitions and divorce decrees for 1800–1805. Only the divorces that were granted are included.

Published Primary Sources

Alcott, William A. *The Young Man's Guide.* 10th ed. Boston: Perkins and Marvin, 1836.
———. *The Young Wife or Duties of Woman in the Marriage Relation.* Boston: George W. Light, 1837; reprint, New York: Arno Press, 1972.
Armes, Ethel, ed. *Nancy Shippen, Her Journal Book.* Philadelphia: J. B. Lippincott, 1935.
Clarke, M. *The Memoirs of the Celebrated and Beautiful Mrs. Ann Carson, Daughter of an Officer of the U.S. Navy and Wife of Another, Whose Life Terminated in Philadelphia Prison,* 2nd ed. Philadelphia, 1838.
Jennings, Samuel K. *The Married Lady's Companion or Poor Man's Friend,* 1808; reprint, New York: Arno Press, 1972.
The Lady's Magazine and Repository of Entertaining Knowledge. 1 (1792); 2 (1793).
Laws of the General Assembly of the State of Pennsylvania. Harrisburg, 1848.
Myers, Albert Cook, ed. *Hannah Logan's Courtship.* Philadelphia: Ferris and Leach, 1904.
The Pennsylvania Gazette. 1728–1790.
The Pennsylvania Magazine 1 (1775); 2 (1776).
The Royal American Magazine 1 (1774).
The Statutes at Large of Pennsylvania from 1682 to 1801. Harrisburg, 1896–1908.
Wainwright, Nicholas B., ed. *A Philadelphia Perspective: The Diary of Sidney George Fisher, Covering the Years 1834–1871.* Philadelphia: Historical Society of Pennsylvania, 1967.
Werner, Raymond C., ed. "Diary of Grace Growden Galloway." *Pennsylvania Magazine of History and Biography* 55 (1931), 32–94. 58 (1934), 152–189.

Secondary Sources

Auwers, Linda. "The Social Meaning of Female Literacy: Windsor, Connecticut, 1660–1775." *Newberry Library Papers in Family and Community History.* No. 77–4A. Chicago, 1977.
Basch, Norma. "Invisible Women: The Fiction of Marital Unity in Nineteenth-Century America." *Feminist Studies* 5 (1979), 436–466.
Bernard, Jessie. *The Future of Marriage.* 2nd. ed. New Haven: Yale University Press, 1982.
Bloch, Ruth H. "The Gendered Meanings of Virtue in Revolutionary America." *Signs* 13 (Autumn 1987), 47–52.

Blocker, Jack S. , Jr., ed. *Alcohol, Reform and Society: The Liquor Issue in Social Context.* Westport, CT.: Greenwood Press, 1979.

Chambers-Schiller, Lee Virginia. *Liberty, A Better Husband: Single Women in America: The Generations of 1780-1840.* New Haven: Yale University Press, 1984.

Clement, Priscilla Ferguson. *Welfare and the Poor in the Nineteenth-Century City, Philadelphia, 1800-1854.* Rutherford, NJ: Fairleigh Dickinson, 1985.

Cohen, Sheldon S. "The Broken Bond: Divorce in Providence County, 1749-1809." *Rhode Island History* 44 (1985), 67-79.

Cott, Nancy F. *The Bonds of Womanhood: Woman's Sphere in New England, 1780-1825.* New Haven: Yale University Press, 1977.

———. "Divorce and the Changing Status of Women in Eighteenth-Century Massachusetts." *William and Mary Quarterly* 33 (1976), 586-614.

———. "Eighteenth-Century Family and Social Life Revealed in Massachusetts Divorce Records." *Journal of Social History* 10 (1976), 20-43.

Cott, Nancy F. and Elizabeth Pleck, eds. *A Heritage of Her Own: Toward a New Social History of American Women.* New York: Simon and Schuster, 1979.

Dayton, Cornelia Hughes, "Women Before The Bar: Gender, Law, and Society in Connecticut, 1710-1790." Ph.D. diss., Princeton University, 1986.

Degler, Carl N. *At Odds: Women and the Family in America from the Revolution to the Present.* New York: Oxford University Press, 1980.

Duberman, Martin, "Male Impotence in Colonial Pennsylvania." *Signs* 4 (Winter 1978), 395-401.

Fliegelman, Jay. *Prodigals and Pilgrims: The American Revolution Against Patriarchal Authority, 1750-1800.* Cambridge: Cambridge University Press, 1982.

Freedman, Estelle B. "Sexuality in Nineteenth-Century America: Behavior, Ideology, and Politics." *Reviews in American History* (December 1982), 196-213.

Gilligan, Carol. *In a Different Voice: Psychological Theory and Women's Development.* Cambridge: Harvard University Press, 1982.

Glenn, Myra C. *Campaigns Against Corporal Punishment: Prisoners, Sailors, Women, and Children in Antebellum America.* Albany: State University of New York Press, 1984.

Gordon, Michael. "Mate Choice and Domestic Life in the Nineteenth-Century Marriage Manuel." *Journal of Marriage and the Family* 32 (November 1970), 665-674.

Griswold, Robert L. *Family and Divorce in California, 1850-1890: Victorian Illusions and Everyday Realities.* Albany: State University of New York, 1982.

Grossberg, Michael. *Governing the Hearth: Law and the Family in Nineteenth-Century America.* Chapel Hill: University of North Carolina Press, 1986.

Gunderson, Joan R., and Gwen Victor Gampel. "Married Women's Legal Status in Eighteenth-Century New York and Virginia." *William and Mary Quarterly* 39 (1982), 114-134.

Hartman, Mary S. *Victorian Murderesses*. New York: Schocken Books, 1977.

Hirsh, Alison Duncan. "The Thrall Divorce Case: A Family Crisis in Eighteenth-Century Connecticut." *Women & History* 4 (1982), 43–75.

Hoffer, Peter C. , and Natalie E. H. Hull. *Murdering Mothers: Infanticide in England and New England, 1558–1803*. New York: New York University Press, 1984.

Howard, George E. *A History of Matrimonial Institutions*. Chicago: University of Chicago Press, 1904.

Jensen, Joan M., *Loosening the Bonds: Mid-Atlantic Farm Women, 1750–1850*. New Haven: Yale University Press, 1986.

Kerber, Linda K. "Separate Spheres, Female Worlds, Women's Place: The Rhetoric of Women's History." *The Journal of American History* 75 (June 1988), 9–39.

————. *Women of the Republic: Intellect and Ideology in Revolutionary America*. Chapel Hill: University of North Carolina Press, 1980.

Klepp, Susan Edith, "Philadelphia in Transition: A Demographic History of the City and Its Occupational Groups, 1720–1830." Ph.D. diss., University of Pennsylvania, 1980.

Koehler, Lyle. *A Search for Power: The 'Weaker Sex' in Seventeenth-Century New England*. Urbana, IL.: University of Illinois Press, 1980.

Landale, Nancy S. and Guest, Avery M., "Ideology and Sexuality Among Victorian Women." *Social Science History* 10 (Summer 1986): 147–170.

Lantz, Herman R. *Marital Incompatiblity and Social Change in Early America*. Sage Research Papers in the Social Sciences. Beverly Hills: Sage Publications, 1976.

Lantz, Herman R. et al., "Pre-Industrial Patterns in the Colonial Family in America: A Content Analysis of Colonial Magazines." *American Sociological Review* 33 (June 1968), 413–426.

Lebsock, Suzanne. *The Free Women of Petersburg: Status and Culture in a Southern Town, 1784–1860*. New York: W. W. Norton, 1984.

Lender, Mark Edward, and Martin, James Kirby. *Drinking in America*. New York: The Free Press, 1982.

Lewis, Jan, "The Republican Wife: Virtue and Seduction in the Early Republic." *William and Mary Quarterly* 44 (October 1987), 689–721.

Lopez, Claude-Anne and Herbert, Eugenia W. *The Private Franklin: The Man and his Family*. New York: W. W. Norton, 1975.

Masters, William H. and Virginia E. Johnson. *Human Sexual Inadequacy*. Boston: Little, Brown, 1970.

May, Elaine Tyler. *Great Expectations: Marriage and Divorce in Post-Victorian America*. Chicago: University of Chicago Press, 1980.

Meehan, Thomas R. " 'Not Made Out of Levity': Evolution of Divorce in Early Pennsylvania." *The Pennsylvania Magazine of History and Biography* 92 (October 1968), 441–464.

Norton, Mary Beth. "Eighteenth-Century Women on Peace and War: The Case of the Loyalists." *William and Mary Quarterly* 33 (1976), 386–409.

――――. *Liberty's Daughters: The Revolutionary Experience of American Women, 1750–1800*. Boston: Little, Brown, 1980.

Paul, Norman L. and Paul, Betty Byfield. *A Marital Puzzle: Transgenerational Analysis in Marriage Counseling*. New York: W. W. Norton, 1975.

Pleck, Elizabeth. *Domestic Tyranny: The Making of American Social Policy against Family Violence from Colonial Times to the Present*. New York: Oxford University Press, 1987.

――――. "Wife Beating in Nineteenth-Century America." *Victimology* 4 (1979), 62–74.

Rose, Phyllis. *Parallel Lives: Five Victorian Marriages*. London: The Hogarth Press, 1984.

Rothman, Ellen K. *Hands and Hearts: A History of Courtship in America*. New York: Basic Books, 1984.

Rotundo, Edward Anthony, "Body and Soul: Changing Ideals of American Middle-Class Manhood, 1770–1920." *Journal of Social History* 16 (Summer 1983), 23–38.

――――. "Manhood in America: The Northern Middle Class, 1770–1920," Ph.D. diss., Brandeis University, 1982.

Rowe, G.S. "The Role of Courthouses in the Lives of Eighteenth-Century Pennyslvania Women." *The Western Pennsylvania Historical Magazine* 68 (1985), 5–23.

――――. "Women's Crime and Criminal Administration in Pennsylvania." *Pennsylvania Magazine of History and Biography* 109 (1985), 335–368.

Ryan, Mary P. *Cradle of the Middle Class: The Family in Oneida County, New York, 1790–1865*. Cambridge: Cambridge University Press, 1981.

――――. *Womanhood in America: From Colonial Times to the Present*. 3rd ed. New York: Franklin Watts, 1983.

Salmon, Marylynn. "Equality or Submersion? Feme Covert Status in Early Pennsylvania." In *Women of America: A History*, 92–113, ed. Carol Berkin and Mary Beth Norton. Boston: Houghton Mifflin Co., 1979.

――――. *Women and the Law of Property in Early America*: Chapel Hill, University of North Carolina Press, 1986.

Scott, Joan W. "Gender: A Useful Category of Historical Analysis." *The American Historical Review* 91 (December 1986), 1053–1075.

Shamas, Carole. "The Domestic Environment in Early Modern England and America." *Journal of Social History* 14 (1980), 3–24

Smith-Rosenberg, Carroll. *Disorderly Conduct: Visions of Gender in Victorian America*. New York: Alfred A. Knopf, 1985.

Smith, Billy G. "The 'Lower Sort': Philadelphia's Laboring People, 1750–1800." Ithaca: Cornell University Press, 1990.

――――. "The Material Lives of Laboring Philadelphians, 1750 to 1800." *William and Mary Quarterly* 38 (April 1981), 163–202.

Soderlund, Jean R. *Quakers and Slavery: A Divided Spirit*. Princeton: Princeton University Press, 1985.
———. "Women's Authority in Pennsylvania and New Jersey Quaker Meetings." *William and Mary Quarterly* 44 (October 1987), 722–749.
Stansell, Christine. *City of Women: Sex and Class in New York, 1789–1860*. New York: Alfred A. Knopf, 1986.
Straus, Murray A. "Wife-Beating: How Common and Why?" in *The Social Causes of Husband-Wife Violence*, ed. Murray A. Straus and Gerald T. Hotaling. Minneapolis: University of Minnesota Press, 1980.
Thompson, Roger. *Sex in Middlesex: Popular Mores in a Massachusetts County, 1644–1699*. Amherst: University of Massachusetts Press, 1986.
Ulrich, Laurel Thatcher Ulrich. *Good Wives: Image and Reality in the Lives of Women in Northern New England, 1650–1750*. New York: Oxford University Press, 1982.
Waciega, Lisa Wilson. "A 'Man of Business': The Widow of Means in Southeastern Pennsylvania, 1750–1850." *The William and Mary Quarterly* 44 (January 1987), 40–64.
———. "Widowhood and Womanhood in Early America: The Experience of Women in Philadelphia and Chester Counties, 1750–1850." Ph.D. diss., Temple University, 1986.
Weisberg, D. Kelly. " 'Under Greet Temptations Heer': Women and Divorce in Puritan Massachusetts." *Feminist Studies* 2 (1975), 183–191.
Zuckerman, Michael, ed. *Friends and Neighbors: Group Life in America's First Plural Society*. Philadelphia: Temple University Press, 1982.

Index